I0813830

LIFE along the TRACKS

S P
MW
3248

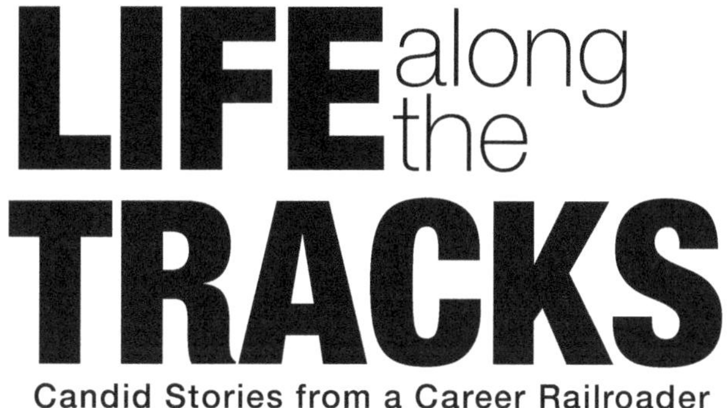

Candid Stories from a Career Railroader

MIKE MCLAUGHLIN AND
JIM PROVIDENZA

MAPS BY DAVID R. CLEMENS

Basalt Books
Pullman, Washington

Basalt Books
PO Box 645610
Pullman, Washington 99164-5910
Phone: 800-354-7360
Email: basalt.books@wsu.edu
Website: basaltbooks.wsu.edu

First printing 2025

Basalt Books is an imprint of Washington State University Press.
The Washington State University Pullman campus is located on the homelands of the Niimíipuu (Nez Perce) Tribe and the Palus people. We acknowledge their presence here since time immemorial and recognize their continuing connection to the land, to the water, and to their ancestors. WSU Press is committed to publishing works that foster a deeper understanding of the Pacific Northwest and the contributions of its Native peoples.

Frontispiece: Siskiyou Summit, December 1960, by Richard Steinheimer.
Steinheimer Collection, DeGolyer Library, Southern Methodist University.
Cover design by Patrick Brommer
Interior design by Tracy Randall

DEDICATION

To Uncle Walter
from one Rock Island man to another.

"Hernia bulging, lift the rear end of the car, stumble over the timbers and ties, set it down on the rails." A Rock Island section gang puts their motor car back on the mainline after the Corn Belt Rocket goes by in a flash; Malcom, Iowa, July 3, 1961. *Photographed by Philip R. Hastings, Philip Ross Hastings, MD, collection, California State Railroad Museum.*

LIFE ALONG THE TRACKS

1

INTRODUCTION

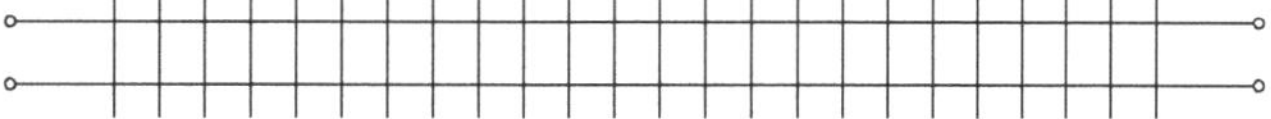

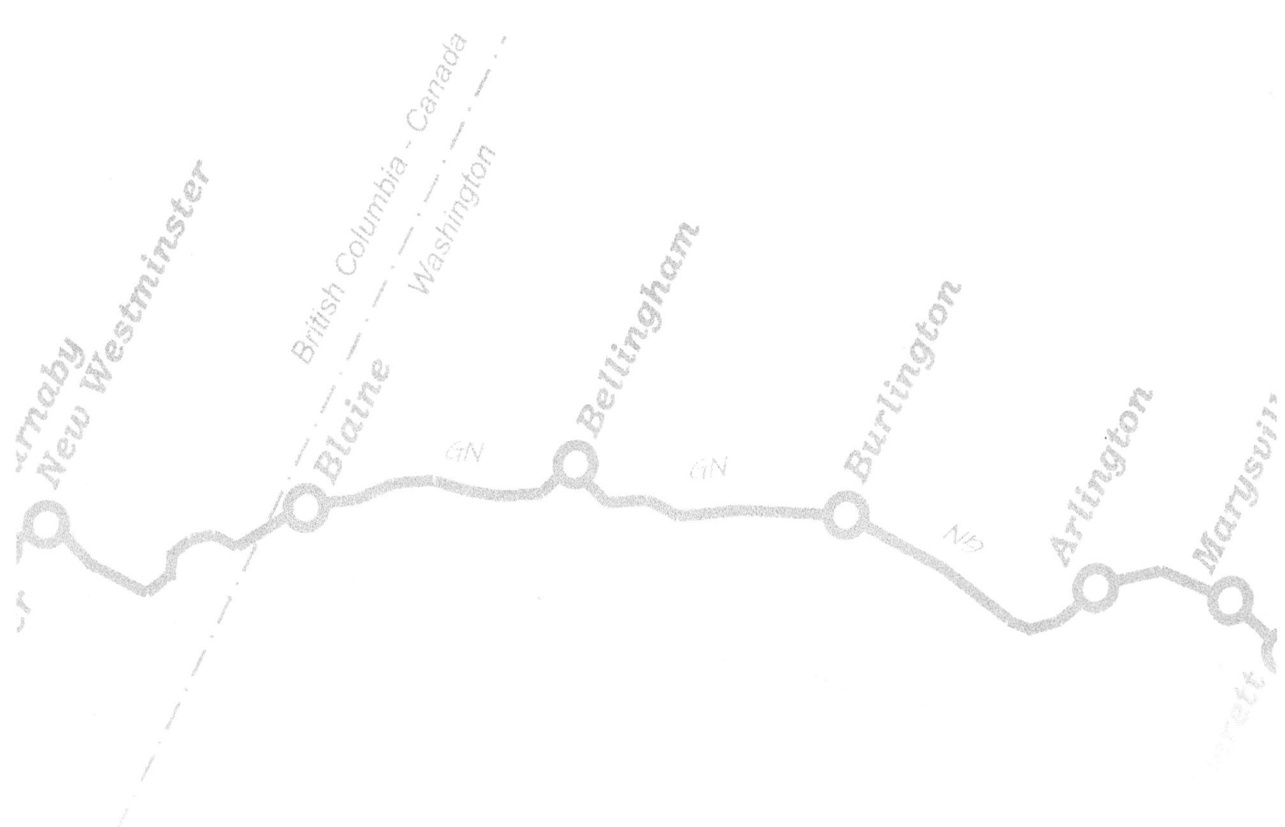

New Westminster
British Columbia - Canada
Washington
Blaine
GN
Bellingham
GN
Burlington
Arlington

INTRODUCTION

FOLLOWING MIKE'S FOOTSTEPS

It seems Mike McLaughlin was just about everywhere in the US at one time or another—at least when it concerned railroading. And as we think you will find, he had a talent for distilling what he saw or experienced into writings that were at times humorous, sometimes very personal; occasionally expository—but almost always entertaining.

He was also a collector of information; railroad "paper", ephemera…and an occasional coal stove. And Mike was generous with the information he had gathered regardless of whether it was about the history or operations of a particular prototype or information that answered a specific question of how something was done on a railroad and how that might be applied on a model railroad. Often such info was accompanied by his opinions…the Correspondence section of this book contains portions of some of Mike's letters and emails to us.

But Mike was not a photographer. While several of his "vignettes" as he liked to call them have been published over the years in various railroad historical society magazines, Mike always hoped to put them all together in a book—this book—which he titled *Life Along the Tracks*. Mike had no photographs or maps to support or illustrate his vignettes and he believed the book could not be published without them. Mike talked to us about the book, asking us to help get the book in print if we were able to.

Dave Clemens met Mike in late -1990 as the newly appointed Editor of the Layout Design Special Interest Group (LD SIG) quarterly magazine/journal. The LD SIG focuses on making model railroads more "railroad models"; looking like and functioning like actual railroads. Mike first submitted a Letter to the Editor; this was followed by a series of model railroad plans of actual railroad locations around the greater Seattle area. As a Burlington Northern and Milwaukee Road devotee, Dave immediately connected with Mike about the joint Milwaukee/Pacific Coast Railroad operation directly below his office at the City of Renton, Washington—see Chapter 13: A Day on the Pacific Coast.

Dave introduced Mike to Jim through early correspondence and as fellow travelers in the Layout Design world. Correspondence by letter morphed into infrequent (pre free-cell phone) long distance calls, then email as the technology became more reliable and readily available. Dave met Mike and his wife Carol in Denver in June 1996 after riding Amtrak's Zephyr from California on "the longest day of the year" for Dave's 50th birthday. Eventually Mike ventured to California on one of his trips as a customer service 'spotter' for Amtrak, finally meeting Jim face to face. Dave, Jim, and Mike spent Mike's free hours talking railroading and railroad modeling.

Mike gave each of us a copy of his draft of *Life Along the Tracks*. It was really only a collection of photocopies of texts. The earliest stories were typewritten; he graduated to a Brothers word processor and later to computer. With the printed material were photocopies of three photographs—a single sheathed outfit car in the snow, a section crew putting a motor car back on the track at a station, and a caboose lettered Pacific Coast. Mike had printed the book title on the outfit car photocopy.

Mike passed away unexpectedly the summer of 2012. And so began the journey with encouragement from Mike's family—talking to railfan and modeling friends, contacting museums and archives in person, by phone or via the internet, reaching out to possible sources, rereading books in our personal railroad libraries, always looking for photos that would illustrate what Mike wrote about.

The outfit car and motor car photocopies set the tone for the photo selection. Each turned out to be by a preeminent railfan photographer—the outfit car photo by Richard Steinheimer and the photo of the section crew with motor car by Philip R. Hastings. Photographs needed to be good in their own right as well as give a visual presence to Mike's text.

Many of Mike's vignettes are about a time of tremendous change in US railroading—the tail end of the "transition era" when the last steam locomotives went to the scrap yard. As has been often noted, many fine railfan photographers simply stopped taking pictures, sometimes forever, when diesels replaced steam. As you read on you will see the photos chosen to illustrate what Mike writing about are often from the 1940s for steam or late 1960s through the 1980s for diesel. Suitable photos from the mid 1950s through the mid 1960s were often not to be found.

And yet...following Mike's footsteps brought us photos and comments. Brian Holtz, our early collaborator and a traffic manager himself—"Mike's stories about Coors and Larry Parsons reminds me of..." From Mike Chandler—"I'm sure that is the same snowplow Mike wrote about." Or John Charles—"Well I don't remember Mike specifically, but he and I were working at Thistle at the same time." Chuck Conway—"Sure, happy to help. Mike and I met years ago, then we sort of lost track of each other." And Mark Amfahr—"Is that the Mike M who used to live in Denver?" Ah yes, personal connections across the years!

Mike McLaughlin early in his railroad career. Clearly working as a signal maintainer, but where? Considering the open shirt and dark tan, probably Utah rather than Seattle! *Photographer unknown, Trigg family collection.*

Where Mike worked. *Map by David R. Clemens.*

Chris Rockwell and the rest of the staff at the California State Railroad Museum Library, Gary Tarbox and Bob Kelly at the Pacific Northwest Railroad Archive, Stephanie Gilmore at the Colorado Railroad Museum, Cherie Christensen of the Saltwater People Historical Society, Paul Swanson of the Lake States Railway Historical Association, Melissa Dawn at the Museum of the Rockies, Anne Peterson of the DeGolyer Library of Southern Methodist University, and Steve Smith at NCRails.net, helped not only in answering questions and filling requests for photos in their collections but often suggested leads to new resources. As a group they remain excellent examples of librarians, curators, and archivists at their best.

Special thanks to Kim Morris for her illustrations of things we could not obtain photos for; an acknowledgment to Joe McMillan of McMillan Publishing and to Chuck Conway who happily made introductions to "the desert photographers" when Jim cold-called them for help. Another thank you is due Chuck Conway and one to Mac McCulloch, who helped fill in many blanks regarding interchange in Denver and Seattle, respectively.

And a final "thank you!" to Christine Trigg, who believed her father's stories were worth telling to a wider audience.

Jim Providenza, San Rafael, California, January 2025
Dave Clemens, Rocklin, California, January 2025

Other Departments Use Shovels

I was working as a gandy, long hot hours with shovel, lining bar, occasionally a brush hook and other instruments of extreme physical labor, the normal accoutrements of my "profession." At 17, the exalted positions of brakeman or fireman were unobtainable and engineer/conductor unthinkable. We moved up and down the line, performing all those tasks appointed by the Roadmaster, when I noticed an individual who coasted up to signal locations either in a truck or on a motor car. A casual dismount, approach to the relay case, and the door was opened. Certain arcane rites were performed and the maintainer moved on.

Ah hah! I noticed right away he did not carry a shovel. My engineer father and my high school shop classes had given me more than the average level of familiarity with electricity. Why, I was already nearly over-qualified for my new job description. The following spring, I applied for a job in the signal department. Not only was I accepted with alacrity, I was given to believe that future train operations on the Great Northern would be dependent in part on the performance of my new duties as a signal helper. As an indication of my new importance in the railway hierarchy, I was given a pass to ride the morning train to Blaine on the Canadian border.

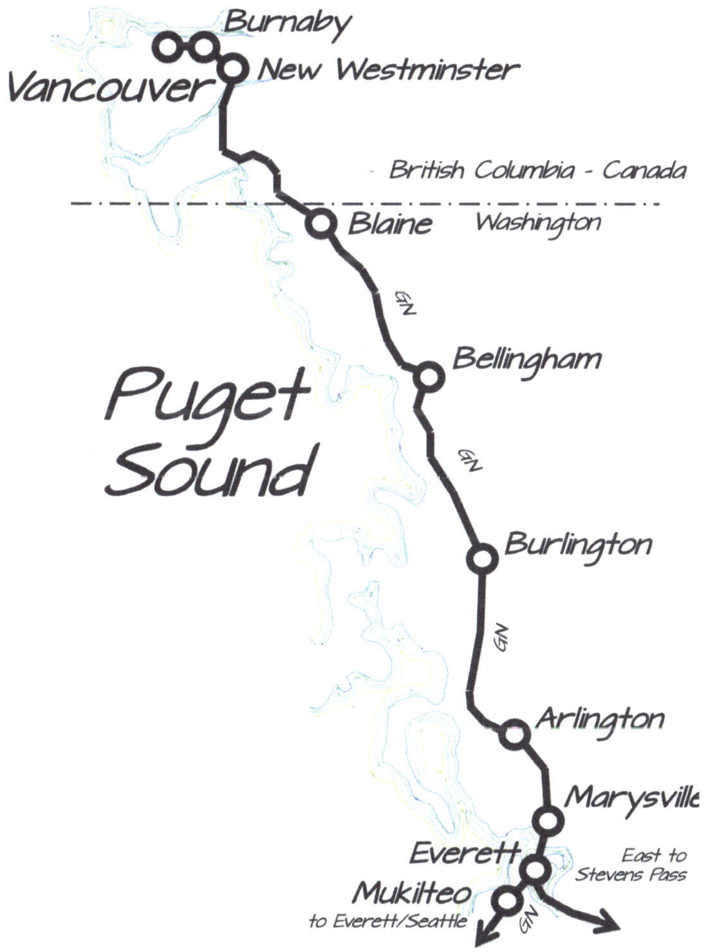

The signal gang had just arrived, and the foreman had put the men to work cleaning the outfit cars. The following day we would start our daily commute to the suburbs of Vancouver, BC to remove the interlocked crossing of the BC Electric "Burnaby Lake" line and the GN. Well, I could wash down walls and clean the kitchen car for an afternoon. Tomorrow, I would undoubtedly be handed a meter and be introduced to those mysteries behind the signal case doors.

In the morning, we all piled into our gang truck which resembled—and was called—the "bread truck." Because the job was of short duration, it was supposed to be cheaper for us to drive back and forth every day than to pay Canadian customs duty on the outfit. Following the highway to Surrey, across the Fraser River bridge to New Westminster, we proceeded to the site of the Ardley Interlocking. When we pulled up, a variety of supplies and equipment was unloaded and—oh, oh, under that pile were shovels. And picks. The foreman directed

Great Northern: Mukilteo, WA to Vancouver, BC.
Map by David R. Clemens.

the signalmen to various tasks and then turned to the assistants and helpers. "Track wires from there to there and there and there. Cables from there to there and there and there." Wait a minute! Those things have to go into a ditch. Dug by the lower echelon of the gang—us! Where's my meter? My wiring diagrams?

The awful truth sinks in, damn near everything in a signal system is connected to every other thing by wires, cables, multiple cables, buried anywhere from eighteen inches to three feet below the surface.

Furthermore, to avoid the wrath of the Roadmaster and Division Engineer, this plebian exercise must be carried out so that the ballast will not be contaminated with plain old dirt. Nor must the ditches alongside the track pose any hazard to train crews that might stop and work in the area. And the ground is hard! Countless trains pound the subgrade into a compactness totally out of character with the swampy surroundings.

An education in soil engineering and mechanics is assimilated in one percent of the time it would take at the University of Washington. To dig this deep, it has to be this wide. Pick through, then clean out. Ditch digging, like so many other tasks, has its own science.

Learn how to scoop and leverage the shovel over your knee. Move the dirt back far enough so that it doesn't cascade into the ditch when a train passes by. Damn, you even learn that the angle of the shovel blade to the handle makes a difference. Twenty years from now, I'll probably walk into a hardware store, and with a critical eye, reject a shovel as being "not right." A pick is not just a pick—the head has to be long and sharp and even the handle has to "be right."

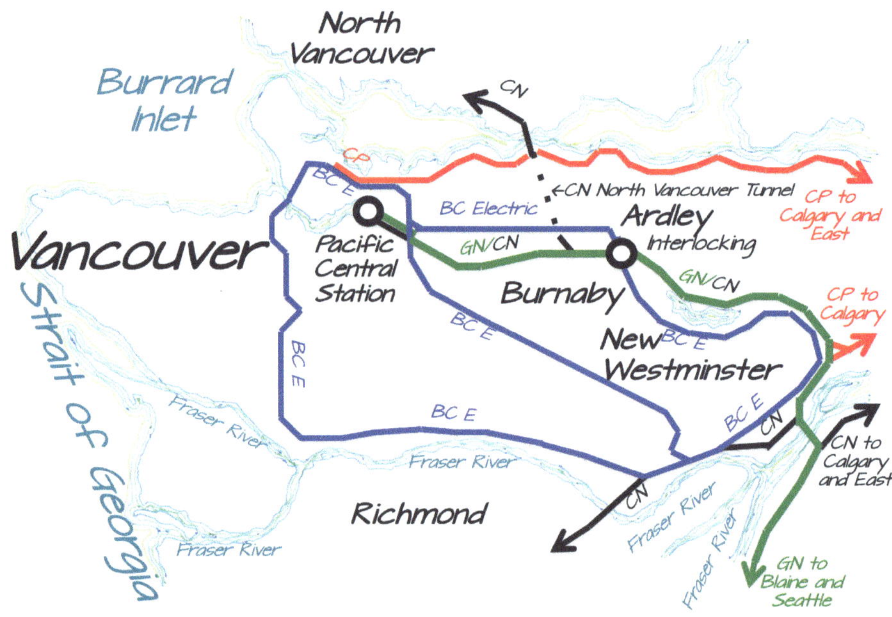

GN/BCE Ardley Interlocking and surrounding lines, circa 1955.
Map by David R. Clemens.

Of course, you can also use a pick handle to bat rocks (not ballast, Mr. Roadmaster) during the lunch break. Shovels dig trenches from signal cases and battery boxes to the bootlegs that complete the track circuits with their connections to the rails. Cables are buried to slide fences, high-water detectors, crossing signals, you name it. Particularly crossing signals.

Not only picks and shovels, but jack hammers are required to install the signal circuits across streets. The inevitable awakening—I've only traded one type of shovel for another. Although, a long-handled, spade shaped shovel is easier to use than the short-handled, square-bladed gandy variety. But—that's ditch digging—not tamping.

Daily we drive back and forth between Blaine and Burnaby, the major differentiation between each day's labor being a ditch across the tracks vs. a ditch alongside the tracks. The area really is a peat-bog, so some of the ditches become canals. Indeed, the entire right-of-way undulates under approaching trains. As the job progresses, the signalmen test, connect, and retest again the various circuits. Here are the meters and wiring diagrams, but they're not in my hands. My hands only fit shovels. The ultimate in shoveling will come when the gang buries several miles of underground cable in the slide areas along Puget Sound. Every day, the same old ditch, just a thousand feet farther down the track.

"Finally, Ardley Interlocking is no more..." On July 14, 1971, a westbound CN transcontinental passenger train goes through the crossovers as a BN southbound freight waits on double track for it to clear. The high voltage overhead transmission lines are on BC Electric's abandoned right of way and therefore mark the location of Ardley between the two trains. *Photograph by Mike Chandler.*

Finally, the Ardley Interlocking is no more and the gang moves to Mukilteo. The only change in my duties appears to be a trade of digging in peat to digging in clay as we install "mud" fences to detect slides in the bluffs along the track. But one thing is for sure—I'm in damn good physical shape! Even if I'm developing a permanent crouch and my feet are always one ahead of the other rather than side by side due to the narrowness of the ditch. When the summer is over, I'm going to pitch this shovel over the sea-wall or under a train and never touch one again!

Little do I know it, but before I'm through, I'll dig ditches at 10,000 feet, in swamps, in the ghettos of Chicago, under the blistering desert sun, in the Back Bay area of Boston, below sea-level along the Salton Sea, in ground frozen so hard that dynamite has to be used to start the hole. I'll dig along tracks and across tracks in the wheat fields of Kansas, the bayous of Louisiana, the Salt Lake valley, the corn fields of Iowa, the Berkshire Mountains, the Rocky Mountains, the Cascade Mountains, the Wasatch Mountains, the Blue Ridge Mountains. Cable will be buried on bridges and in tunnels, in sand, in water, in rock, in mud, in ice and snow, amid bugs and flies, accompanied by hostile canines and even more hostile humans. Ditches alongside the Atlantic, the Pacific, the Gulf, downtown and 250 miles from the nearest downtown; in forests, in canyons a thousand feet deep, alongside raging rivers, in orchards, behind steel mills, next to universities, at piers and at mines.

I'll get out of my ditch to watch the passing trains of the Great Northern, Northern Pacific, Rio Grande, Rock Island, New York Central, Boston & Albany. I'll highball the crews of the Southern, Norfolk & Western, Conrail, Southern Pacific, Burlington Northern, Union Pacific, Kansas City Southern, Grand Trunk Western, Illinois Central,

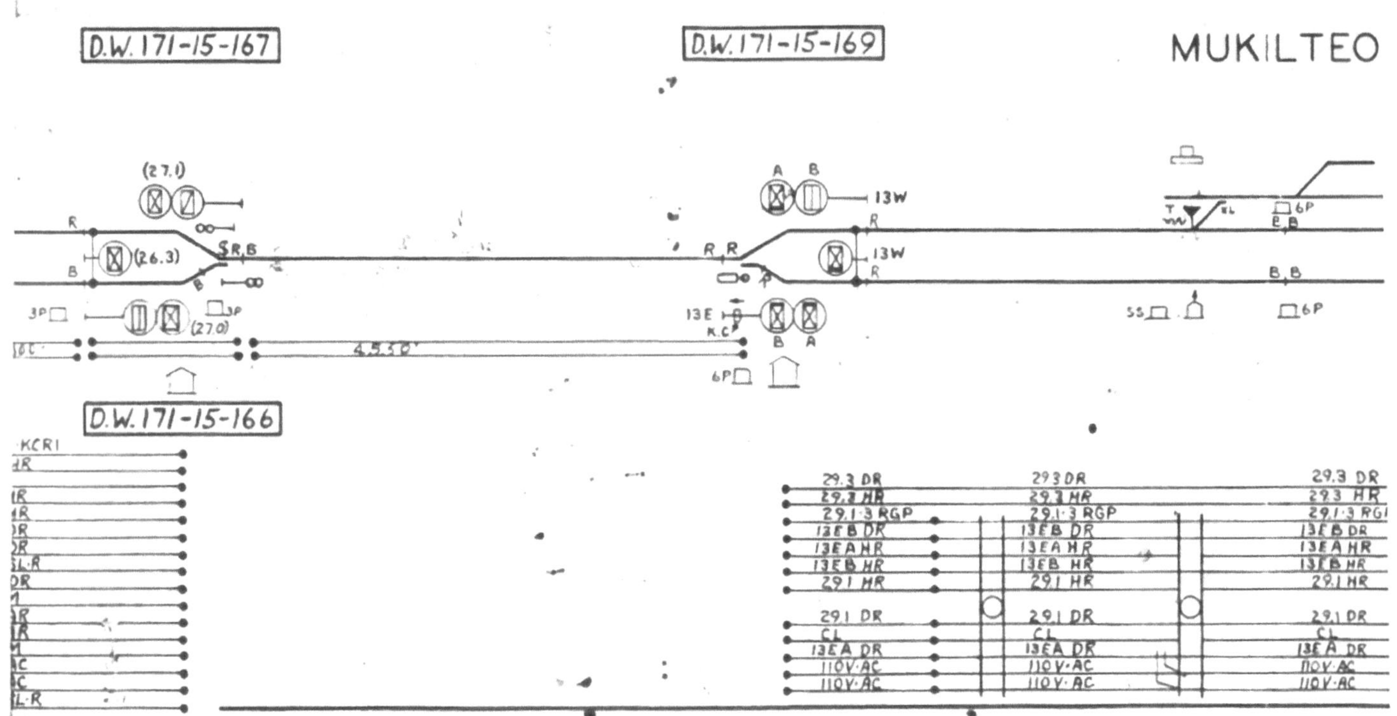

"A signal pole diagram from the Great Northern at Mukilteo, WA… very archaic circuitry… also 110v power, the line loss must've been horrendous! Between MP 27 and 28 the line is buried in a cable through the single track mud slide area." Mike McLaughlin, 8/19/1992. *Michael J. McLaughlin collection.*

Peoria & Pekin Union, Western Pacific, Missouri Pacific, Chicago & West Pullman, Boston & Maine, Sabine River & Northern, Utah, Santa Fe, Baltimore & Ohio, Nickel Plate, New Haven—an endless parade observed because my hands fit a shovel.

Oh sure, I'll trade my digging implements for the hooks and belt of a lineman, but line gangs also carry shovels—long ones for digging pole holes. Even as a management employee, I'll frequently pick up a shovel—and no union employee ever filed a grievance because I helped with the digging.

Have shovel, will travel.

1

LIFE ALONG THE TRACKS

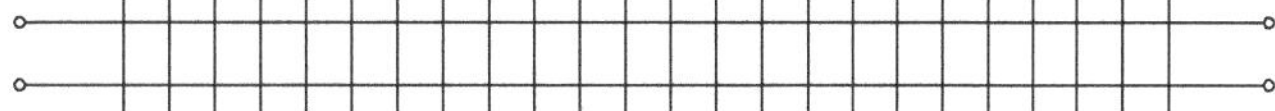

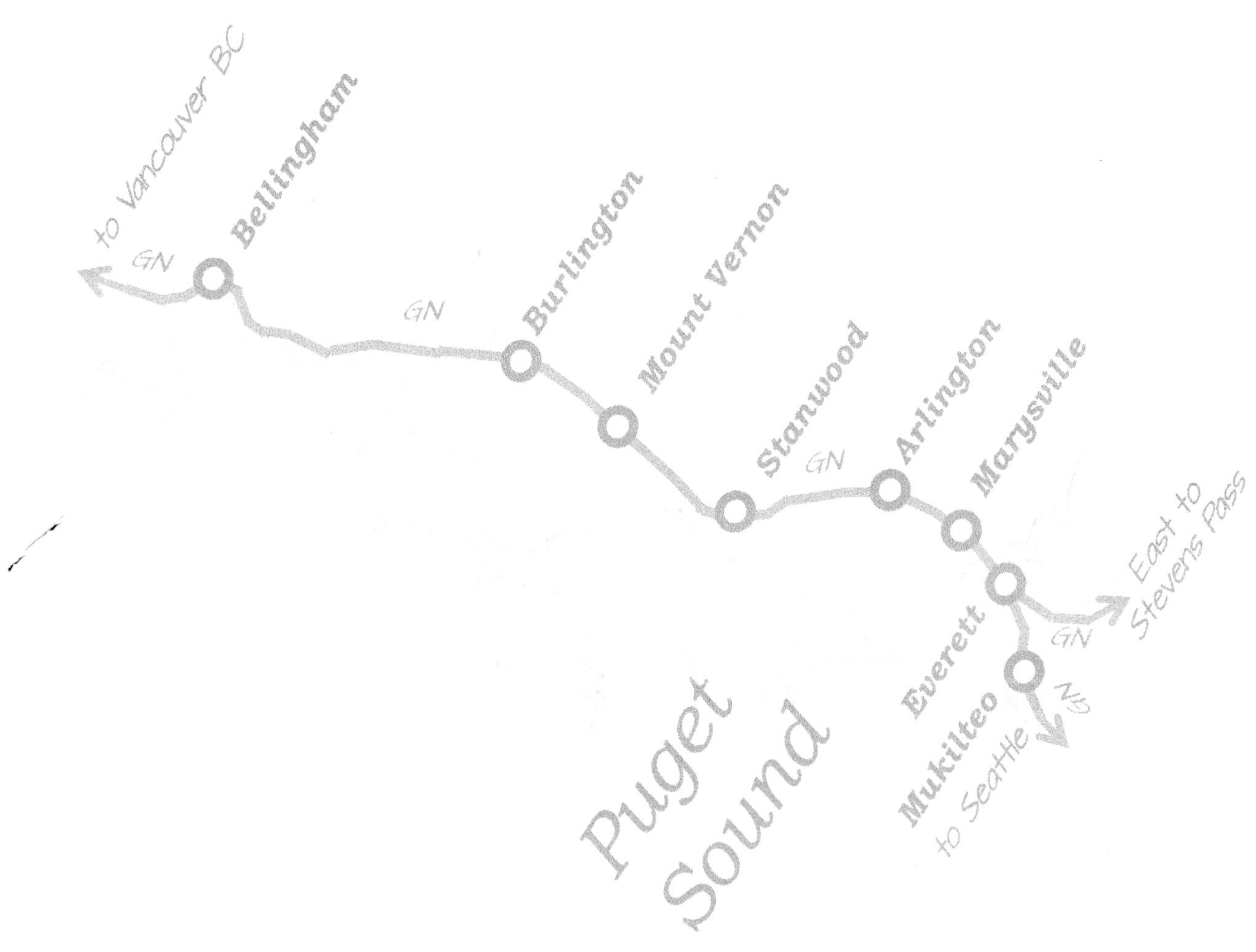
to Vancouver BC
GN
Bellingham
GN
Burlington
Mount Vernon
Stanwood
GN
Arlington
Marysville
East to
Stevens Pass
GN
Everett
Mukilteo
GN
to Seattle
Puget
Sound

Life Along the Tracks

Railroad gangs of all types live along the tracks in outfit cars, the members performing all the usual domestic duties and functions that other employees engage in, in the more normal habitats firmly anchored to concrete foundations—not merely mobile quarters placed temporarily on a spur waiting for the next moving day. Arrival after work, showers, either a meal prepared in the outfit or eaten "uptown" while "housekeeping" maintains a reasonable level of life style. Card games, reading, radio, even TV in some locations, then lights out until workday activities renew in the morning.

Whether in the mountains, along the seashore, in the city, desert or farm country, life along the tracks becomes addictive. Certain comforts are based on seniority: upper bunks are warmer in the winter, and if the windows are cut high in the side of the car, as cool as can be hoped for in the summer desert sun. Signalmen are closer to the stove—but not too close—than helpers. Other aspects of outfit life are dealt out on a more random basis. The spur is on a grade, and so the foot-cupboard becomes a low clearance head cupboard. Last week's view of the Sound on the beach side becomes next week's vista of urban industry with an intervening mainline. No matter what the circumstances, it "averages out" and the occupants enjoy, accept—or abandon forever, scarcely remembered—the regimen imposed by a railroad career in the more mobile, away-from-home ranks.

There are people who equate living "by the tracks" with being within a couple of blocks, half a mile, or even viewing across a broad valley, the mainline, a branch line, or—depending upon mentality—within hearing distance of a twice-weekly switching secondary. A railroader living along the tracks can literally reach out of an outfit side door and touch a passing train. A spur holding bunk cars may only be fifteen feet from the mainline, or it may be located with an intervening siding or yard tracks, but everything from hotshots to switch cuts to engine terminal movements are a part of bunk car existence.

TThe run-of-the-mill populace considers trains passing by as noise—to railroaders and others along the tracks, passing trains are a way of life. Routine, accepted, noticed when wanted to be noticed, ignored when other activities or sleep take precedence. It is the abnormal that suddenly attracts attention. A train stops instead of passing, the rattle of wheels over a break in a rail—people living along the tracks become acutely attuned to the sounds that herald entertainment, overtime, or even disaster.

A track supervisor bunks down three nights a week in the rooming house/beanery at Thistle and prefers the trackside, west ("railroad direction") corner room on the second floor. The Zephyr, hotshots, the Marysvale branch Salina Turn, Utah Railway drags, dead freights, unit train loads and empties pass by without disturbing his slumber. Suddenly, in the middle of the night, a westbound stops on the compound 7½-8-6 degree curve in front of the depot. The track supervisor immediately awakens, puts on the minimum clothing requirement, and runs downstairs to the telegraph operator's office where the third trick op informs him that a half-frozen hobo had been sighted on a TTX flat.

A signal gang outfit sits on a spur between the Rock Island roundhouse and the Blue Island commuter branch in that same suburb of Chicago. Between the "dummies" carrying suburbanites from and to the city, and all the noises of the freight yard, engine house, and turntable/ready tracks, it would seem that the occupants of the bunk cars would find it impossible to sleep, yet it is only the early morning yells of the cook that awakens them. Another signal gang has its cars parked on a spur in Hidvale, Utah adjacent to one leg of the Bingham Branch wye and junction, alongside the mainline, and with a major arterial street crossing the tracks. Trains inbound to Roper Yard or eastbounds from the UP–WP–SP interchanges slam past, whistles blaring the standard --o- grade crossing warning, the crossing gate bells clang, and the gang members sleep through the clamor.

A third gang is situated less than a train length south of the Canadian border at Blaine, Washington. Every southbound freight train stops for customs inspection alongside. Car doors being slid—forced—swung open and slammed back, accompanied by vocal descriptions of the cars' contents. The gang sleeps through these sounds and those of ships, foghorns, and even the siren at the customs house a part of daily existence. However, all of these men are aware of their location, attuned to the railroad operations near, next to, or surrounding them, and if questioned, would vehemently deny that there is any positive aesthetic quality involved in their lifestyle.

But railroading once absorbed in the blood will not out. Two businessmen request rooms "on the fourth floor at the back" over the recommendations of the desk clerk — they want to observe the activity on the MOP yard leads in Ft. Worth. A vacationing family "happens" to find itself in a motel backing up to the NP mainline in Bismarck, ND. A section foreman lives between the mainline and the Aspen Branch in Glenwood Springs. Railroaders, ex-railroaders, or just those who like railroading find their ways to reside along the tracks, for a night, a season, a lifetime, or in more than one location, forever in a cemetery next to the right-of-way.

Blizzards in Chicago or Buffalo, heat ranging from the high, dry desert to the bayous of Louisiana, tornados, hurricanes, avalanches, dust storms, floods—and unbelievable nights under Rocky Mountain skies, vistas of green-clad islands in Puget Sound, a mainline arrowing through Iowa corn fields, commuter trains arriving precisely on schedule: railroading attracts its people who have lived, live, or want to live along the tracks.

This photo of Black River Junction on the Pacific Coast is looking south, with Mount Rainier in the background. It's the view I had looking out my apartment window the first three months I was living in the Renton area. Little did I know that Renton and these tracks would lead to a life-long friendship with Mike McLaughlin.

The UP/ex-MILW joint track is crossing the BN/ex-NP right under the locomotives. What appears to be a turnout is in fact a moving points crossover because of the extremely skewed angle. Photographer Dave Houston is standing on the PC/UP/Milwaukee right-of-way heading north for Van Asselt. The line going left is the PC through Renton and out to Maple Valley. MILW's Black River Yard is around the corner 200 yards to the left. Behind the interlocking equipment shed, forming the third leg of the wye, the Milwaukee swung from the PC across the BN ex-NP headed south for Tacoma.

I would park near the yard and watch westbound MILW trains set-out Seattle-bound cars in Black River Yard. After putting their train back together, they would continue around the south leg of the wye, cross the BN, and proceed to Tacoma. The Seattle-bound cars were picked up by a Transfer Crew out of Stacy Street Yard, who brought with them Seattle traffic for an eastbound train to pick-up. The Transfer would take the Seattles back to Stacy Street.

My apartment was on the bluff right above the yard. But there was no way to see directly through all of the heavy vine maple and alder foliage. I could hear them working the middle of the day or in the middle of the night, but couldn't see trains from my balcony. But boy could I see Rainier, and on a sunny day, it was magic.

Dave Clemens

In the post-Burlington Northern merger era of the 1970s, the BN and Southern Pacific developed run-through trains between the SP's major yard at Eugene, Oregon, and the BN in Seattle. Nearing the end of its run here is run-through symbol LAS, running as BN 112, at Black River Junction in 1980. 1980 was also the "end of the run" for the Milwaukee Road in the West. *Photograph by David Houston.*

Outfits

No, not what one wears, or how one equips himself for an expedition, but rather what one lives in when working out on-line for the railroad.

An outfit is usually a collection of old revenue cars—both passenger and freight—converted to sleeping, cooking, shower, supply, tool, storage, and machinery transport use. An outfit can be one lone car for a signal helper assigned to follow a steel gang, or the multitude of cars belonging to the rail gang itself. Welders, communications gangs, machine operators, B&B gangs, water service, signal gangs, rail/tie/surfacing gangs, and anyone else required to be away from home during the work week have outfits. They range from the elegant, to the acceptable, to the barely passable, to unspeakable roach boxes. They are found alongside the mainline, tucked away in yards, in the middle of cities, and at locations so remote that the railroad itself is the only access.

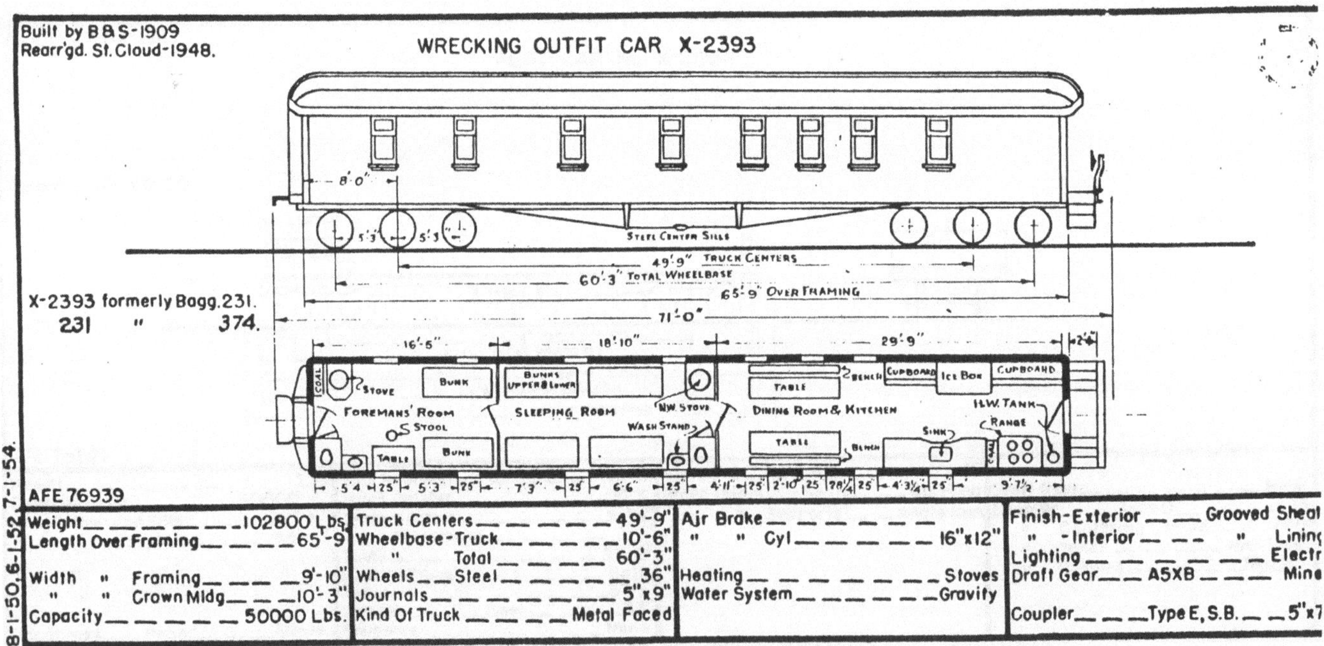

Diagram of GN outfit car combining Foreman's room, sleeping quarters, dining room and kitchen. *GN Work Equipment Diagrams, Vol 2, 12-1- 1956, PRNArchive collection at Burien, WA.*

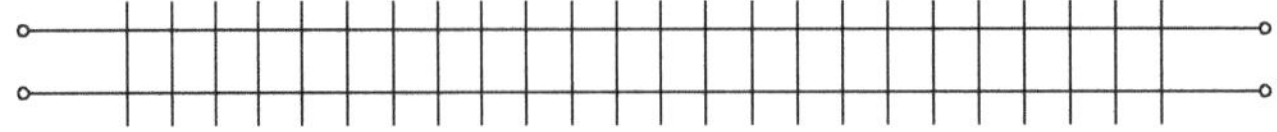

GN outfit 03266. The blanked-out arched windows and clerestory roof speak to a more elegant past life.
Photograph by Dan Perkins. DRP003-070, PNRArchive collection at Burien, WA.

Generally speaking, signal gang outfits are a cut above the ordinary. But they vary, from railroad to railroad, and gang to gang. Signal gang #17 on the Great Northern had quarters that could only be described as elegant. The bunk car was a converted Pullman with a foreman's office / bedroom at one end and individual bunks for the men with cupboards and foot lockers, even reading lights. The kitchen car was another ex-passenger car with a dining area, propane stove and refrigerator, hot water heater, and cooks' quarters. The shower car was a more plebeian wooden ex-boxcar, but with two showers, coal stove/hot water heater, and lines for drying work clothes. These cars were painted two-tone green inside and were kept spotless. The bunk and kitchen cars were heated by oil stoves, and all windows were screened against the Northwest's flying insect population. The kitchen car was equipped with serviceable heavy china and all the necessary pots, pans, cutlery, and silverware.

Water for the outfit was provided by an old steam locomotive tender body mounted on a flat car. Coal for the shower car was kept in the obvious location, while the opposite end of the car extending beyond the tender had low sides for storing signal masts, ladders, and other paraphernalia. The balance of the outfit was several old wooden boxcars converted to tool and storage cars. Work benches, storage bins, and other conveniences were installed in the interiors. Small windows were supplemented in the more important cars by connection to the bunk car's electrical system.

At the other end of the spectrum of Great Northern outfits was a single boxcar assigned to a signal helper following a steel gang. Storage area at one end, the "living quarters" consisted of an army surplus steel bunk, a coal stove, table and chair, a water can, an enamel wash basin, sink/cupboard without water, and nails driven into the wall for clothes hooks. Lighting was by kerosene lamps, or one long extension cord.

Signal gang #3 on the D&RGW was an "extra" gang with an appropriately "extra" outfit. A couple of typical tool / equipment / storage cars, and two living cars. The gang car was an old, small wooden boxcar converted by adding windows and replacing the boxcar doors with normal house-size doors. The interior was a series of double-deck, army-style bunks, and a coal stove. Lighting was kerosene lamps until an assistant signalman "wired" it over a long weekend with twisted pair and drop lights. The second habitat was the foreman's car which contained an office, bedroom, and center area with coal stove/water heater, kitchen and shower, plus a dining table and benches. This was a somewhat more modern car, higher, still wood-sided but

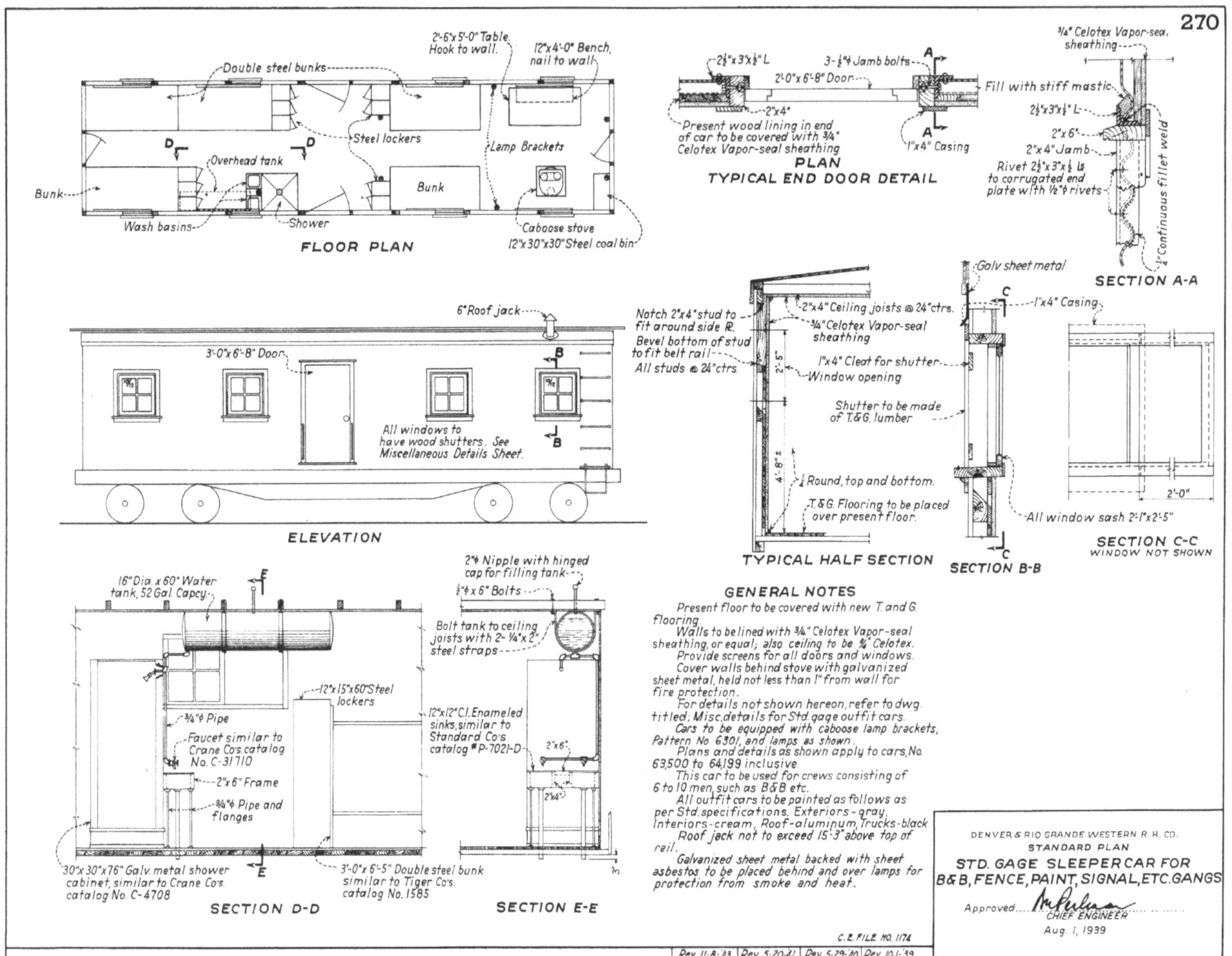

D&RGW plan for standard gauge outfit sleeper car, 1939. Michael J. *McLaughlin collection.*

with dreadnought steel ends. As with all converted boxcars, access to the side doors was through portable wooden steps that were hung off the door sills and hopefully reached the ground at a reasonable angle.

Now signal gang #2 on the Grande was a 'permanent' gang and its outfit displayed a more substantial position in the signal department hierarchy. The bunk car was an ex-army steel troop sleeper with Allied "full cushion" trucks. The inside contained an also-ex-army, coal fired space heater, shower stall, and several double-deck, government-surplus bunks. While the bunk car was only marginally superior to gang #3's accommodations, gang #2 had a full-fledged kitchen car with a coal stove large enough to feed a complete steel gang. Sinks, hot water tank with its contents heated by coils in the stove, refrigerator, and electrical wiring designed rather than added-on completed the amenities. Most winter nights, the gang sat around the dining table, playing cards, arguing, and bitching about all the past-present-and-future grievances imposed upon them by an uncaring management. One of the tool cars usually held a fresh strung-up venison; life is at least acceptable in bunk cars along the Colorado River.

The Rock Island, in common with many other Class I railroads, provided accommodations varying from "okay" to "why did I take this job?" A dilapidated old bunk car and the associated tool cars housed a signal gang in Kansas. Converted from a one-time first-class passenger car, the bunk car had fallen on hard times. The unprepossessing exterior was matched by the neglected interior—the occupants only

D&RGW steel gang outfit cars—former WWII troop sleepers—in Monument, CO.
Photograph by Chuck Conway.

interested in the next long weekend. However, the big gang at Blue Island in Chicago occupied living quarters that were cleaner and more organized; it is a product of "economy of scale." When a gang has 23 members, a full-time cook, and a flunky or two—bull cooks—can be justified to provide minimum domestic services. As the size of the "gang" degenerates to "crew" to "signalman and assistant," the quarters also diminish to the barely acceptable boxcar to a tiny trailer parked by a depot.

But elegant or disreputable outfits have been disparaged—even reviled—by generations of railroad employees, and simultaneously remembered as living quarters aesthetically unsurpassed. Time, season, and labors all color gang members' recollections of their temporary domiciles, but few would trade their past or present railroad car habitats for a life that had never known moving day as a local switcher rather than a Mayflower moving van.

The temperature remains stuck below freezing, attested to by the icicles formed along the sides of the string of Canadian Pacific outfit cars at Yoho, BC, "a location so remote that the railroad itself is often the only access." The silhouettes of the engineer and fireman in the warm cab of CP SD40-2 5952 stand in sharp contrast to the working conditions of the occupants of the outfits. *Photograph by Mike Chandler.*

Moving Day—GN

CRASH!!!

The Omaha-orange-and-Pullman-green geep couples into the maroon outfit at the extreme north end of Mukilteo. It's moving day for signal gang #17 and the "Oiler" will take the cars into Delta Yard at Everett where they will be put on a train for Bellingham. One signalman is in the bunk car and—knowing that sleep is now impossible—he dresses and walks back to the crummy to talk to the train crew

The Oiler moves swiftly along the shore of Puget Sound only to be held at Everett Junction while a long freight moves off the Vancouver line onto double track. Soon the local is threading its way past the myriad paper plants and lumber mills, the rank odor of pulp processing overriding the smells of the harbor. Through the interlocking at Delta Junction and onto the lead, the short train comes to a halt in Delta Yard. Immediately three more members of the signal gang climb on the outfit and greet the man already aboard. The quartet will ride to Bellingham on the cars while the balance of the gang, who will be commuting by automobile, finishes a small job near Stanwood.

Soon an SW8 pulls the outfit off the yard track and backs through Delta Jct. to Long Siding where it is placed on the rear of the pick-up spotted for Second 7ll, the next northbound freight. The gang members spend the waiting time observing the activity at the lumber mills and making a last-minute inspection of their "home."

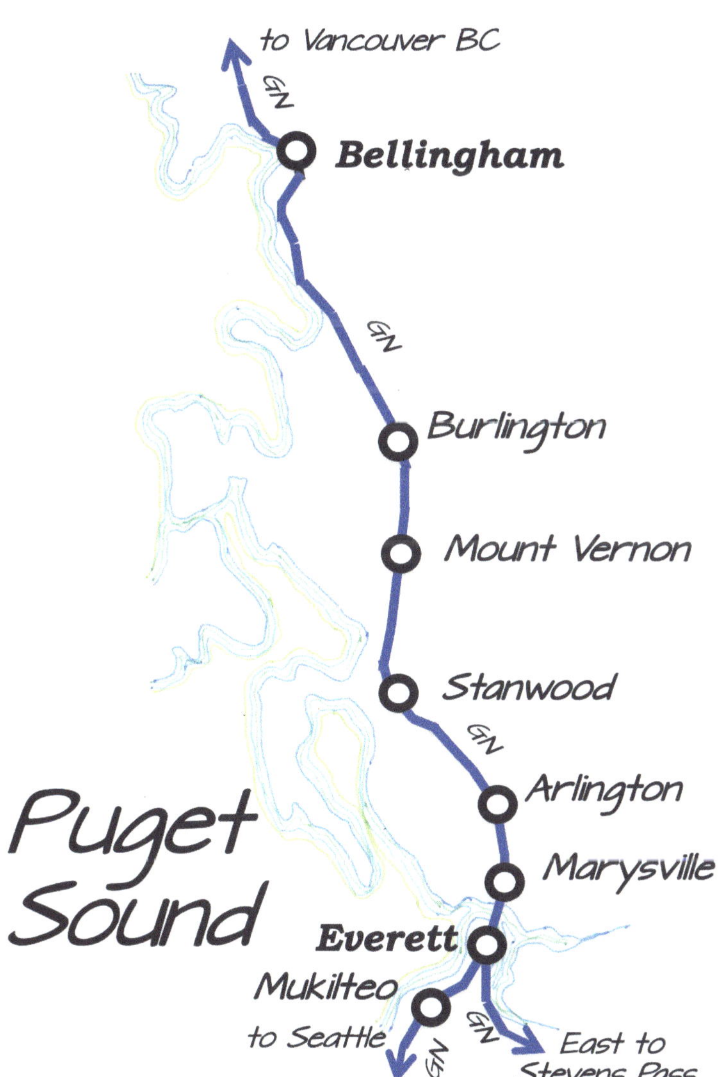

Great Northern RR—Mukilteo to Bellingham. *Map by David R. Clemens.*

Finally, the sound of an air horn blowing for the succession of street crossings on the Everett waterfront announces the approach of 2nd 7ll. A trio of typically Great Northern F-3's grinds to a halt on the mainline. The road freight crew's disgust upon sighting the signal gang consist is as vocal as it is justified: instead of merely making a normal pick-up with the cut being placed on the head end, the outfit—stenciled "rear end only"—must be cut in ahead of the caboose.

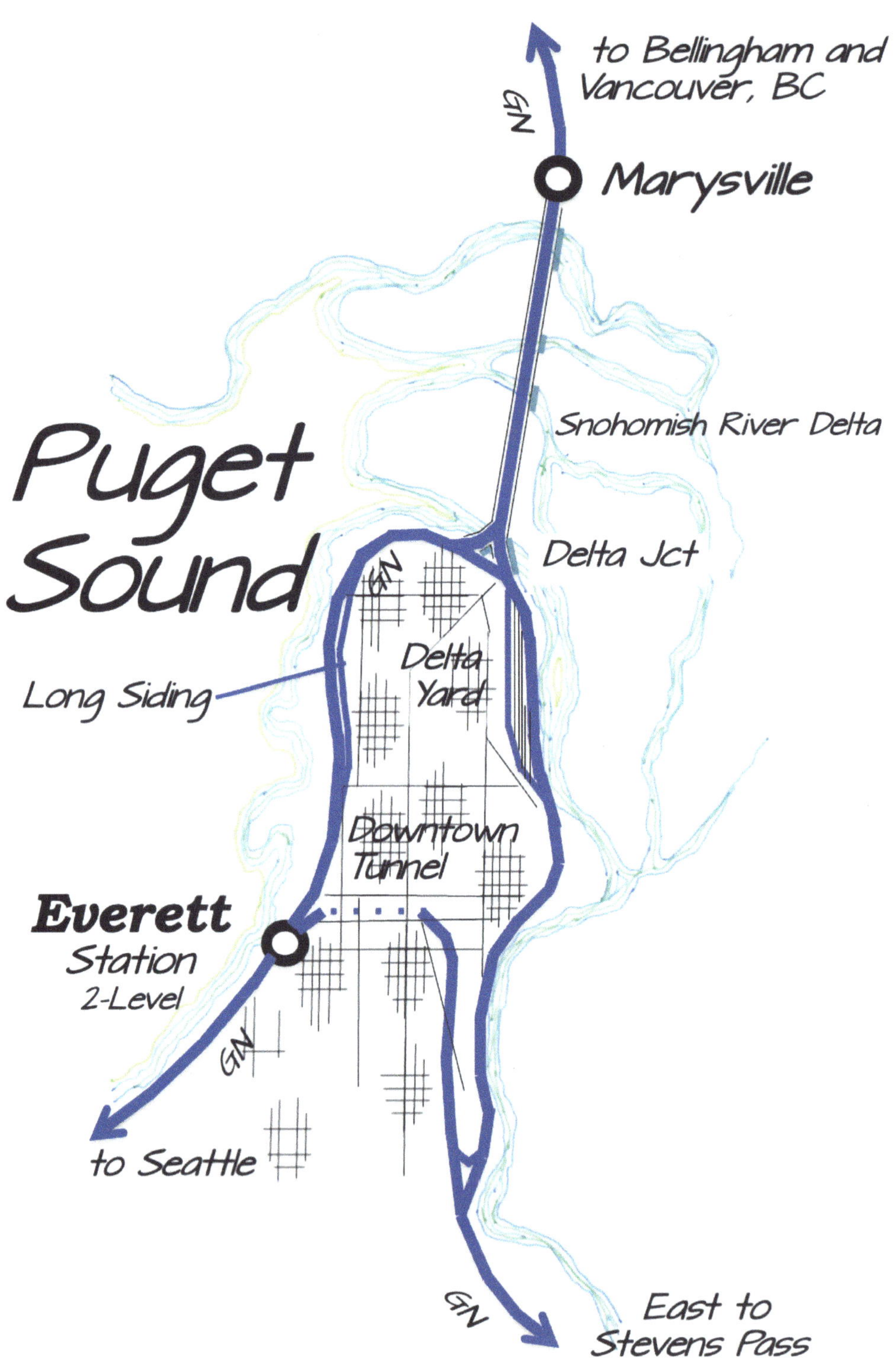

GN Everett Yards and Delta Junction. *Map by David R. Clemens.*

Work completed; the F's start the freight with the rolling crash of slack running out until the hack leaps forward in instant acceleration. Curving north through Delta Jct., 2nd 711 clatters over the NP crossing and onto the first of three swing bridges over the various channels of the Snohomish River. The waterways are lined with log rafts, raw material for the huge Weyerhaeuser mills. Although the line is laid with heavy steel supported by solid rock ballast from the Belleville pit north of Burlington, the speed is held to 20 mph in deference to the draw spans. At last, a radioed highball indicates that the rear end has cleared the final bridge at Marysville and the northbound freight picks up speed through the western Washington farmland.

Outfit car GN 03106, a former heavyweight observation, at Delta Yard, April 1971. *Photograph by Dan Perkins. DRP011-066, PNRArchive collection at Burien, WA.*

The green fields are dusted by the passage of the train as it approaches Stanwood. In the outfit, the gang members make preparations for greeting the balance of their crew. All water faucets are opened and pots are filled in the kitchen car. As the freight bears down on the signal location being worked by their compatriots, the men stand in the side doors with their water containers. Shouts, laughter, and flying water from the doors and the drains beneath the outfit greet the men on the ground. Congratulating themselves on a magnificent bit of chicanery, the signalmen decide to reward themselves with popcorn made in a roasting pan on the gas stove. The first attempt ends in disaster, the pan full of nearly-popped corn flipping to the floor as slack runs in when the freight brakes for Mount Vernon. Undaunted, the crew fills another pan and the white kernels on the floor are swept out onto the right-of-way. Soon the kitchen car is the scene of high hilarity as popcorn and cokes are consumed amid much laughter over the highly successful water episode at Stanwood.

As the train grinds to a halt in Burlington, two of the men swing down to watch the train crew at work. During the activity No. 359, the southbound Noon International, flashes past on its way to Seattle. Set-outs and pick-ups completed, Second 7ll clatters over the 6th subdivision crossing and moves across the fields toward the shoreline. Curving along the base of the Chuckanut Cliffs, the train skirts the beaches of Puget Sound. In the outfit, the gang members sit in the open doorway on the west side, absorbed by the view of the green islands spotted on the sparkling blue salt water. Through two short tunnels and back along the shore, the F-3's move their tonnage north. The train crosses a small bay on a rock fill and proceeds through a curved tunnel, then slows for South Bellingham. The men catch a brief glimpse of the spur that will be their home for the next few weeks.

The freight reduces speed and bangs over the NP crossing and then the wheels rattle across the two Milwaukee diamonds at the south end of their yard. An orange-and-black switcher waits on the car float lead for the Big G to clear. As the caboose moves past, a switchman swings the gates and work resumes. High above the yard, the Chicago road's engine terminal is flanked by the even higher NP line crossed earlier. A third CMStP&P crossing, leading to the Georgia-Pacific mill, is crossed and a fourth, also protected by gates, is negotiated as Second 711 passes the depot and stops just south of Pine Street. The Bellingham set-out is cut off the head end and, after dropping it in the yard, the road engine moves down to pluck the outfit from the rear end.

The signalmen watch as their cars are added to an industrial job that will return them to South Bellingham. It soon becomes apparent that their new crew not only isn't on the job; it hasn't even been called. Assured that no move will be made before six PM, the men wander uptown. As they return, they express profane thanks that their new location will be far to the south of the G-P pulp mills and their sulfurous odors. A green-and-orange switcher couples onto the train made up in the yard and, air pumped up, moves south. A halt in front of the depot as the Milwaukee Sumas Turn blocks the crossing at the north end of that road's yard and, in motion again, the industrial job continues along the shore.

Arriving at South Bellingham, the outfit is spotted on the "chain spur" and the gang members start to hook up the lights. Observing their efforts, the switch foreman advises them not to make any permanent connections. It seems that the log chain factory that gives the spur its name is switched three or four times a week, requiring moving the bunk cars each time. Glumly, the men consider the inevitable chaos resulting from each switch, acknowledging that relief will not be obtained until the next moving day.

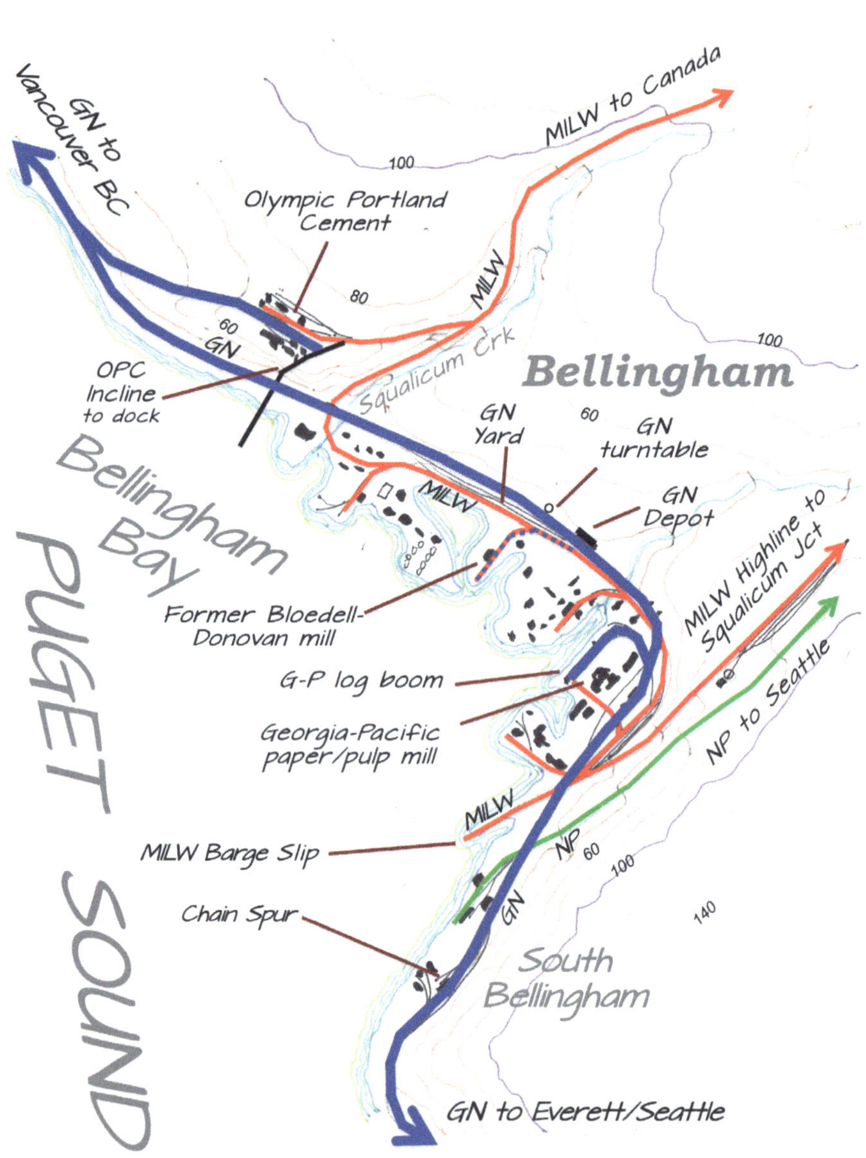

The Bellingham spaghetti bowl. *Map by David R. Clemens.*

Moving Day—D&RGW

Three silver D&RGW outfit cars, Plainview, CO. *Photograph by Philip R. Hastings, Philip Ross Hastings, MD, collection, California State Railroad Museum.*

CRASH!!!

The three silver cars comprising the signal gang outfit roll off the hump at Grand Junction and come to an abrupt halt against the cut already in bowl seven. Cries of anguish fill the night air as the inhabitants of the bunk car express their displeasure at such cavalier treatment. The crew has finished a minor pole line repair job at Grand Valley and is on its way to the next project, extension of the local CTC at Soldier Summit to include Kyune and Gilluly. The FM switcher-and-slug set grinds down through the retarders, couples into the cars, and growls back up the hump. With the cut hanging over the crest, slack runs in and then jerks out as the hump engine builds the westbound extra. The crummy is tacked on and one of the signalmen asks a switchman how big their train is. Upon being informed that they have the dubious honor of bringing up the rear of 105 cars of dead freight, the signalman groans and comments that "dead" will probably be an apt description of the bunk car's occupants by morning.

Air test completed, the carmen take down the blue flags, slack runs out with a crash, the train threading through the power switches at Tenth Street and around the curve next to the ice house. Past the station, then the stockyards at Durham, the F-units on the head end roar as they attempt to accelerate out of town. The rear end surges through the sag at Rhone and then rolls easily past the depot at Fruita. In the dark interior of the bunk car, the men lie in their bunks, grimly holding the sides as the outfit pitches first one way and then another. Brake shoes grind against wheel treads and the drag heads into the clear at Mack. Number 8, the eastbound Prospector, slams past. Two sharp blasts from the engine and the approaching thunder of slack running out causes the men to brace themselves, an action that they will have to perform all too often through the night ahead. Curving through Ruby tunnel, the smell of diesel exhaust enters the open windows. Soon the train is following the Colorado River, winding continuously through the red rock canyon. Again, the familiar braking action as the main line is cleared at Utaline. This time the wait is lengthy before an eastbound rumbles past. The dispatcher, knowing that the drag was too long for the siding at Westwater, has decided not to risk the delay that would undoubtedly occur climbing Cottonwood hill.

The Grand Junction hump yard: D&RGW 5304, an SD9, is working as the hump engine in October 1979. *Photograph by Chuck Conway.*

Picking up speed, the extra returns to the main line and continues down the river. At the west end of Westwater the tracks turn away from the Colorado and start climbing into the desert. The chant of 567's fills the land as the units struggle up to old Cottonwood. Speed down to a walk, the train crests the grade at the site of the siding the gang had helped remove earlier in the summer. Slack slams in, adding to the chaos in the outfit. Past Agate and slack runs out as 105 cars snake around some rock outcroppings and start the climb to Cisco. The sound of a diesel horn drifts back as the engineer blows for the highway crossing. The faded yellow paint of the Cisco station is briefly illuminated by the headlight. Again, brakes are felt as the mainline is cleared at Whitehouse.

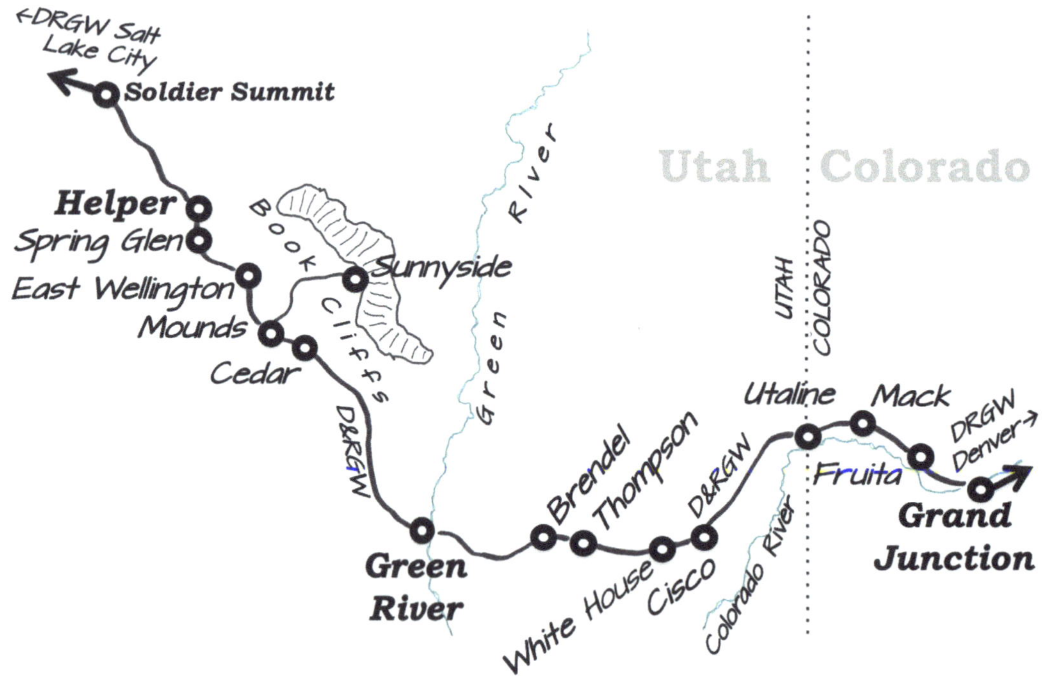

D&RGW: Grand Junction, Colorado to Soldier Summit, Utah. *Map by David R. Clemens.*

The signalmen drop off to sleep, only to be awakened as #7 crashes past in the night. With the familiar clash of couplers, Extra 5502 West grinds out of the pass as the dwarf blinks from red to amber. The next signal will have turned to green long before the drag reaches it. Elba and Sagers are passed as the grade holds forward motion to a walking speed. In the cab the ammeter is in the red and the odor of hot traction motors becomes noticeable before a series of sharp curves near Vista is negotiated and the grade levels at Thompson. Descending again on the roller coaster grade, the train rambles through Brendel. The stars shine brilliantly in the desert sky as the long freight rumbles across the Green River bridge and into the siding in front of the brick depot.

The silver bunk car is quiet, occupants sleeping as the train crew walks up town to eat in an all-night cafe. A passing train, then once again the extra west is in motion. Dawn breaks across the land, the Book Cliffs to the north a contrast of yellow highlights and purple shadows. A man in the bunk car gets groggily to his feet and stumbles to the side door where he stands in his shorts until he realizes that the highway at this point is only a few yards from the tracks.

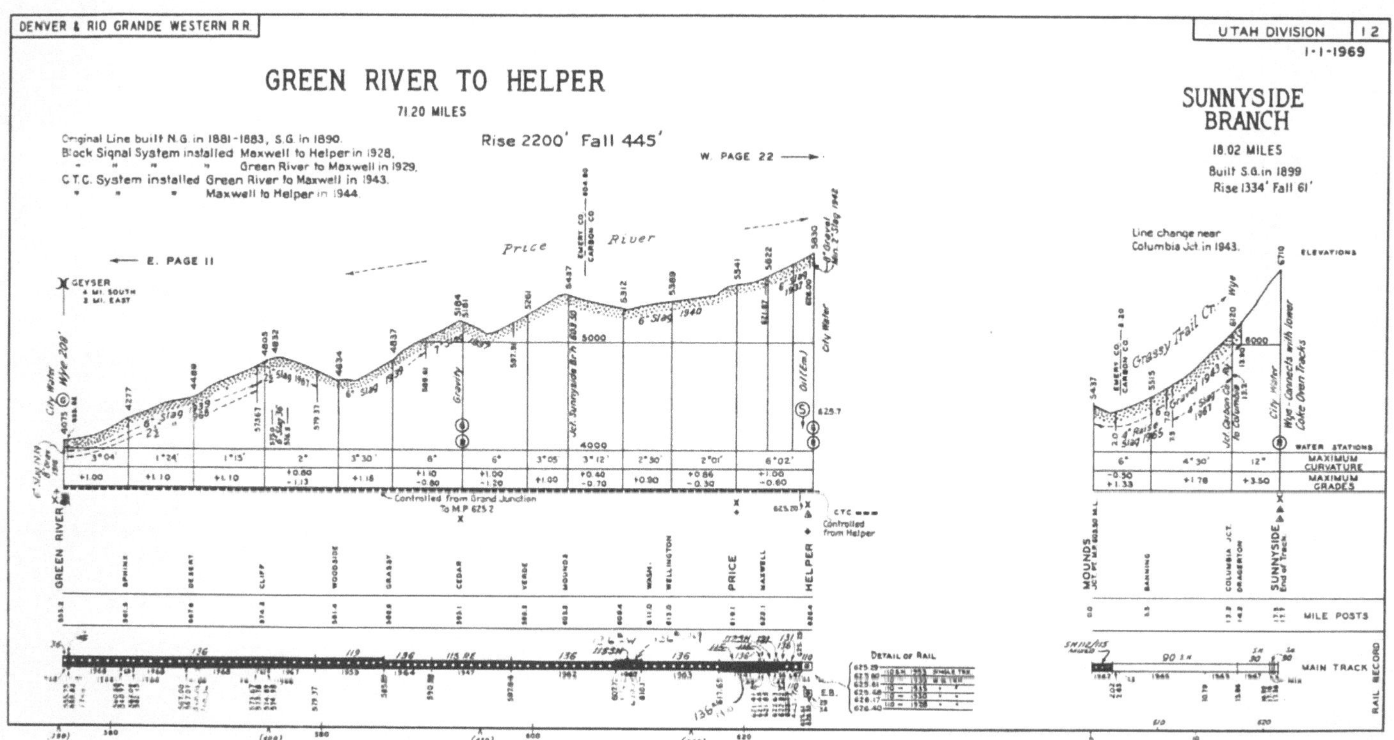

D&RGW 1969 track chart, Green River to Helper. *Michael J. McLaughlin collection.*

The long train crawls around the sharp curves and tips over the summit at Cedar. Although moving downgrade, the speed remains low as more curves cause the outfit to lurch from side to side. Up to Mounds, junction of the Sunnyside Branch, down to old Farnham, and up past the U.S. Steel coal washing plant at East Wellington. The inside of the bunk car is a shambles and the men are numb from lack of sleep and the incessant pounding they have received. At long last, the drag rattles through the switches at Spring Glen and, brake rigging clattering, comes to a halt in front of the Helper depot. Wearily the signalmen enter the brick building and ask the agent about their paychecks. He informs them that the gang is "supposed to be up at Summit," so that's where the checks are. The freight the men arrived on is to be switched and no other train is due for several hours. In ill humor from their long night ride, they demand to be paid immediately.

The roadmaster overhears their loud complaints and offers a ride to Soldier Summit in the back of a truck. Soon men and luggage are climbing the east slope of the Wasatch Mountains, high above the main line. The truck driver bounces down a dirt road and stops next to the station. Inside, the operator dispenses pay checks and, humor restored, the men inquire about eastbound trains.

Being informed that an SPF is approaching and will cut out its helper just west of the depot, the gang troops out to board the caboose as the hotshot comes to a halt. One member, whose father is a signal maintainer at Soldier Summit, will stay behind. The rest, it being Friday, will return home to Grand Junction, their starting point some fifteen hours earlier.

Moving Day—CRI&P

CRASH!!!

"What the..."

Oh, yeah, it's "moving day." Today is Saturday and, work done, your signal gang is being moved from Belleville, Kansas to Omaha. The rest of the gang has gone home for the weekend. However, since you are from Seattle, you stay with the outfit. It will be a chance to observe the operations on this part of the Rock Island system and become more familiar with granger railroading.

Stumbling out on the platform of the coach-converted-to-a-bunk-car, you're greeted by the train crew picking you up. "Hell, if we'da known you were in there, we'da hit it harder." The tempo of the journey has been established. The agent had estimated departure for "about 8:30," but the local is two hours early. Or twenty-two hours late...

Chicago, Rock Island and Pacific outfit lettered RIMW 96181, photographed at Altoona, Iowa, while assigned to the "Steel Bridge" gang. It was converted to maintenance of way service from CRIP 2909, a 79-seat heavyweight coach built by Pullman in 1930. *Photographer unknown, Steven Hile collection.*

Two decrepit F units in fading maroon paint pull the outfit out of the back track and insert it in the train just ahead of the caboose. Following the air test, the slack runs out with a crash and the local leaves Belleville. You walk back to the crummy and climb up into the cupola at the conductor's invitation. The train struggles up the grade toward Munden with a surging notion as the speed drops and finally forward progress comes to a halt. Cursing, the conductor and brakeman descend to double the hill.

After picking up a couple of cars at the Co-op elevator at Munden and reassembling the train, the local rambles across the Kansas countryside. Another pickup at Mahaska and a meet with a westbound freight. You walk through the outfit to see how it's traveling and discover slack action is beginning to take its toll. Replacing belongings and closing locker doors, wandering through the cars, you wonder what is going to happen in the next 130 miles. Speed picks up on the downgrade and the cars lurch as they clatter across the "Q" crossing. Through Thompson without pausing, up a slight grade, and down to Fairbury, slowing for the UP crossing and finally coming to a halt by the depot, the local works its way into Nebraska.

Checking the time, you come to a quick decision—four hours, thirty-five miles… While the crew is setting out and picking up, a short trip across the street to a corner grocery nets provisions for what promises to be a long journey: a half case of beer, a loaf of bread, and assorted lunch meats. Hurrying back to the outfit proves to be a waste of energy as switching is still in progress. The UP cow-and-calf working in the adjoining yard provides a counterpoint to the Rock activity.

Finally, the two weary F's reassemble their train and pump up the air. Struggling out of town, the train grinds up the grade. Soon a surging motion becomes apparent and the crew prepares to double another hill. However, before the drag comes to a halt, it crests at Jansen and picks up speed. Plymouth: the order board is blinking an amber imperative and orders are picked up on the fly.

"Damn…" The conductor passes the flimsies to the flagman and yourself. The reason for his disgust is obvious: the local is ordered into the pass at De Witt to let 60 by. "Over tonnage and we go into the hole at the bottom of the grade." Maybe you should have picked up a full case of beer. Sure enough, after 60 roars by, the local struggles out of the siding and, the familiar surging getting more pronounced, barely makes Clatonia. Here the crew switches the elevator and doubles to Hallem. Once reassembled, the local heads downgrade and you make another tour of the outfit.

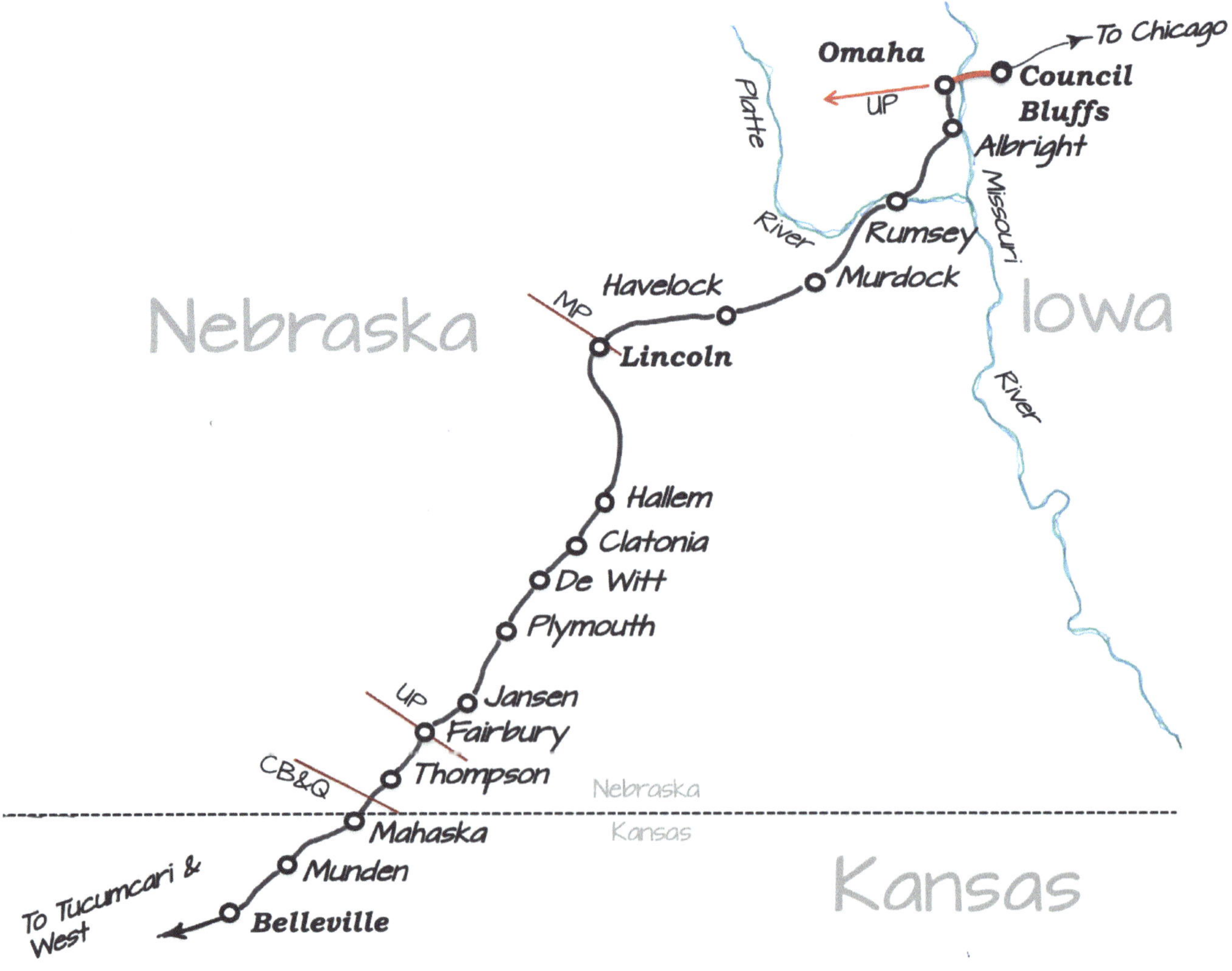

Chicago, Rock Island & Pacific across Nebraska. *Map by David R. Clemens.*

Surveying the mess, you make mental note that if you ever become a traffic manager, you'll never ship via a Rock Island local over this district! A couple of sandwiches and more beer and the train ambles into Lincoln threading through industrial and residential areas, crossing innumerable streets. Pulling into the yard, the air goes out with a finality that is mirrored by the conductors "We're gonna eat an' I don't care if we ever come back." However, after an hour passes, the men straggle back to their train.

Setouts and pickups made, the two disreputable EMD's drag their train out of town and clatter over the MOP crossing. Through Havelock and a roller-coaster ride to Murdock where more switching occurs. You open the beer purchased at Lincoln and it's getting dark outside. If this is typical "granger railroading..."

Bright sun light streams in the window and you immediately notice that the outfit is not moving. A glance outside reveals more Nebraska farmland and the mainline. While you wash and dress, a freight rumbles past and you reflect that your last memory before falling asleep the previous evening was of doubling yet another hill. Wandering into the caboose, you find no trace of the crew. Well, they're probably up at the head end switching. Listening, you discover all that is audible is the sound of a couple of idling 567's. Strolling up to the point, you pass a signboard reading "Rumsey." The two F's are devoid of personnel and, noting the absence of the reverse lever in the control stand, it's assumed that the crew "died" during the night and has been taken to some unknown place of rest. Well, they forgot one body.

Walking back along the tops of the cars, you note that whatever Rumsey is, it's not a town. Slowly the morning hours pass until voices interrupt the ubiquitous sound of birds and insects. The returning crew laughs about your abandonment and the local lurches out of the pass. Up one more hill and down into Albright, the destination for the outfit. However, the train goes through, picking up clearance on the fly.

The conductor explains that all switching in the South Omaha district is done by crews out of Council Bluffs, so you'll have to go there and then backtrack 10 miles. The local clatters across the UP diamond and negotiates the turnout onto the UP double main line. Through the stockyards and up the hill. Soon the surging of an incipient stall is felt and, once again, the local comes to a halt. This time however, help is immediately procured from a UP transfer run immediately behind. Boosted over the hump by the yellow and gray units, the local moves down through the depot and out onto the massive bridge over the Missouri River while the crew discusses the merits of a claim for additional pay based on the UP transfer's help. Undoubtedly, the UP crew is making similar computations.

Slowly the train moves past the UP icing dock and into Council Bluffs. Through the junction and into the yard, the local grinds to a halt. You wearily plan on further delays in the return to Albright but the arrival of a GP7 behind the crummy brings about the first purposeful movements in your journey. In short order the outfit is switched onto the South Omaha transfer and the terminal crew pulls out back over the bridge into Nebraska. Passing through the station, they move swiftly back down the hill to South Omaha. Threading through the stockyards and packing plants, your train moves back onto Rock Island rails and up the hill to the CRI&P depot.

At long last the faded orange cars are spotted on the house track below the J. Neils packing house and across the main from the blood processing plant. A brief glance at the employee timetable confirms that the journey you have just made in something like 38 hours is covered by #8, the Rocky Mountain Rocket, in just 2 hours, 24 minutes. As you drag out the twisted pair and hook up the outfit lights to the nearest signal case, the rest of the gang arrives, back from their weekend. "Hey, haven't you got the power hooked up yet? What you been doin' for two days?"

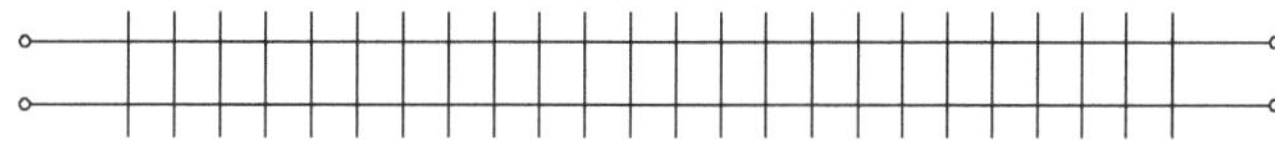

The Stove

Few people on the passing trains realize the battle for survival engaged in by the occupants of the gray bunk car seen so briefly on the spur at Dotsero in the Colorado Rockies

The evening's warfare begins with the arrival of the motor car carrying the signal gang back to the snow-covered outfit after a day of installing CTC on the cutoff. With some trepidation, the men open the side door and confront the malignant organism lurking in the center of the car, known darkly as The Stove.

The Stove sits quietly, awaiting the battle... At first, a direct frontal assault is attempted; wood, coal and kerosene being dumped into the battered interior of what was once merely a surplus army space heater. A match is thrown in, a ball of flame belches into the room, a cloud of black smoke fogs the outfit, and the fire goes out.

D&RGW Denver to Glenwood Springs. Dotsero was the western and Bond the eastern junction of the Dotsero Cutoff linking the Rio Grande's Pueblo–Grand Junction main with the former Denver & Salt Lake line, providing the railroad with a more direct Denver–Salt Lake City route. *Map by David R. Clemens.*

Surplus US Army WWII space heater—The Stove. *Illustration by Kimberly Hoverter Morris.*

A flank attack is next. The grate is shaken thoroughly – but gently, to prevent total collapse of the fire bed into the ash drawer. More kerosene, which turns into a billowing white cloud upon contact with the coals. A match ignites this vapor and the resulting explosion adds more holes to The Stove's battered hulk. A few feeble flames flicker beside the blackened coils and smoke pours out of a multitude of cracks.

During the night, these flames will either extinguish completely or, at some terrible hour, burst forth with maniacal fury, heating The Stove red hot and driving the inhabitants of the car into the cold. As a third alternative, it will send great clouds of black smoke belching forth until the outfit is filled with choking, reeking billows. In all cases, The Stove will cease to function at dawn.

Once in a while, to add variety, The Stove will immediately burst into cheerful flame, heating the car to a cozy temperature, lulling all into a false sense of security. Promptly at lights out, all heat ceases to radiate, the bunk car becomes icy cold and despite the renewed attacks, The Stove refuses to ignite.

Indeed, the only time The Stove is observed to function properly is when the last exhausted combatant stumbles out into the bitter morning air, leaving behind a warm fire that will not extinguish until the precise moment calculated to return the car to its normal frigid condition before the men return from their day's labor.

Silver D&RGW outfit cars in winter stand out in the snow on a distant spur in Bond, Colorado. *Photograph by Philip R. Hastings, Philip Ross Hastings, MD, collection, California State Railroad Museum.*

Night Meet

The silver bunk car rests on the stock yard spur next to the Cisco siding, windows open to the night breeze. Inside, the gang members lie sleeping on top of their blankets, the blistering heat of the desert sun still lingering in the outfit.

From the west comes the low whine of a diesel engine in dynamic braking and a long freight drifts down grade and into the siding. The engine makes but a low rumble as it rolls past in the darkness, headlight briefly illuminating the cluttered interior of the bunk car. The steel wheels of the cars thump over the rail joints, punctuated by an occasional rasp of flange against rail-head. Slowing to a crawl, the dirty, work-worn freight cars creak as they sway over the uneven rails of the siding. With a jangle of draft gear, the cars are abruptly checked, brake rigging clattering as the worn shoes halt the long drag. A momentary silence and then, with a low-pitched groan, the brakes release and with air hissing softly, the train waits.

Suddenly the quiet is shattered by the raucous shout of an air horn, blowing for the highway crossing at the east siding switch. A passenger train, diesels thundering, slams past the waiting freight and disappears into the desert night.

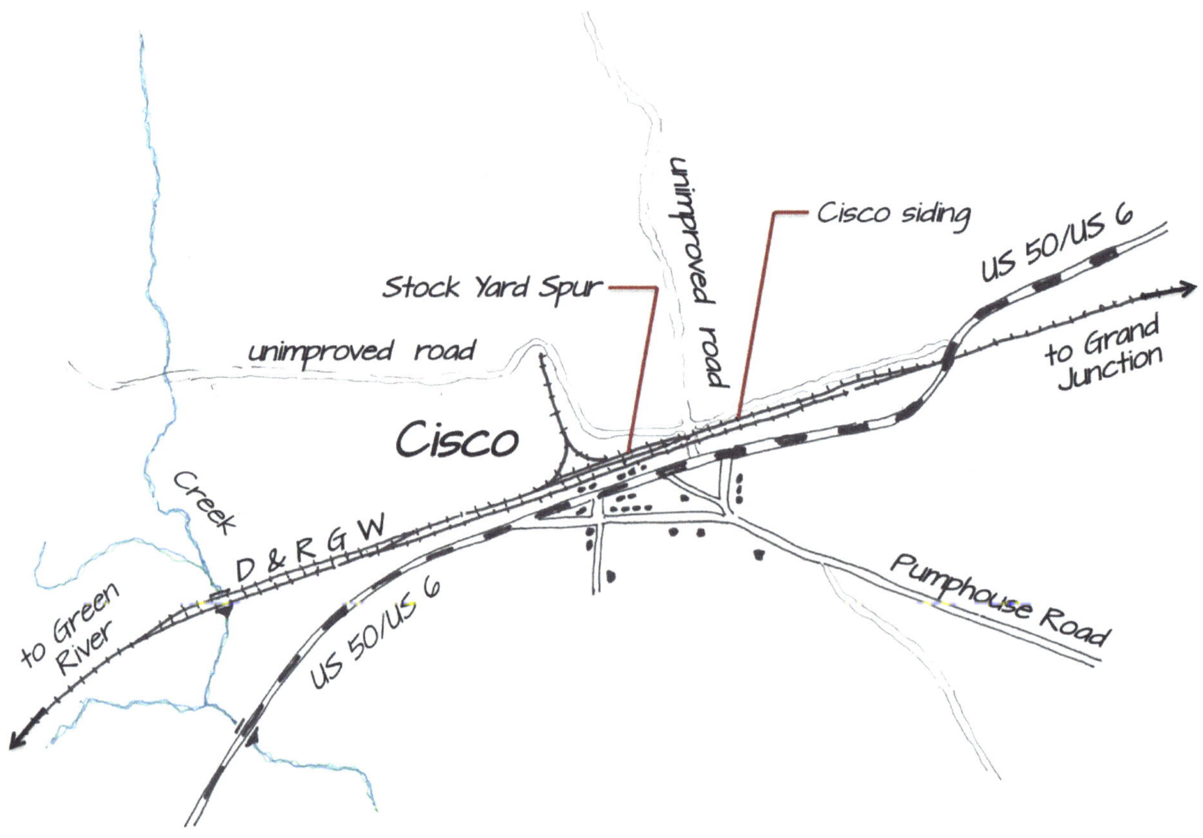

Denver & Rio Grande Western station at Cisco, Utah. *Map by David R. Clemens.*

June 12, 1992, night meet, Helper, Utah. *Photograph by Mike Chandler.*

The dwarf signal at the siding end changes from red to amber; two quick blasts from the head end, and with a rolling, jarring crash, slack runs out and the freight begins to move, following the passenger train down towards the Colorado River. The click of the wheels over the joints becomes a rapid chatter as the engine roars, exhaust echoing across the rolling wasteland. Couplers clash again, and the caboose, markers glowing in the darkness, rolls by the outfit and through the siding switch onto the mainline. Gradually the clamor of the engine fades, the individual sounds of the train merging into a low rumble as it hurries towards its Denver connections.

Inside the bunk car, the men are still sleeping, used to the sounds of trains passing in the night. A faint, far-away whistle, and the desert is again quiet.

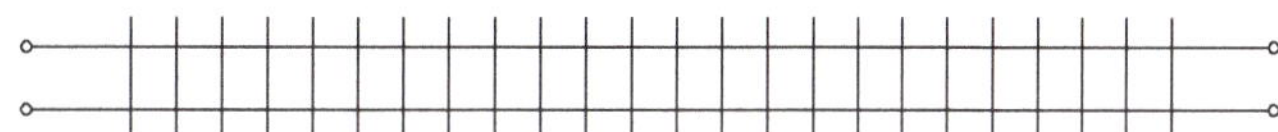

Ballard Bridge

Life along the tracks ranges from an existence imposed by economic straits to a location carefully chosen by those who consider an adjacent mainline to be - in the words of an unheralded English railfan - "God's Wonderful Railway." Whether along beaches, in forests, above canyons, on deserts, or in urban settings, an overview of a railroad is a thing to be cherished.

If life along a track can be good, life along two tracks is better and, with a major waterway thrown in, life becomes truly great. Such a location is found in the Ballard section of Seattle, where a duplex sits high on the south-facing hill overlooking the Lake Washington Ship Canal, the Great Northern Railway Ballard branch on the north bank of the waterway, and the huge, double-track bascule bridge carrying the GN mainline over both canal and branch. The bridge dominates the scene, both visually and in activity. But the canal locks and the nightly "Ballard Job" provide their own counterpoint to the mainline action viewed from the kitchen window. Indeed, the rail and marine activity are interlinked, each having an absolute effect on the other.

Ballard Bridge (also known as the Salmon Bay Bridge or Bridge No. 4) and environs. *Map by David R. Clemens.*

The canal serves to connect the length of Lake Washington along Seattle's east side, and Lake Union - wholly within the city - with the salt waters of Puget Sound. The two lakes have numerous shipyards, saw mills, pier complexes, a major fishermen's terminal, and other marine-oriented industries that provide traffic literally ranging from rowboats to naval vessels. Although the rail bridge is some 50 feet above mean sea level, all the larger ships, the bigger fishing boats, and a surprising number of weekend sail boats have superstructures or masts high enough to require opening the bridge in amounts ranging from a few feet to the full, vertical upright position. High tide exacerbates the problem, and train-boat right-of-way conflicts occur around the clock. The bridge tender has his normal railroad line-up information provided by the dispatcher on a regular basis, time-table schedules, and more up-to-date movement information gleaned from the dispatchers' wire. The marine movements are more random - a vessel arrives and expects passage. Only the week-end parades of pleasure craft out of the lakes, all returning summer Sunday afternoons, are predictable.

The bridge tends to be left in its last position unless a train is due and it is then lowered to provide the least amount of delay to the rail traffic. However, it is inevitable that the mere act of lowering the span to the horizontal results in the approach of boats requiring greater clearance. The vessels blow the appropriate request for bridge opening on a variety of horns and whistles ranging from the high-pitched squeak of portable compressed-air tanks carried aboard sailboats through the typical electric horns on large pleasure cruisers to the multitude of tones produced by tugs, fishing boats, and other commercial craft. Occasionally, a stentorian blast heralds the arrival of a truly large vessel: an Alaskan ferry on route to a shipyard, a small freighter, or a Navy or Coast Guard ship on some obscure mission.

If a train is approaching, the bridge tender replies with a signal on his horn that the vessel will have to wait. Otherwise, a different signal indicates that the span will be lifted to provide passage. Following this audio communication, the bridge tender operates the mechanism unlocking the ends of the span. A soprano grinding of gears echoes from the canal banks, and then the main lifting motors are engaged. A heavy-duty, no-nonsense bass announces that the span is ascending, and the massive concrete counterweight descends toward the track on the north approach span. Depending on traffic, the lift span may stay up, or immediately descend, coming to rest with a resounding thump. Again, the high-pitched ringing of the locking mechanism and trains are once again free to cross over the canal.

The Empire Builder, Train No. 1, crossing Ballard Bridge in 1937. *Photograph by James A. Turner, JTLoco_2504d, PNRArchive collection at Burien, WA.*

Rail movements over the bridge are restricted to 20 mph, but eastbound trains are working upgrade out of Interbay yard, and the diesels provide a respectable chant as they pull a long freight around the curve and out onto the bridge. The rail gaps at the joints between fixed and moving spans are necessarily opposite each other, not staggered as normally found in open track construction. Even though the rail ends are cut at an angle, each wheel set of each truck at each end of each car whacks across the gap and is clearly heard along the canal. The sounds of westbound trains are blocked by intervening hills until they are actually out on the approach girders and moving across the canal.

First-class rail traffic along the Great Northern's shore line is provided by three streamlined Internationals each way between Seattle and Vancouver, BC; the mostly-head-end-traffic Western Star; and the flagship of the GN fleet, the Empire Builder. Interspersed with these premier trains is a variety of freights carrying every conceivable commodity that can fit on or in a myriad of boxcars, flatcars, gondolas, tank cars, auto racks, log cars, hoppers, and reefers, all followed by the inevitable bright red caboose. Trains 83 and 97 from the east arrive at the bridge in the early evening and just after midnight, respectively, with a variety of loads for the industries of the Puget Sound area, plus large numbers of empties to feed the insatiable appetites of the paper and lumber mills. Their eastbound counterparts, 82 and 88, again depart in the late evening and early morning hours loaded with forest products for the middle western and eastern markets.

GN 1105, a class F-5 2-8-0, running tender first, is crossing Ballard Bridge eastbound with the "Oiler." *Photograph by James A. Turner, JTLoco_1105f, PNRArchive collection at Burien, WA.*

Additional sections of the mainline trains, plus first, second, and third 711 and 712 between Vancouver and Seattle add to the heavy freight traffic across the bridge. The "Oiler," the local between Seattle and Everett bounces back and forth with an endless string of tank cars to and from the tank farms and oil piers at Richmond Beach, Edmonds, and Mukilteo, plus handling any other switching duties at the intermediate stations.

The green-and-white Foss tugs, buff-white-and-black tugs of Puget Sound Tug & Barge, green-and-orange American Tow Boat vessels, Island Tug & Barge, Washington Tug & Barge, and an incredible number of independent towing operators move a ceaseless stream of barges, ships, log booms, and other floating objects into and out of the canal locks. The distinctive sound of marine diesels echoes off the banks in a definite contrast to the EMD 567's and Alco 251's moving overhead.

Suddenly, a deep, melodious steam whistle brings knowledgeable canal dwellers out into back yards and onto sidewalks and paths. The chow-chow-chow exhaust of a stern wheeler announces the arrival of the Army Corps of Engineers "snag boat," the W. T. Preston. Clearing dead-heads (no, not train crews moving to a new assignment, but half-sunken logs and other debris) all along Puget Sound from Washington Ship Canal to the Nisqually waterway,

US Army Corps of Engineers' *W. T. Preston* pulling deadheads from the water. In service 1929–1981, she is preserved today at the Anacortes Maritime Heritage Center in Anacortes, Washington. *Photographer unknown, Saltwater People Historical Society collection.*

the classic river boat brings all other commerce to a halt as people stop to watch, listen, and enjoy a total anachronism in the diesel age.

In the late afternoon, the "Ballard Job" makes its appearance on the bridge. Caboose first, it moves around the curved bridge approach backing out of Interbay. It is normally powered by an EMD SW-series switch engine, and the consist has empties for Seattle Cedar Lumber, loads for the appliance warehouses, and loads and empties for Northwest Steel Rolling Mills who will switch them with their own small diesels and self-propelled cranes. Inbound tank cars of petroleum products for Bardahl, fertilizer, reefers for Ballard Cold Storage, cars for Fentron, Rail-to-Water Transfer, and other industries, the Ballard Job is a microcosm of all railroading everywhere.

The cabooses (cabeese?) leading the movements across the bridge add to the variety of the switch run. Bright red or "Big Sky Blue" mainline crummies, cupola-less short wooden transfer units with the large mountain goat herald adorning their sides, the job draws whatever is available on the "hack track" just below the Interbay yard office at the north end of the yard. Occasionally, the X-180 will appear in Ballard, outweighing most of the loads it accompanies. While having the typical "outhouse-on-a-raft" appearance of many transfer cabooses, in this case the platform is a cast-steel underframe from an old Baldwin diesel switcher, and the 135,000 lb weight depresses the rail joints into the mud and sawdust of the Ballard industrial trackage.

Backing across the bridge, "gum ball" warning light on cab roof flashing in the dusk, the small train disappears into the mainline cut at the site of the old Ballard station, now a signal maintainer's residence. Soon it reappears on the industrial track on the north side of the canal and ducks under the bridge it has just crossed. It continues on into the Ballard business area, engine first in deference to the numerous street crossings. Soon it is switching the multitude of spurs, following the instructions left by the agent in the tiny white yard office sandwiched between the team tracks and the cold storage building. When the work is finished, the job will appear again, engine leading, on the north bank track past the locks, accelerate through the dip beneath the draw bridge, and climb the ramp back to the mainline. Caboose first, the switcher will back across the bridge and down to Interbay Yard.

Canada
Vancouver
Bellingham
Mt Vernon
Marysville
Snohomish
Monroe
Gold Bar
Index
Skykomish
Scenic
Chumstick
Mountains
Cascade
Cascade Tunnel
Cashmere
Wenatchee
Trinidad Loops
Quincy
Ephrata
Wilson Creek
Odessa
Harrington
Fairchild
Spokane
Dean
Newport
Spokane R
Columbia River
Wenatchee River
Puget Sound
Skykomish R
Seattle
Washington
Idaho

2

SEATTLE
1948–1959

Pacific Coast caboose 53 and crew near Maple Valley, WA, March 1943.
Photograph by Harold A. Hill, WWAPC0281, PNRArchive collection at Burien, WA.

A map for three stories! "A Day on the Pacific Coast," "Riding the Van Asselt Transfer," and "Addendum: Extra GN 83 East" each look at different aspects of railroading along the Pacific Coast RR tracks. This overview map should help keep the comings and goings of the various railroads in perspective. *Map by David R. Clemens.*

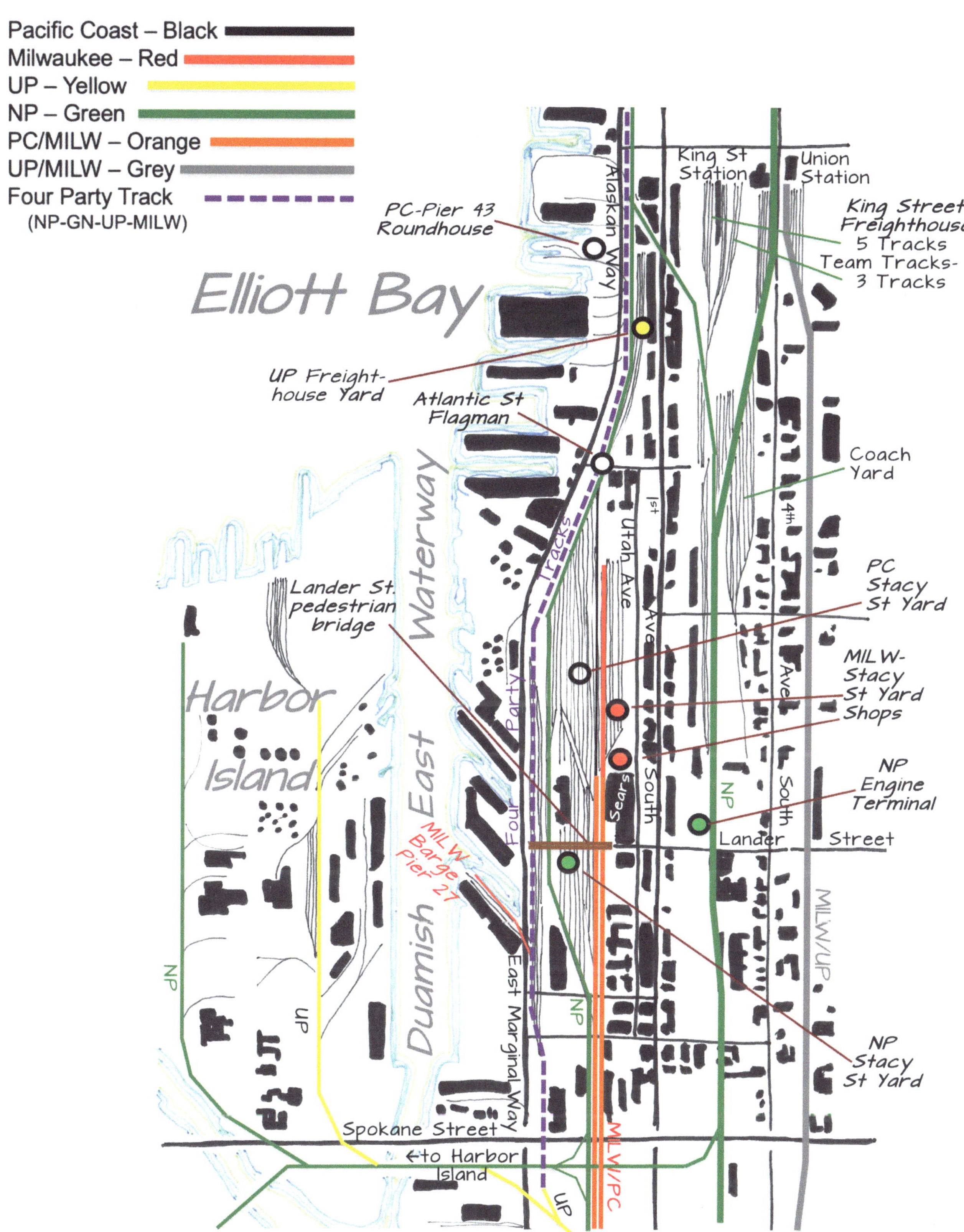

Railroading in South Seattle from King Street south to Spokane Street: four trunk lines and a short line side by side! This more detailed map helps with three more stories: "Route of the Sea-Going Hiawathas," "Wash the Builder," and "Seattle Engine Terminals."
Map by David R. Clemens.

Doodlebug B-23 picking up orders at Marshall, Washington, August 1950. *Photograph by Philip R. Hastings, Philip Ross Hastings, MD, collection, California State Railroad Museum.*

Gus and The Ghost

In the middle 1950's, railroad passenger service was undergoing major changes. Not only were local operations being eliminated wholesale, but long-distance through trains were being cut back. Each visit to the station revealed a further-reduced departure board. In the Pacific Northwest, the last rail logging shows were disappearing at an even faster rate. An opportunity to combine a branch-line trip to investigate the only recently abandoned headquarters of a logging railroad was definitely not to be ignored.

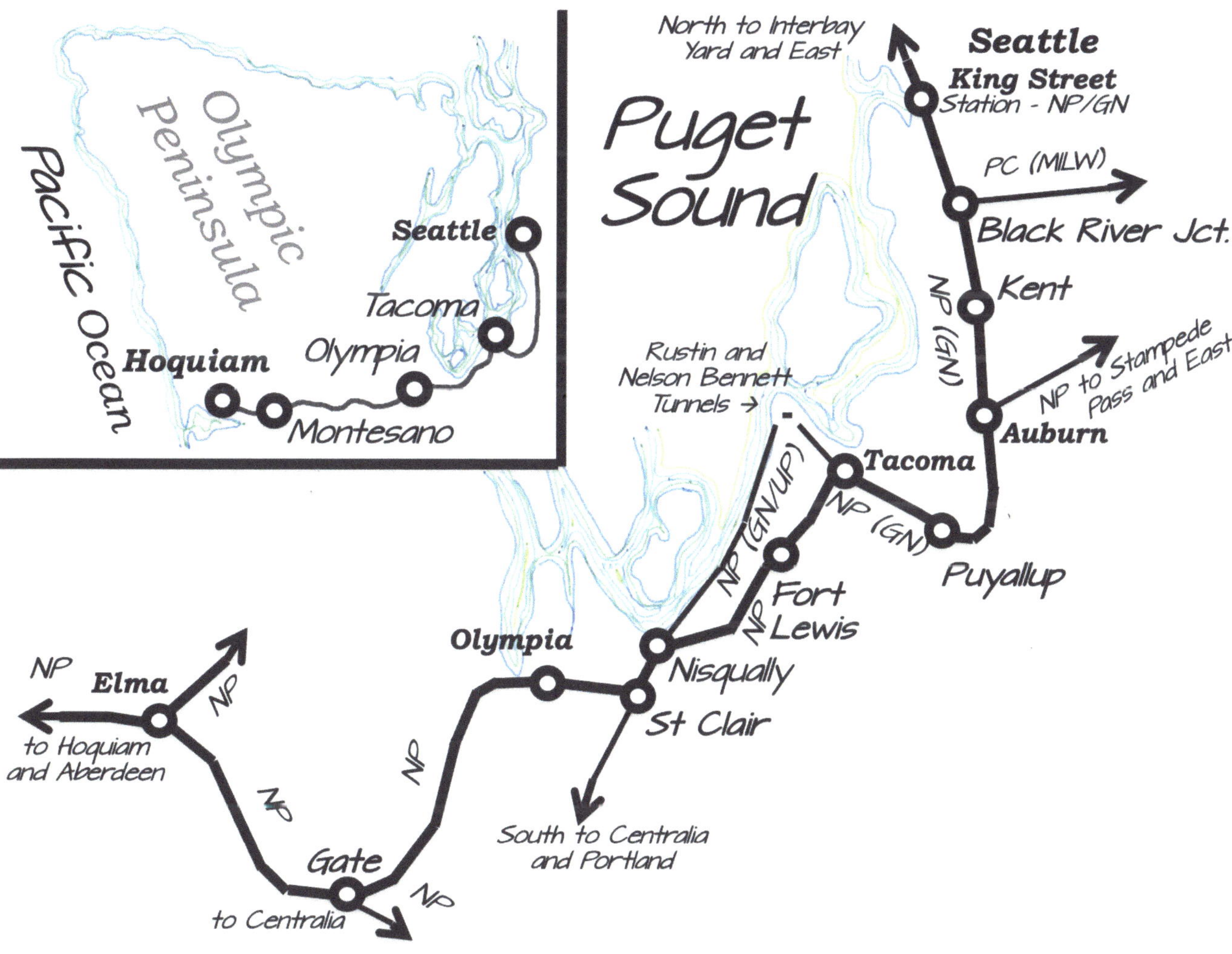

Route of the "Grays Harbor Doodlebug": NP #422-461 from Seattle to Hoquiam, WA.
Map by David R. Clemens

In late 1955 or early 1956, my friend Ken and I decided to take Northern Pacific Railroad train #422-461 from Seattle to Brady (near Montesano) to inspect the remains of the Schaeffer Brothers logging show, which had been headquartered at that point until being bought out by Simpson Timber Co. A substantial added benefit would be that the trip would be in one of the last gas-electric cars. These cars were being scrapped system wide as the various regulatory schedule discontinuances were received. The Seattle-Hoquiam run was the last remaining in the Puget Sound area and time, as they say, was of the essence.

Car B-23 was the assigned unit for the run on what was a typically gray, cold winter day. There were few passengers out of Seattle, and the last of them left the run at Olympia. Well, there was one through passenger—a corpse in the baggage section going to the Gray's Harbor area for burial. At Tacoma, the conductor (known as "Gus") discoursed at length about his intense dislike of transporting bodies in general and on "his" train in particular. As the train moved up South Tacoma hill and through Fort Lewis, we noticed that Gus spent most of his time on the rear platform of the B-23—as far from the coffin as possible—in spite of the weather, and the run continued along the branch from Tacoma back to the mainline at Nisqually.

Electromotive Division Doodlebug B-23 on NP train #422 during a station stop at South Tacoma. *Photograph by J.M. Fredrickson, JMF01-03582.0, NPRHA collection at PNRArchive at Burien, WA.*

After a brief sprint along the Seattle-Portland main, we left the high iron at St. Clair and headed toward Olympia. I rode on the rear platform with Gus for a while. I noticed that he was protecting himself from the spirit in the baggage compartment with some more prosaic spirits from a pint concealed in the pocket of his overcoat.

I returned to the substantially warmer interior of the car at Olympia, while Gus maintained his self-imposed exile on the rear platform. The B-23 snaked up the line through Belmore and Little Rock and came to a halt at the junction/train register station of Gate. We noticed that the engineer and telegraph operator were wandering around, apparently looking for some misplaced object. Finally, the engineer swung up onto the rear platform and entered the passenger compartment. He asked if we had seen Gus, and more importantly, when.

Doodlebug B-19, sister to the B-23, on the Grays Harbor train along Airport Way in 1939.
Photograph by James A. Turner, WWANL-T02-265, PNRArchive collection at Burien, WA.

We replied that Gus had been riding the platform for most of the trip and that the last time we really noticed him was somewhere around Little Rock. Trailing the engineer as he left the car and walked into the station, we listened as he discussed the problem with the operator. There was little doubt that Gus had been flipped off the platform on one of the numerous curves, with a little help from the spirits residing in his overcoat pocket. Just as the operator was preparing to take his car and check back along the route for the missing crewman, the phone rang. He answered it and after a brief conversation, handed it to the engineer.

"Gus! Gus, where the hell are you?... You can't be at Montesano, we're only at Gate! Okay, okay, how'd you get there? Yeah, okay, I'm on my way."

Quickly, the engineer said that Gus had indeed fallen from the rear platform of the B-23, had made his way to the highway, and had been picked up by a passing State Patrol officer. The officer had driven directly to Montesano, thinking that we had already left Gate, and Gus was in no condition to remember the train register. As we ran to the gas-electric, Ken and I asked to be dropped at Brady and picked up on the return trip. The engineer agreed to slow down enough for us to unload, then the B-23 was moving down the line with all the determination of the North Coast Limited making up time. There is no doubt that we set a record for gas-electric travel over the 27 miles from Gate to Brady. The station stop at Elma barely qualified as such, and we unloaded at Brady without stopping.

After exploring and photographing the Schaeffer Bros. camp, we returned to trackside to wait for the eastward trip of the B-23. Promptly at 3:15 it stopped in front of us with full crew plus one passenger. Gus was substantially worse for wear: glasses, false teeth, and conductor's hat were lost in the right-of-way brambles, and a borrowed pair of bib overalls covered the shredded remains of his uniform. A multitude of scratches and abrasions were visible, and he moved slowly and most reluctantly. We started to ask about his great adventure, but he moved down the aisle with what for him was great alacrity, leaving us with the other "passenger" who turned out to be the Trainmaster.

The TM questioned us repeatedly, and at great length about the morning's occurrence. All we were able to say was that Gus had been riding the platform, apparently because of the corpse, and must have lost his balance on a curve. Had there been any drinking? In the best traditions of Harry Bedwell's narratives, where the Trainmaster was the enemy, we were shocked at the suggestion. Indeed, if the Roadmaster would improve maintenance along this line, both passengers and crew would fare better. The Trainmaster eyed us most suspiciously all the way to Olympia where he finally left the B-23 to catch a freight back to Aberdeen.

I promptly joined the engineer in the cab of the gas-electric for the run to Tacoma. At that point, I rejoined Ken in the passenger compartment for the mainline journey to Seattle. We were nearly hysterical with laughter over the day's activities, particularly the overly-suspicious Trainmaster. For some reason, Gus in his new raiment didn't appear to be amused.

Almost twenty years later, I ran into Ken at a convention and we agreed that the Trainmaster was undoubtedly convinced to his dying day that we really had thrown Gus bodily off the rear platform of train #422-461.

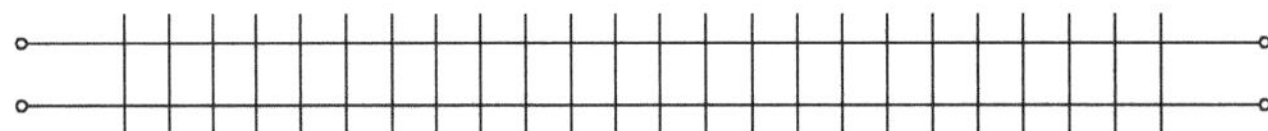

Route of The Sea-Going Hiawathas

The Pacific Northwest lumber industry is scattered along a wide selection of waterways that are used for both inbound raw materials and outbound finished products. Logs are dumped in rivers and the salt chuck, rafted to the mills, and once reduced to marketable form, shipped out in carload quantities. Other commodities are railed from producing locations -- coal mines and even limestone quarries -- to either piers or plants on the Sound, and then those products distributed, as are the forest loadings, by barge to the mainline terminals at Seattle and Tacoma.

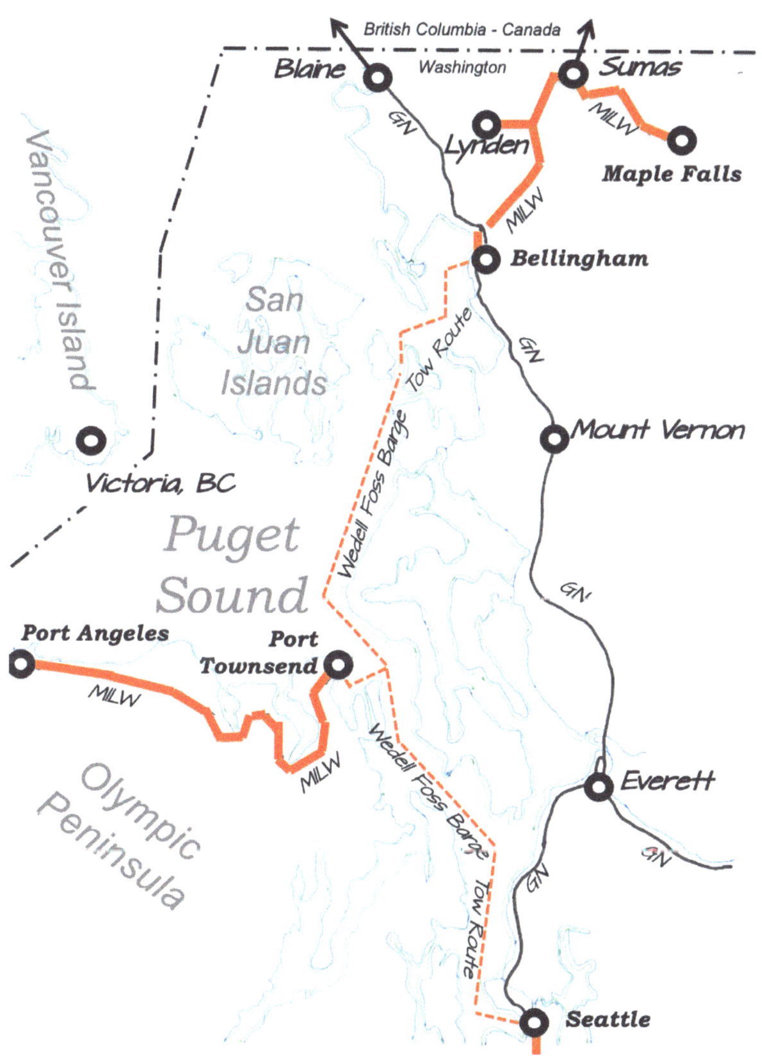

CMStP&P barge routes on Puget Sound from Seattle Pier 27 to Port Townsend and Bellingham. *Map by David R. Clemens.*

The Seattle barge pier serves the isolated Chicago, Milwaukee, St. Paul & Pacific Railroad branch lines extending from Port Townsend to Port Angeles and from Bellingham to Maple Falls. Pier 27 is a combination of fill and piling at Forest Street. A hand-full of tracks not much longer than the barges they service occupy the fill, and on the land end, a lead curves across busy Marginal Way to connect with the tracks paralleling the waterfront. The yard narrows at the harbor end of the fill to a lead and then fans out to three tracks on the barge apron. The apron itself is supported by an elaborate gantry spanning the slip. Although electrically operated now, the huge old hand wheels and chains remain in place as a standby. Rows and clusters of pilings provide both guidance into the slip and, on the outer side, dolphins for mooring a couple of car barges. A tiny gray yard office about the size of a boxcar fronts on Marginal Way, perched on piling over the oily waters of Elliott Bay. An orange-and-black EMD switcher idles on the lead alongside as the crew consults with the Yardmaster about their upcoming chores. Sea gulls and pigeons flock in the area, and the harbor odors of salt water, rotting seaweed, and other flotsam permeate the air.

Foss tug *Wedell Foss*, winner of the 4th Annual Maritime International Tugboat Race, Seattle, 1951. Built in 1904, it was photographed in the Washington Ship Canal, possibly en route to the Foss dock a short distance away. *Photograph by Marine Salon, Seattle. Saltwater People Historical Society collection.*

Under damp gray skies, the green-and-white Foss tug *Wedell Foss* approaches the pier with a barge from one of the branch lines. Although towed down the Sound, the barge has been shifted in mid-harbor and is now lashed alongside the tug for maneuvering into the slip. The barge itself looks as if it had been manufactured in the Milwaukee Road shops in its name-sake city. The horizontal ribs on the hull sides mirror countless boxcars bearing the "Route of the Hiawatha" logo. A two-story deck house spans the stern and supports the couplers helping to hold the cars in place. Each of the three tracks holds about five boxcars or flats of forest products. The barge is guided into the slip and made fast to the apron. The tug casts off, moves to a previously loaded barge moored to the dolphins north of the slip, and begins preparations for a trip back up-Sound. The tide is too low to begin switching the newly-arrived car float, but the crew begins removing the jacks and chains securing the cars to the deck as the overcast becomes a chilling drizzle.

Soon the rising water level covers a majority of the piling barnacles and the angle of the apron connection makes unloading feasible. The switcher moves down the lead and couples into the string of old wooden flat cars used as idler cars to keep the acceleration/braking forces of the engine off the apron. The idlers are shoved across the apron onto the barge and coupled into the standing cars on the starboard side. Air hoses are joined and the line charged. When the wheezing brakes are pumped off, the deck house coupler pin is pulled. A back-up sign, and the switcher slowly pulls the cut off the barge deck. The creaking of the gantry and apron provide a counterpoint to the click of the wheels over the various joints between the barge and land. As each load moves toward the solid pile/fill of the pier, first the stern of the barge starts to lift, then the whole starboard side. The weight of the port side loads causes the barge to list alarmingly and the apron to develop a surprising twist to accommodate the off-center barge trim.

When the apron switch is cleared, the cut is reversed and pushed back out onto the opposite side and coupled into the port cut, causing an even greater distortion in the apron. Air is again cut in and this time as the cut is pulled from the float, the list is righted, the apron loses its twist and the original downgrade onto the barge deck becomes nearly level. Back over the apron to the center track cut and as it is pulled onto the pier, the barge rides high in the slip. The switch engine crosses the wet pavement of Marginal Way and moves onto the paralleling running track, dragging the entire barge load out of the pier yard until the lead switch is cleared. A reversal, and the inbound loads are shoved into a transfer track to await another switch engine that will move them to the Stacy Street yard for movement east or even back to the waterfront interchange tracks to be turned over to the GN, NP or UP.

The pier crew pulls down to clear the lead switch and moves back into the little yard where the outbound barge load is waiting. These cars are mostly empties, and the three loads are shoved into the center barge track along with a couple of empty boxes. The movement of other empties across the outer apron tracks results in only a slight list when compared to the opposite movement of loads. The reverse movements to the land end of the pier to switch these cuts interrupts traffic on Marginal Way as a switchman flags the crossing.

In the waterway, the Puget Sound Tug & Barge tug *Goliah* shepherds a tramp freighter to its berth on Harbor Island. The last steam tug working the Seattle waterfront, it recalls an era when both water- and rail-borne commerce was moved by the energy generated in boilers and utilized in single, double, and triple expansion engines.

Soon the barge is loaded and the cars are firmly anchored in place by the crew in oilskins working on the slippery deck. Before long, a passing tug of the Foss fleet will appear out of the mist and pull the car barge, moving it alongside the slip to await the next up-Sound tow to Bellingham or Port Townsend.

The tug *Wedell Foss* lashed alongside an empty Milwaukee Road barge along the north side of Pier 27. The gantry supporting the pier's apron is visible behind the barge deck house. *Illustration by Kimberly Hoverter Morris.*

Sea gulls wheel overhead and freighters pass on the east channel between Harbor Island and the mainland piers. Inside the little yard office, clerks sort waybills in the warmth of the coal stove and the Yardmaster plans the loading for the next movement of the Hiawatha Navy.

The Pacific Coast and Milwaukee Road trains operating on trackage rights over this portion of the Pacific Coast Railroad between Seattle and Maple Valley, Washington, on August 15, 1952, are described in the "Day on the Pacific Coast" section. *Map by David R. Clemens.*

CMStP&P: A Day On The Pacific Coast

Not a day on the "Pacific Extension," or even on the western Washington network of main and branch lines reaching to the docks of Seattle and Tacoma and extending to the branch lines on the Straights of Juan de Fuca and the Pacific Ocean harbors in the southwestern area of the state, but a day on the Pacific Coast—Railroad that is.

My good friend Dave Clemens lived in Renton, Washington for a brief period, and during his exile in "soggy Sound" country, befriended Ralph Ozura, a BN (Pacific Coast RR) railroad dispatcher at Maple Valley. As a result, Dave acquired a dispatcher's train sheet from a generation earlier, squirreled it away, and then retrieved it to send me a copy, knowing of my intense interest / first-hand experience with the PC dating back to junior high school days circa 1950. Also, I have long been fascinated by the Chicago, Milwaukee, St. Paul & Pacific operations in the era / area. Thus, I have attempted to decipher the train sheet information so as to accurately depict a day of Milwaukee operations on the Pacific Coast a half century ago. Whether this day was typical or not is lost to history, but my recollections of those times lead me to believe it is.

In this 1953 image, a pair of Milwaukee Road bipolars, led by the E2, have train No. 16, the eastbound Olympian Hiawatha, moving at track speed under the covered bridge at Allentown, Washington. It is just about 3:00 pm if No. 16 is on time, and the Hi will be off the Pacific Coast in about 15 minutes. In the 70 years since John Illman captured this action, this once rural location has become a suburb in the Seattle/Tacoma metro area. *Photograph by John C. Illman, WWAPC0341, PNRArchive collection at Burien, WA.*

When the Milwaukee Road built into the Pacific Northwest in 1908, it negotiated trackage rights over the Columbia & Puget Sound RR, a Seattle-area coal-hauling short line that later became the Pacific Coast Railroad, from Maple Valley to Seattle, some 20 miles. Operations split at Argo, with freight traffic continuing to Spokane Street Tower on the C&PS, and then a short distance to the Stacy Street yard in the central waterfront industrial area. Passenger trains ran from Argo to Seattle Union Station (a joint MILW-UP facility) on Union Pacific trackage rights. The Milwaukee main line to Tacoma diverged from the C&PS at Black River and continued south to Tacoma on right of way owned jointly with the UP. The MILW electrified the line in 1919, installed electric light automatic block signals on the C&PS from Maple Valley to Argo to replace the semaphores originally built in 1912, and extended the catenary to Union Station over the UP. These arrangements, minus the overhead wire circa 1974, lasted until the demise of the Milwaukee's "Lines West" in 1980.

Prior to the GN purchase of the Pacific Coast RR, Engineer Fritz Soderback on PC 14 meets MILW E 50 on a westbound freight at Renton. *Photograph by Harold A. Hill, WWAPC0078, PNRArchive collection at Burien, WA.*

By the 1950s, the basic operating pattern resulted in the CMStP&P passenger trains running west to Union Station where any cars for Seattle were switched out. The road engine ran around the consist and towed it backwards to Tacoma. During the brief period when the electrics were replaced by FM cab diesels and the trailing unit was a B unit or an A unit facing the wrong direction, the trains were wyed at Black River and towed backwards to Seattle by steam/diesel engines, or headed into Union Station and then towed back to Black River to head around the wye and proceed to the end of its run at Tacoma.

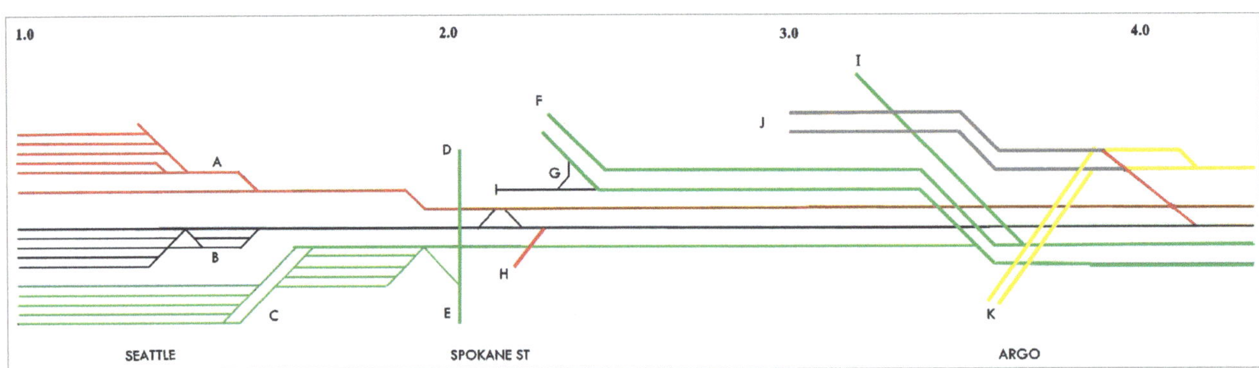

Schematic track diagram, Seattle to Maple Valley, circa 1952. See legend on page 59 for detailed information. *Drawn by Mike McLaughlin, digitized by Jim Providenza.*

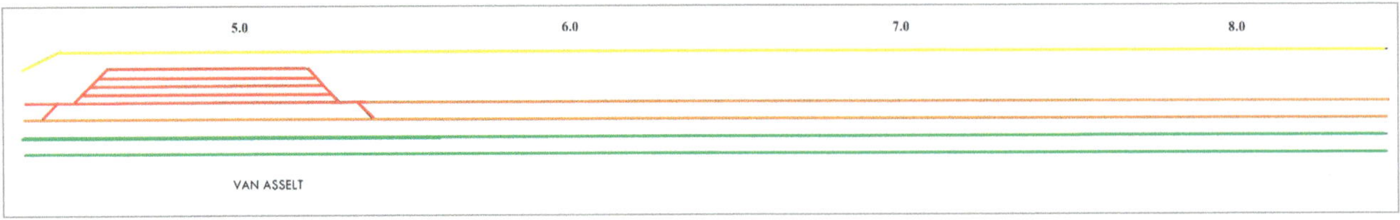

Freight movements varied even more as the newest brass came up with "innovative" scenarios to cut train hours/miles, crew times, and penalty time slips, but rarely improved equipment utilization or customer service. The base plan was to drop the Tacoma portion of westward trains at Black River, grab the Seattle set-out, run to Van Asselt Yard (just south of Argo), and highball back to Black River, pick up the Tacoma cars and head down the valley for the last 28 miles and tie up in Tide Flats Yard. Unfortunately, a plethora of details were introduced/rescinded as experiments were made with which was cut where for forwarding to while setting out what and when for connection to—usually the crews ended up doing it their way; cabooses hauled along, left behind, mostly a decision based on least hours for the most miles. The Seattle traffic was handled between Van Asselt and the Stacy Street Yard by long distance yard moves entirely within yard limits. Obviously, eastbound movements were a mirror image of the westbound traffic.

The Pacific Coast RR had an employee timetable special instruction that undoubtedly helped the dispatcher maintain control during heavy traffic levels: "yard engines and extra trains are not permitted to use Main Tracks within Seattle Yard Limits east of Argo Tower except upon train order authority."

While moves to Harbor Island and/or the cement plant aren't tracked, the instruction does allow insight as to typical train operations and car handling fifty years ago in and out of the Seattle terminal as documented by the dispatcher's train sheet. Using the information available, it is possible to reconstruct the train movements for Friday, August 15, 1952, with a reasonable degree of accuracy.

Pictured here are the dispatcher's sheet, a copy of the applicable Pacific Coast RR employee timetable (No. 12), a schematic track diagram, and a "string line" diagram of all the recorded train movements taking place on the day in question. Certain assumptions have had to be made when the information available is incomplete, but it is believed that the results are indeed an accurate description of the events as they played out.

The assumptions are: (a) since times are not shown at Van Asselt, running time from that point to Black River is 15 minutes and to Spokane Street 12 minutes; (b) orders are received at Black River for moves to Van Asselt and return; (c) eastward trains from Tacoma pull through the MILW wye into the MILW sidings and the engine only appears on the PC train sheet after it cuts off and returns to the tower to proceed to Van Asselt; (d) the engine and fill arrive back at Black River at the time shown, add the cars to the train, and depart at the time registered; (e) westbound trains arrive at the time indicated, cut off the Seattle set-out, depart for Van Asselt at the time shown, return to Black River and disappear onto the MILW (f) car counts are extrapolated for prior/subsequent figures as necessary; (g) some dispatchers recorded tonnage, some didn't; some consists were recorded routinely as 'loads-empties'(this was probably due to the fact that the MILW was billed on car count, not tonnage); (h) running time Spokane Street/Argo 5 minutes.

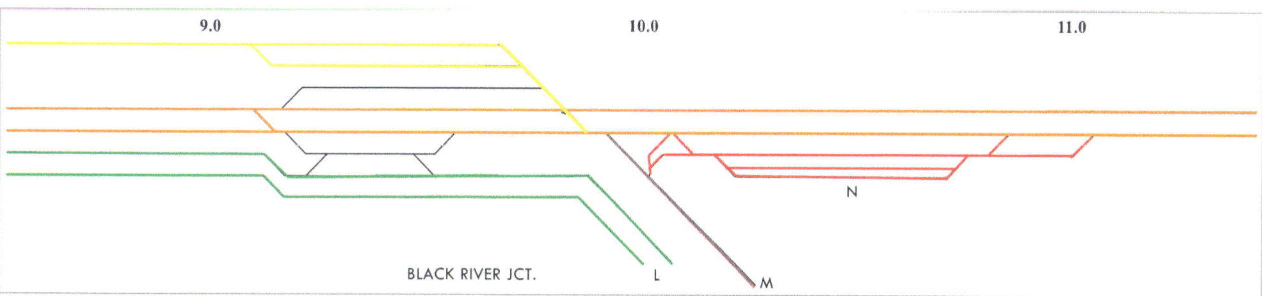

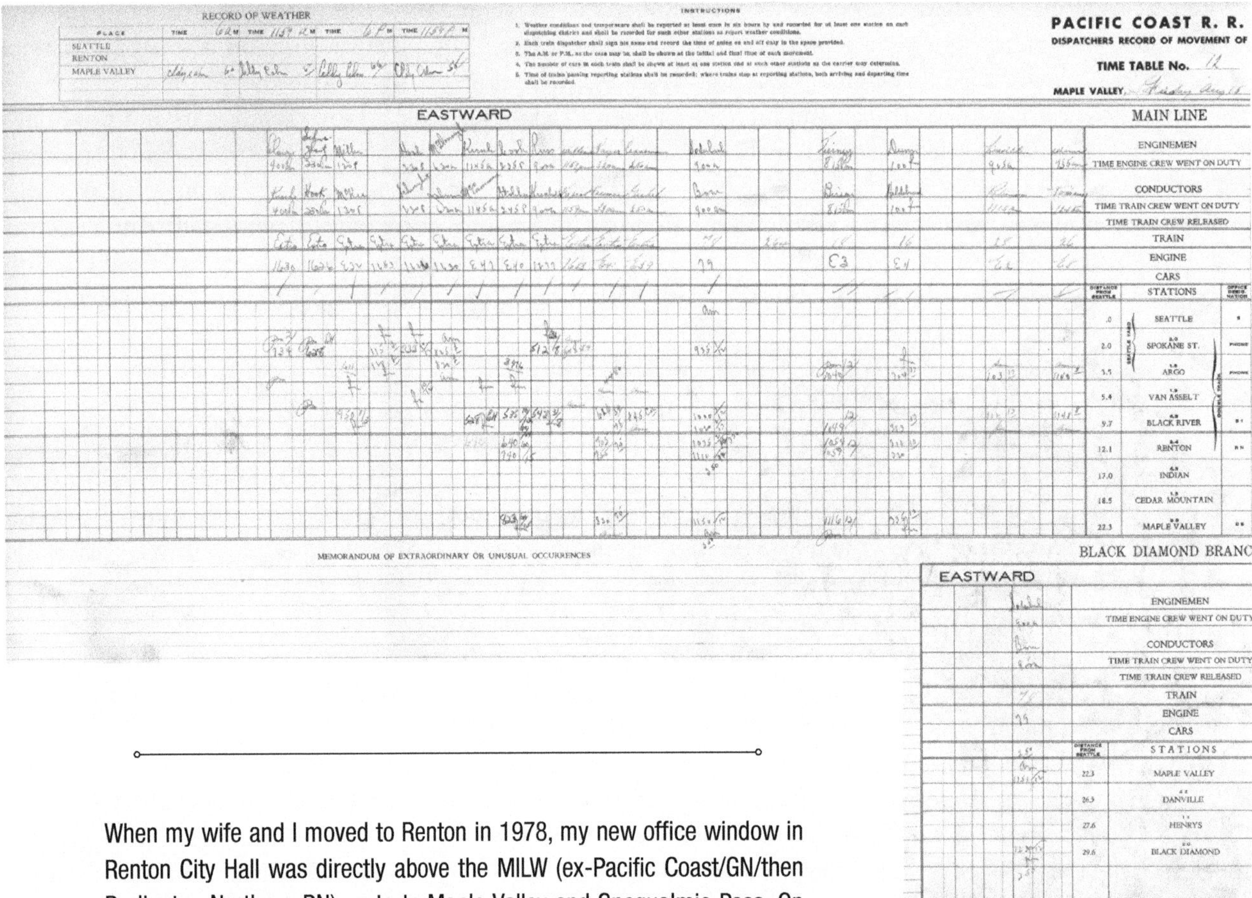

RECORD OF WEATHER

PLACE | TIME | TIME | TIME | TIME

SEATTLE

RENTON

MAPLE VALLEY

INSTRUCTIONS

PACIFIC COAST R. R.

DISPATCHERS RECORD OF MOVEMENT OF

TIME TABLE No. 12

MAPLE VALLEY

EASTWARD

MAIN LINE

ENGINEMEN

TIME ENGINE CREW WENT ON DUTY

CONDUCTORS

TIME TRAIN CREW WENT ON DUTY

TIME TRAIN CREW RELEASED

TRAIN

ENGINE

CARS

DISTANCE FROM SEATTLE	STATIONS
.0	SEATTLE
2.0	SPOKANE ST.
3.5	ARGO
5.4	VAN ASSELT
9.7	BLACK RIVER
12.1	RENTON
17.0	INDIAN
18.5	CEDAR MOUNTAIN
22.3	MAPLE VALLEY

MEMORANDUM OF EXTRAORDINARY OR UNUSUAL OCCURRENCES

BLACK DIAMOND BRANC

EASTWARD

ENGINEMEN

TIME ENGINE CREW WENT ON DUTY

CONDUCTORS

TIME TRAIN CREW WENT ON DUTY

TIME TRAIN CREW RELEASED

TRAIN

ENGINE

CARS

DISTANCE FROM SEATTLE	STATIONS
22.3	MAPLE VALLEY
26.3	DANVILLE
27.6	HENRYS
29.6	BLACK DIAMOND

When my wife and I moved to Renton in 1978, my new office window in Renton City Hall was directly above the MILW (ex-Pacific Coast/GN/then Burlington Northern-BN) route to Maple Valley and Snoqualmie Pass. On one of my first train chases I stumbled across a manned depot/telegraph office at Maple Valley. I was greeted by a pleasant gentleman named Ralph who explained the office dispatched the BN between South Seattle and Maple Valley and served as a MILW Train Order office.

Over the next two years I learned how Chief Train Dispatcher Ralph Ozura and his train dispatchers controlled train movements via tower operators at Spokane Street (South Seattle), Argo Tower, Van Asselt, Black River Jct., Renton and Maple Valley.

A few weeks before the MILW's planned shutdown west of Rapid City, Ralph told me he was retiring after 30 years and change. Two days before the end, I was wishing Ralph my very best in retirement when he reached under his desk and gave me the worn but intact Record of Train Movements presented here. To my astonishment now, 70 years after the fact and 42 years after obtaining the Train Sheet, what did I find? In the inset blow up of the Sheet is the signature RALPH E OZURA as the midnight to 8:00 am dispatcher!

A wonderful and beloved gift from an amazing railroader.

David R. Clemens

:IFIC COAST R. R. CO.
TCHERS RECORD OF MOVEMENT OF TRAINS

TIME TABLE No. 12

E VALLEY, Friday Aug 15 1952

H. V. O'Neil Chief Dispatcher

DISPATCHERS ON DUTY

	from	M. to	M.
Ralph E. Zuur	12:01 a	8:01 a	
H. Vongil	8:00 a	4:00 P	
C.J. Sparks	4:00 P	11:59 P	

MAIN LINE

WESTWARD

Distance from Seattle	Stations	Office Designation
	ENGINEMEN	
	TIME ENGINE CREW WENT ON DUTY	
	CONDUCTORS	
	TIME TRAIN CREW WENT ON DUTY	
	TIME TRAIN CREW RELEASED	
	TRAIN	
	ENGINE	
	CARS	
0	SEATTLE	S
2.0	SPOKANE ST.	PHONE
3.5	ARGO	PHONE
5.4	VAN ASSELT	
9.7	BLACK RIVER	BI
12.1	RENTON	RN
17.0	INDIAN	
18.5	CEDAR MOUNTAIN	
22.3	MAPLE VALLEY	MV

WORK TRAINS

DELAYS

BLACK DIAMOND BRANCH

WESTWARD

Distance from Seattle	Stations	Office Designation
	ENGINEMEN	
	TIME ENGINE CREW WENT ON DUTY	
	CONDUCTORS	
	TIME TRAIN CREW WENT ON DUTY	
	TIME TRAIN CREW RELEASED	
	TRAIN	
	ENGINE	
	CARS	
22.3	MAPLE VALLEY	MV
26.5	DANVILLE	
27.6	HENRYS	
29.6	BLACK DIAMOND	PHONE

FORM 27—11-49 1M N.L.CO.

DISP

Ralph E. Zuur

H. Vongil

C.J. Sparks

H. V. O'Neil Chief Dispatcher

WESTWARD

Top previous page and above | Pacific Coast Railroad, Dispatcher's Record of Train Movements, August 15, 1952.

At right | August 15, 1952, the first movement: Extra MILW E41 West, 10 loads, 1 empty to Van Asselt from Black River Jct.

Operations Begin

The first movement on the train sheet was extra MILW E41 at Black River, an eastbound freight, but the first physical move was the engine and 11 cars westbound to Van Asselt leaving at 5:37 am. Normally, traffic from Tacoma to Seattle was handled by the daily local, but this day the 10 loads and 1 empty appear to be a priority move that couldn't wait for handling later in the day. Arrival at Van Asselt was 5:52 am. In the meantime, engine MILW 1653 left Spokane Street at 5:48 am with 39 cars and arrived at Van Asselt at 6:00 am. The train and switch job swapped cars and the 1653 headed back to Spokane Street at 6:20 am with the hot 11 cars brought in by the E41.

The E41 returned to Black River at 6:11 am with the 39 cars from Stacy Street, arriving at 6:26 am. After adding the Seattle cars to its consist, Extra E41 East departed at 6:59 am with 75 cars and arrived at Renton at 7:05 am, where it went into the clear for Extra E39 West. Following E39's passage at approximately 7:25, Extra E41 East departed 30 minutes later (breakfast?) at 7:55 am and left PC rails at Maple Valley at 8:30 am with 4480 tons.

Note: Extra E41 East may actually have been Number 264. Nos. 263 and 264 ran every day, but if it became apparent that a train would be ready to depart early, or was already running early, the schedule was annulled and the trains run as extras, as indeed both 263 and 264 were this day. In the instant case, the E41 was called for 3:30 am, and arrived Black River approximately 5:30 am. Still, the E41 East was off the Pacific Coast at 8:30 am, an hour before #264's listed time.

During Extra E41's travel across the railroad, Extra E39 West left Maple Valley at 7:00 am with 48-3, met Extra E41 East at Renton as described, and arrived Black River at 7:31 am. 34 loads and 2 empties were cut off and the E39 departed west at 7:50 am arriving Van Asselt at 8:05 am where the cars were dropped. The E39 returned cab hop at 8:30 am, arriving at Black River 8:45 where it later departed for Tacoma with 14-1.

At 8:25 am, MILW 1630 departed light from Spokane Street and arrived Argo 8:30 am, presumably for Union Station. It later returned leaving Argo at 12:40 pm, arriving Spokane Street at 12:45 pm with 2 cars. This would put a switch engine at Union Station while #17 arrives with 12 cars and departs with 8.

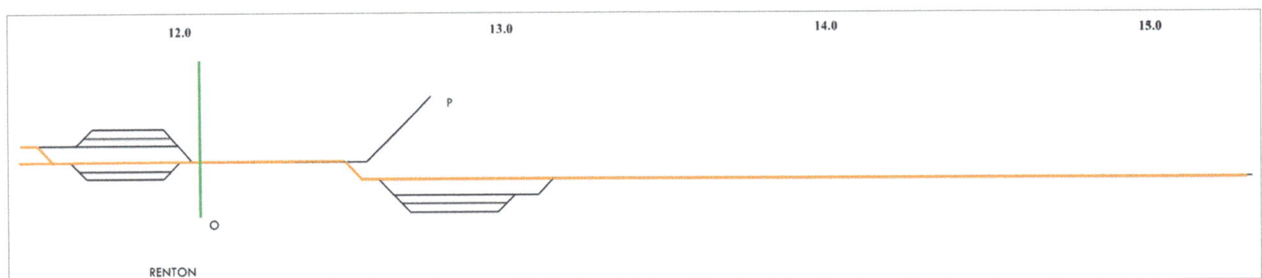

A Mid-Morning Lull

Pacific Coast train #78, the "Renton Rocket," left Spokane Street at 9:35 am with 1 load and 12 empties behind engine GN 79, arriving at Black River at 10:00 am. They picked up 1 load and 1 empty, departed Black River at 10:20 am, and arrived at Renton at 10:35 am with 2-13, 330 tons. They set out the two cars picked up at Black River and the one load from Seattle, meeting #17, the Columbian, during the process. At 11:10 am they left Renton with 0-12, 250 tons (probably all PC GS gons for coal loading), arrived at Maple Valley at 11:50 am and pulled onto the Black Diamond branch at 11:51.

Number 17, the westbound Columbian, passed Maple Valley with engine E5 and 12 cars at 10:30 am, four hours late. It arrived at Renton at 10:44 am and after a four-minute station stop, departed at 10:48, a further 3 minutes down. It passed Black River at 10:53 am and left PC rails at Argo at 11:01 am for the run to Union Station over the UP, 3 hours 56 minutes late. #17 reappeared at Argo at 11:40 am as number 26, now being towed backwards by the E5 for the run to Tacoma, reduced to eight cars and running 3'41" late. It returned to Milwaukee rails at Black River at 11:48 am, having made up 3 minutes on the schedule.

In 1947 Harold Hill caught PC 15 meeting the Olympian Hiawatha led by BiPolar E3 at Renton.
Photograph by Harold A. Hill, WWAPC0352, PNRArchive collection at Burien, WA.

Number 17 was followed an hour and a half later by #15, the Olympian Hiawatha, passing Maple Valley at 11:59 am with 13 cars behind engine E2, 2 hours 29 minutes late. It arrived Renton at 12:11 pm, made a two-minute station stop, and departed at 12:13 pm, 2'20" late. #15 passed Black River at 12:18 pm and Argo at 12:26 pm, 2'13" late. It reappeared at Argo as number 28 with the same 13 cars, now being towed backwards, at 1:03 pm, 2'10" late and left PC trackage at Black River at 1:12 pm, another minute down.

At 1:15 pm, MILW 1653 left Spokane Street light and arrived at Argo at 1:20 pm for Union Station. It subsequently returned to Pacific Coast rails at Argo at 3:10 pm, again light for the trip to home rails at Spokane Street, arriving at 3:16 pm. This would have placed the crew at Union Station while the eastbound Olympian Hiawatha arrived and filled from 11 to 13 cars.

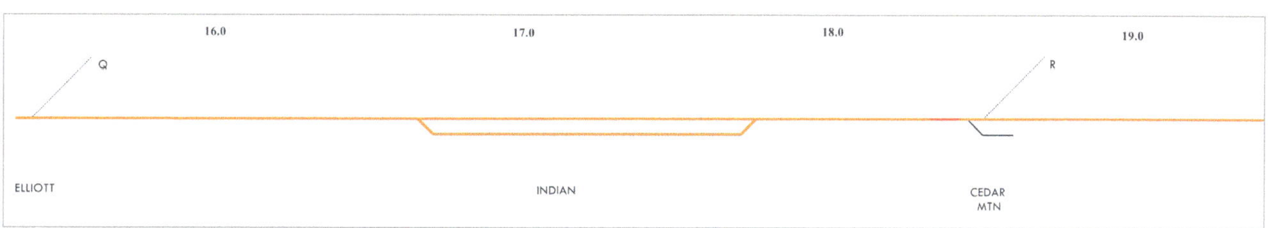

An engineer makes his routine check of BiPolar E1 prior to an early afternoon departure from Tacoma with the Olympian Hiawatha. The E1 will pull The Milwaukee Road's elite passenger train backward to Seattle, run around the train while head end cars are added, and depart from Seattle Union Station with its Pullman-built Skytop sleeper lounge at the end of the train as God and The Milwaukee Road intended. *Date and photographer unknown, photo WWAMP1348, PNRArchive collection at Burien, WA.*

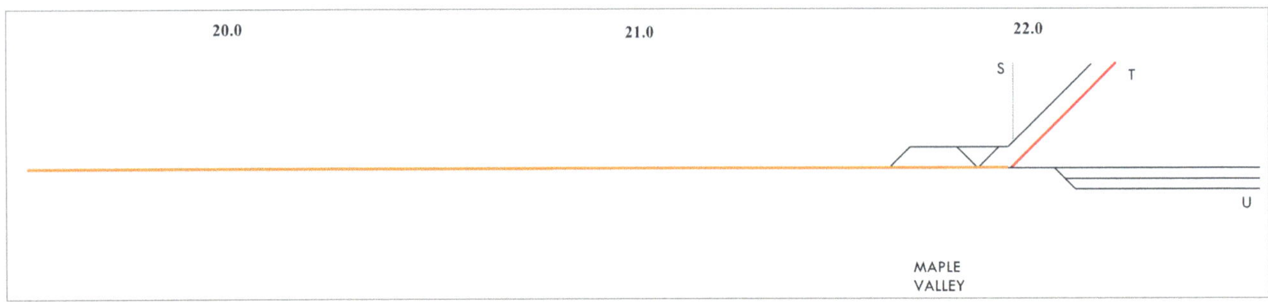

Break for Lunch

The eastbound Hiawatha passed Black River as #27 at 2:18 pm, being towed backwards by the E4, with 11 cars, 11 minutes late, and passed Argo en route to Union Station at 2:27 pm, having made up one minute. The Hi reappeared as #16 at Argo at 3:04 pm, with the consist increased to 13 cars and now oriented with the sky-top at the rear as envisioned by Chicago's public relations corps, still 11 minutes down. Black River was passed at 3:13 pm and arrival Renton was 3:18 pm. A two-minute station stop, departure at 3:20 (now 14 minutes down), and finally off PC rails at Maple Valley at 3:35 pm, the same 14 minutes behind schedule.

With three of the four varnish schedules on the sheet and the fourth not due for some six hours, the railroad belonged to various freight movements. The first was Pacific Coast #79, returning from Black Diamond. It showed up at Maple Valley at 2:50 pm with 18 coal loads, 1350 tons, and held in the clear for #16, departing at 3:35 as the varnish headed east. Number 79 arrived at Renton at 4:15 pm and settled in for several hours of switching Pacific Car & Foundry, Boeing, Gladding McBean, and the other industries in Renton/North Renton.

The next entry on the sheet was MILW 1626 which departed Spokane Street at 3:33 pm with 10-12, arriving at Van Asselt at 3:45 pm. They worked through the set-out of Extra E47 West, and then returned to Spokane Street at 5:44 pm with 29 cars from the extra, arriving at 5:56 pm.

The daily CMStP&P local from Tacoma hit the PC at Black River at 3:20 pm with 13 loads and 7 empties behind MILW 1277, a C5 class 2-8-0, and proceeded to Spokane Street, arriving at 3:37 pm. After turning and beans at Stacy Street, the 1277 departed Spokane Street with 31-8 at 5:12 pm, going back on Milwaukee trackage at Black River at 5:42 pm.

While #79 worked at Renton, the 1626 was at Van Asselt, and the 1277 turned at Stacy Street, MILW Extra E47 West entered PC rails at Maple Valley with 40 loads and 3 empties, 2245 tons, at 4:04 pm. It passed Renton at 4:20 pm, and arrived Black River at 4:25 pm. The E47 cut off 27-3, 1353 tons, and headed down the double track to Van Asselt at 4:45 pm, arriving at 5:00 pm. Dropping the Seattle set-out, they returned cab hop to Black River and onto Milwaukee rails at 5:28 pm where they continued to Tacoma with 13-0, 892 tons.

MILW 1203, a class C-5 2-8-0, was a sister to the 1277. It is southbound crossing onto its own tracks at Black River Junction. As it does so it changes railroad direction from east on the PC to west on the MILW. *Photograph by Harold A. Hill, June 1947, photo WWAMP1924, PNRArchive collection at Burien, WA.*

E47 at MILW's Tide Flats yard in Tacoma, 8/3/66. *Photographed by Al Farrow. WWAMP1611, PNRArchive collection at Burien, WA.*

During E47's stay at Black River, Extra E40 East showed up from Tacoma at 4:52 pm with 50 loads and 2 empties. No further action took place with this train until E47 arrived back from Van Asselt, then the E40 headed for Van Asselt cab hop at 5:35 pm, arriving at 5:50 pm. Why the wait is unknown, the E40 could certainly have advanced to Van Asselt on the double track and been yarded on any convenient track being a caboose-only movement, plus the 1626 would have been there to assist if needed. No other trains would have been involved even if the two mainline freights got snarled up switching, but possibly just to avoid such an event, the E40 waited for the E47. Pick up completed, the E40 left Van Asselt at 6:09 pm with 10-12, arriving back at Black River at 6:24 pm. Ten minutes later at 6:34 pm it left Black River with 60 loads and 14 empties, pulling into Renton at 6:40 pm. The Extra E40 East had a one-car pickup and it would appear that the dispatcher decided to hold it at Renton for the Extra E32 West rather than attempt a meet at Indian. This would be the time the crew of E40 would probably take a meal break as they went on duty at 2:45 pm. On the arrival of the E32, the E40 departed Renton at 7:40 pm with 60-15, 3976 tons, and passed off the PC at Maple Valley at 8:23 pm.

MILW boxcab E32 westbound at Maple Valley in December 1944. It looks like the motor car on the edge of the platform may have a Christmas tree tied to its roof. *Photograph by Harold A. Hill, WWAMP1567, PNRArchive collection at Burien, WA.*

The Extra E32 West passed Maple Valley at 6:55 pm with 13 loads and 51 empties, 1909 tons, and arrived Renton at 7:30 pm. Having gone on duty at 1:30 pm, it appears that they took an hour for lunch, departing Renton at 8:30 pm with the same consist and arriving at Black River at 8:36 pm.

The activities of the two second-trick switchers takes a little examination, but with a couple of "it sounds plausible" scenarios, a reasonable description of their movements can be developed. The crew of 1626 went to work at 2:30 pm and made the first of two trips cab hop to Van Asselt at 6:28 pm, arriving at 6:40 pm. It appears that they spent about three hours switching in the yard, including a meal period. Due to the small size of the Stacy Street yard, cars were frequently left at Van Asselt until needed, at which time they had to be dug out from whatever track the cut was left on. The 1630 crew went on duty at 4:00 pm and eventually headed for Van Asselt at 7:34 pm with two cars, arriving at 7:46 pm. Exactly how much switching was accomplished with two crews in the yard, and how much bs-ing took place is open to conjecture.

Back from Second Trick Beans

While the 1626 and 1630 worked Van Asselt, the Extra E32 West crew finished beans and left Renton at 8:30 pm with 13- 51, arriving at Black River at 8:36 pm, and cut off 7-13, 611 tons, their Seattle set-out. They left Black River at 9:03 pm, arrived Van Asselt at 9:18 pm where the cars were dropped, and returned cab hop to Black River, arriving at 9:50 pm and would ultimately head for Tacoma with 6 loads and 38 empties, 1298 tons.

Pacific Coast #79 finally finished its work at Renton and departed at 9:00 pm with 14-8, 1405 tons, arriving Black River at 9:10 pm. After setting out, they left at 9:55 pm, 8 loads and 6 empties, 852 tons, and arrived at Spokane Street at 10:30 pm.

At 9:32 pm, #25, the eastbound Columbian, passed Black River with 6 cars being towed backward by the E3 and passed Argo onto Union Pacific tracks at 9:43 pm, three and four minutes late respectively. The E3 reappeared at Argo as #18 with the consist doubled to 12 cars, on time at 10:40 pm. They were also on time at Black River at 10:49 pm, arriving Renton at 10:54. After a five-minute station stop, they departed at 10:59, five minutes late, and passed Maple Valley at 11:16 pm, four minutes late.

The two switchers at Van Asselt finished up their work and headed back to Spokane Street. The 1626 departed at 9:51 pm with 34 cars (presumably the loads set out by the E39 at 8:00 am), arriving at Spokane Street at 10:06 pm. The 1630 left at 11:01 pm with 7 cars (probably the 7 loads set out by the E32 at 9:18 pm), arriving Spokane Street at 11:13 pm. The 1630 may have been delayed an hour by the E32 eating at Renton, plus the need to separate the loads from the empties in the set out.

Dan Perkins shot MILW 671, originally the 1653, at the Tacoma roundhouse in October 1971. It was one of the three MILW switchers working on the PC on August 15, 1952. Built in 1940, it was retired in November 1980, after 40 years of faithful service. *Photograph by Dan Perkins, DRP016-035, PNRArchive collection at Burien, WA.*

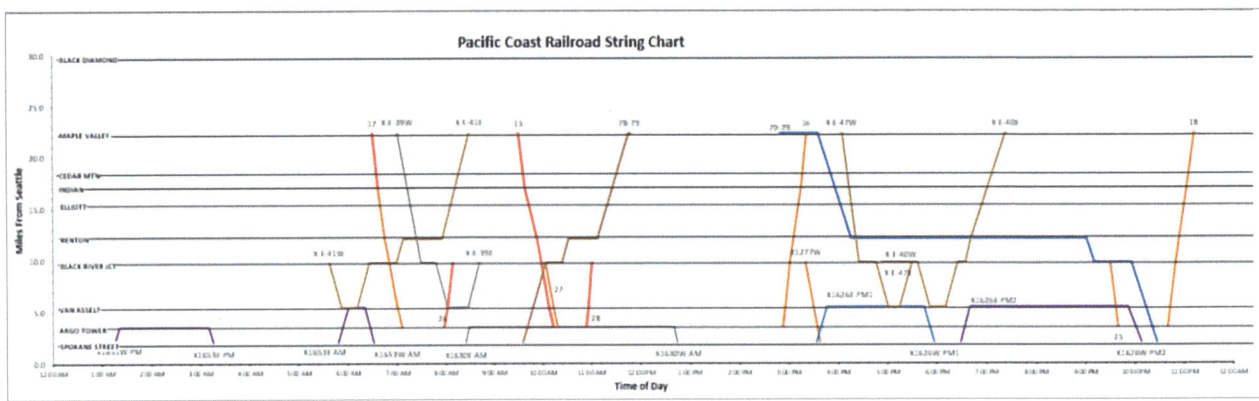

There it is, a day on the Pacific Coast. Two passenger trains each way with additional reverse movements behind four bipolar locomotives; three westbound and two eastbound mainline freights each with a reverse movement and powered by electric freight locomotives (although scheduled freights 263 and 264 were annulled); a round-trip local freight pulled by a steam engine; six round-trip transfer runs pulled by three different diesel switchers; and a Pacific Coast main line local behind a diesel switcher.

The Locomotives:

Eng No.	Class	Type	Builder
E-2	EP-2	Bi-Polar	GE
E-3	EP-2	Bi-Polar	GE
E-4	EP-2	Bi-Polar	GE
E-5	EP-2	Bi-Polar	GE
E-32	EF-5	4 unit	GE
E-39	EF-5	4 unit	GE
E-40	EF-2	3 unit	GE
E-41	EF-2	3 unit	GE
E-47	EF-2	3 unit	GE
1277	C-5	2-8-0	Milwaukee Road
1626	6-ES	SW1	EMD
1630	6-ES	SW1	EMD
1653	10-ES	NW2	EMD
GN 79	----	SW1	EMD

Pacific Coast Railroad
Schematic legend and color code:

A. Milwaukee Stacy Street yard
B. Pacific Coast yard
C. Northern Pacific Middle yard
D. NP crossing to main line
E. NP crossing to West Seattle
F. NP main line to King Street Station
G. Wye for King St Station coach yard
H. MILW to Harbor Island
I. NP Shore Line
J. Union Pacific-MILW to Union Station
K. UP Argo yard
L. NP main line to Tacoma
M. MILW-UP main line to Tacoma
N. MILW Black River yard
O. NP Belt Line crossing
P. PC to North Renton (ex Newcastle Branch)
Q. Abandoned Elliott mine spur
R. Abandoned Cedar Mountain mine spur
S. Abandoned PC Taylor branch
T. MILW main line east
U. PC Black Diamond

Pacific Coast - Black
Milwaukee - Red
UP - Yellow
NP - Green
PC/MILW - Orange
UP/MILW - Grey

H. V. O'NEIL—Chief Dispatcher

R. N. WHITMAN—Trainmaster

L. E. BARNES—Trainmaster

E. T. CARTER—Trainmaster

E. J. GARDNER—Trainmaster

C. A. KEIL—Asst. to Superintendent

TRAIN DISPATCHERS

R. E. Ozura
H. E. Loveless
D. L. Vernor

PACIFIC COAST R. R. CO.

TIME TABLE No. 12

ALSO

PACIFIC COAST R. R. CO.

SPECIAL RULES No. 12

Taking Effect 12:01 A.M. Sunday
November 25, 1951
Pacific Standard Time

This time table is for the government and information of employees only.

The Company reserves the right to vary therefrom at pleasure.

Destroy all time tables of previous date.

I. E. CLARY,
Superintendent

EASTWARD Second Class 78 FREIGHT Except Sunday	EASTWARD Second Class 264 Time Freight Daily C.M.St.P.&P.	EASTWARD First Class 18 PASSENGER Daily C.M.St.P.&P.	EASTWARD First Class 16 PASSENGER Daily C.M.St.P.&P.	EASTWARD First Class 28 PASSENGER Daily C.M.St.P.&P.	EASTWARD First Class 26 PASSENGER Daily C.M.St.P.&P.	Car Capacity Sidings	Car Capacity Com'l. Tracks	Miles from Seattle		MAIN LINE Time Table No. 12 November 25, 1951 Stations and Railroad Crossings		Symbols Rule 6(A)	WESTWARD First Class 17 PASSENGER Daily C.M.St.P.&P.	WESTWARD First Class 15 PASSENGER Daily C.M.St.P.&P.	WESTWARD First Class 27 PASSENGER Daily C.M.St.P.&P.	WESTWARD First Class 25 PASSENGER Daily C.M.St.P.&P.	WESTWARD Second Class 263 TIME FREIGHT Daily C.M.St.P.&P.	WESTWARD Second Class 79 FREIGHT Except Sunday
L 8:30 AM						Yard		0.	D-P	Seattle (Dearborn St.) N.P.—U.P.—C.M.St. P. & P. Crossings, Atlantic St. 2.0	SO	BCKTVWZ						A 5:10 PM
8:50		From U. P.	From U. P.	From U. P.	From U. P.			2.0	DN-P	Spokane St. Tower N.P. Crossing 1.8		DV	To U. P.	To U. P.	To U. P.	To U. P.		4:55
8:55		L 10:40 PM	L 2:53 PM	L 10:53 AM	L 7:59 AM			3.8	DN-P	Argo Tower N.P.—U.P. Crossings and Slip Crossing 1.9	G	DV	A 7:05 AM	A 10:13 AM	A 2:17 PM	A 9:39 PM		4:50
9:00	From C.M.St.P.&P.	10:43	2:56	10:56	8:02	C.M.St.P.&P. Yard		5.4	P	Van Asselt 4.3		X	7:00	10:03	2:14	9:36	To C.M.St.P.&P.	4:45
9:10	L 8:30 AM	10:49	3:01	A 11:01 AM	A 8:10 AM	Yard		8.7	DN-P	Black River Tower U.P. Crossing 2.4	BI	BIJRVX	6:50	9:58	L 2:07 PM	L 9:29 PM	A 3:01 PM	4:25
A 18 9:20 L 11:10	8:43	S 10:54	S 78 3:06	To C.M.St.P.&P.	To C.M.St.P.&P.	78	Yard	12.1	D-P	Renton N. P. Crossing 2.4	RN	BRWXYZ	S 6:45	S 78 9:53	From C.M.St.P.&P.	From C.M.St.P.&P.	2:30	L 18 4:15 A 2:45
11:25	8:56							15.5	P	Elliott 1.5							1:44	2:30
11:30	9:03	11:03	3:14			35		17.0	P	Indian 1.5			6:37	9:38			1:41	2:25
11:35	9:07						5	18.5	P	Cedar Mountain 3.8							1:38	2:20
A 11:50 AM	A 33 9:30 AM	A 11:12 PM	A 3:21 PM			Yard		22.3	DN-P	Maple Valley	DS	BJKRVWX	L 6:30 AM	L 264 9:30 AM			L 1:30 PM	L 2:05 PM
To Black Diamond Branch	To C.M.St.P.&P.	To C.M.St.P.&P.	To C.M.St.P.&P.										From C.M.St.P.&P.	From C.M.St.P.&P.			From C.M.St.P.&P.	From Black Diamond Branch

DOUBLE TRACK (Spokane St. Tower to Renton) — SEATTLE YARD (Seattle to Argo Tower) — AUTOMATIC BLOCK SIGNALS (Argo Tower to Maple Valley)

EASTWARD TRAINS ARE SUPERIOR TO WESTWARD TRAINS OF THE SAME CLASS

EASTWARD Car Capacity Sidings	Car Capacity Com'l. Tracks	Second Class 78 FREIGHT Except Sunday	Miles from Maple Valley		BLACK DIAMOND BRANCH TIME TABLE No. 12 November 25, 1951 STATIONS Railroad Crossings		WESTWARD Second Class 79 FREIGHT Except Sunday	Symbols Rule 6(A)
	Yard	L 11:50 AM	0.	P-DN	Maple Valley 4.2	DS	A 2:05 PM	BJKRVWX
	7	12:05 PM	4.2	P	Danville 1.1		1:50	
	35	12:10	5.3		[illegible] 2.0		1:45	V
	Yard	A 12:20 PM	7.3	P	Black Diamond		L 1:35 PM	XY

EASTWARD TRAINS ARE SUPERIOR TO WESTWARD TRAINS OF THE SAME CLASS

MAXIMUM SPEED PERMISSIBLE: Between Maple Valley and Black Diamond............20 M.P.H.

Westward trains on Black Diamond Branch will come to a full stop just east of Bridge 13 before pulling down to C.M.St.P. & P. junction switch. If necessary to stop for this switch to be lined, trains will stop to clear west switch of P.C.R.R. siding.

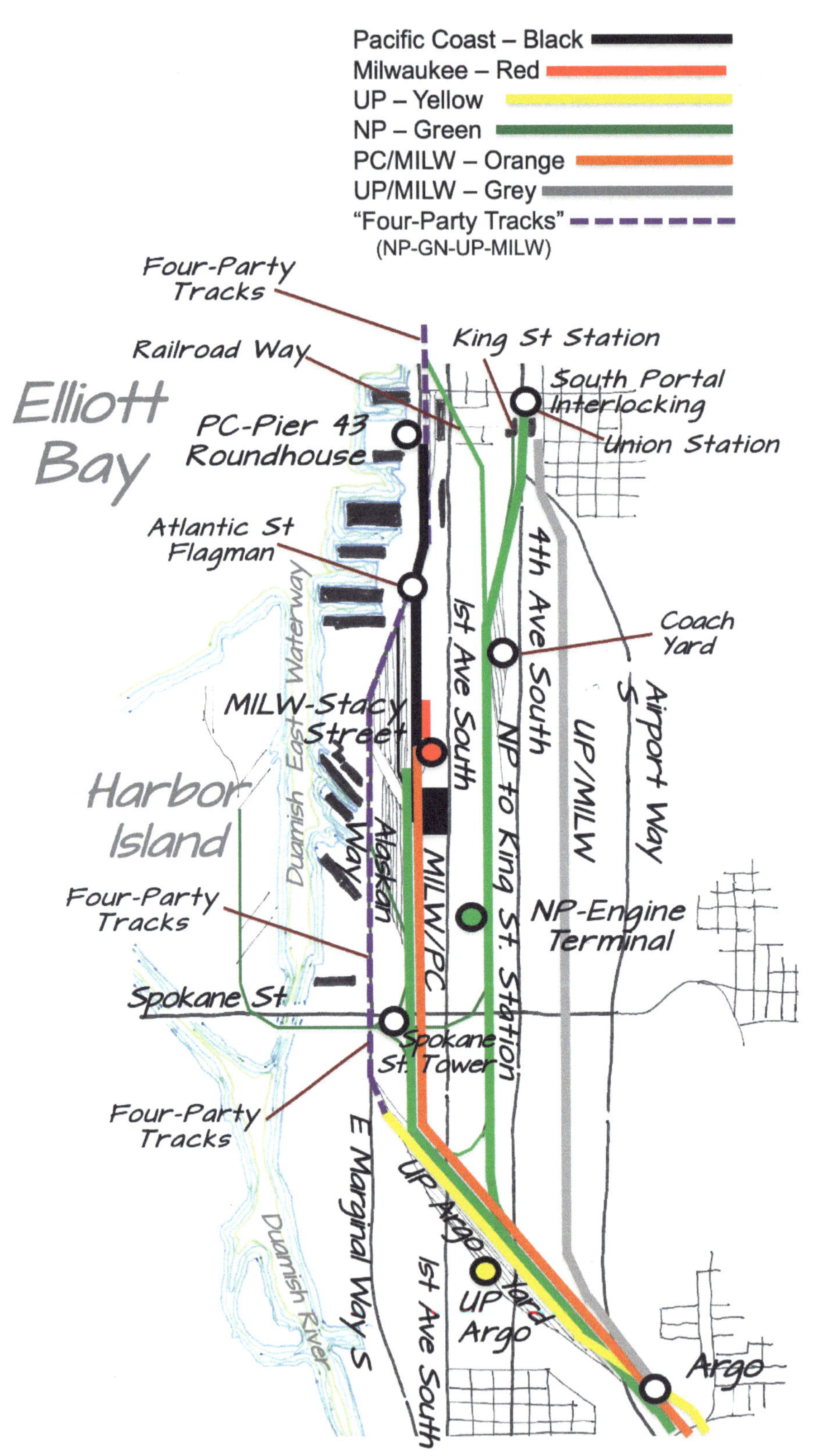

The South Seattle "spaghetti bowl" of tracks south of King Street and the King St. and Union Stations and north of Argo Tower. *Map by David R. Clemens.*

Riding the Van Asselt Transfer

The Milwaukee Road Stacy Street yard in Seattle is a vest-pocket-size facility squeezed in between the Pacific Coast Railroad yard, Sears & Roebuck's northwest retail/distribution complex, Utah Avenue, and the multitude of railroad crossings at Atlantic Street. A few through tracks, a few more stub-end, a couple of rip tracks, turntable, four-track roundhouse, minimal engine service facilities, plus the Sears tracks crossing the turntable/service tracks and switching back into the yard lead at the other end of the building. Overhead, the wooden Lander Street pedestrian bridge spans the tracks of the CMStP&P, PC, NP, GN, UP and joint waterfront lines, offering an incomparable view of yard and road engines working in and out of yard, transfer, and pier trackage. A pair of switch lamps stamped C&PS (Columbia & Puget Sound, the PC's predecessor) mounted on the bent nearest to the PC lead warn switchmen of the close clearance.

The Milwaukee terminal is really a minor appendage servicing the Seattle area, while the "main line" runs south to the Tide Flats yard in Tacoma where traffic is gathered from the Tacoma & Eastern lines to Mt. Rainier, and Milwaukee extensions to further lumber traffic sources at Grays Harbor, Chehalis, Willapa Bay, and Longview. However, a sizable portion of the CMStP&P's transcontinental traffic originates, terminates or moves through Seattle via the waterfront car barge operation serving Port Townsend, Bellingham, and other salt water points. An operating problem was magnified in 1917-20 when the St. Paul Road electrified the Tacoma Division of its Pacific Extension. The main line through Snoqualmie Pass, Maple Valley / Black River via the Pacific Coast RR, and on to Tacoma was strung with wire. However, only the line to Seattle's Union Station on PC and Union Pacific trackage was so equipped. The 3.4 mile freight line between the Stacy Street yard and the mainline connection at Argo was left forever bare of direct-current collection systems for the box-cab freight motors.

To provide the requisite trans-continental connection, the Milwaukee established Van Asselt Yard at MP 5.4, south of Argo, and 4.3 miles north of Black River where the main line leaves the PC right-of-way and becomes the joint MILW/UP line to Tacoma. Van Asselt is eight tracks wide and three-quarters of a mile long, sandwiched between the single-track UP main to the (geographic) east and the double track PC and NP (with GN trackage rights) mains to the west. Immediately across Airport Way west of the tracks is Boeing Field and the multitudinous plants of the aircraft manufacturer. Mainline freights bring their substantial blocks of Seattle traffic to Van Asselt and return to Black River to complete the last leg of their journey to Tacoma. Over time, many operational arrangements have been used for this movement and its counterpart for eastward traffic: leave the train at Black River and handle the Van Asselt cut only; run the whole train to Van Asselt, switch and return; with or without cabooses; and whatever scheme the current Division Superintendent thinks will minimize costs while (a distant second) expediting traffic.

The other end of this equation is the movement of cars between Stacy St. and Van Asselt. As required, yard jobs take transfer cuts to Van Asselt for pick-up by eastbound red ball trains, and - theoretically - bring back blocks left by westbounds. Unfortunately, schedules may not mesh and many one-way-loaded runs are made. To complicate matters, Van Asselt is still inside the Pacific Coast-imposed yard limits. "Yard engines and extra trains are not permitted to use Main Tracks within Seattle Yard Limits East of Argo except on train order authority." Thus, all "Van" transfer turns require clearance and orders to reach the outlying yard.

One such movement is preparing to depart Stacy Street on the morning of June 14, 1951. MILW yard engine 1438, an EMD SW1, has assembled a cut of cars for Van Asselt and connection with the mainline. Complete with caboose, the transfer run pulls down the yard lead, onto the "main" line (in reality, a parallel lead) and approaches

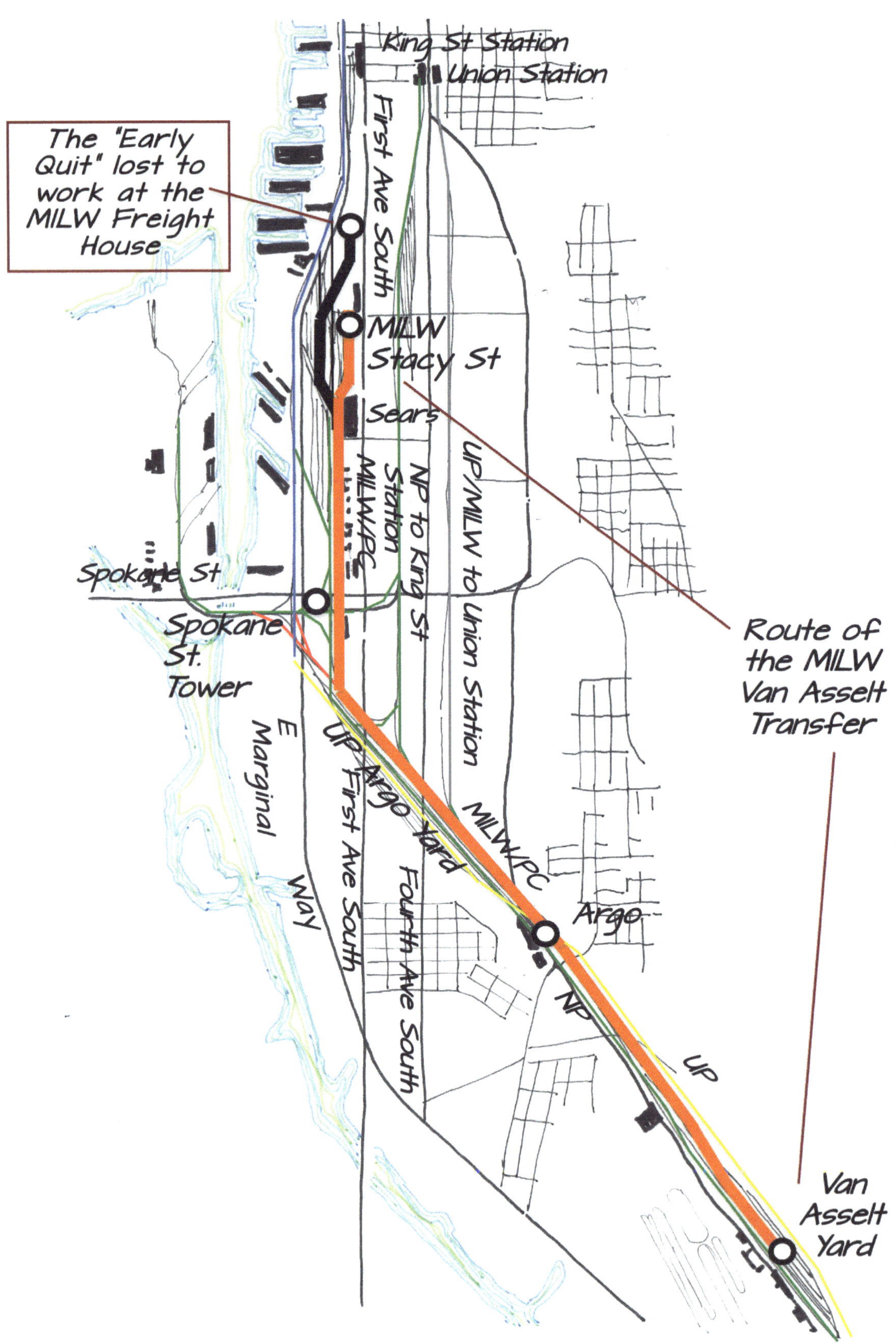

Route of the Van Asselt transfer. *Map by David R. Clemens.*

Spokane Street. To the west, the Pacific Coast and Northern Pacific yard entrance tracks provide the impression of triple-track in an industrial setting. A permanent "approach" semaphore signal with its locked-in 45 degree-angle board is located to the left of the Milwaukee track and provides an unnecessary warning that the train is coming up to the home signals of the Spokane St. interlocking. Here the three separate tracks of the MILW, PC. and NP become the two of the PC (with CMStP&P trackage rights) and the freight line of the NP. In addition, an NP line crosses the three tracks at a 90 degree angle, a connection from the passenger main and roundhouse/engine service facilities that becomes the West Seattle / Harbor island line past the diamonds. A connecting track from the NP freight line (called the "Colorado Avenue Line" in the employee timetable) to the West Seattle line splits off just before the signal gantry over the yard leads.

The Spokane Street Tower is located on the south side of the street and just west of the tracks. It's a diminutive, two-story brick building with just enough mechanical levers to operate the pair of crossovers on the PC tracks, allowing movements to and from the yards with the current of traffic, and the semaphore signals on the triple-track signal bridges plus the additional semaphores on the crossing NP track. In addition, an industrial lead departs from the center (PC eastbound) track just south of the south signal gantry and crosses the NP line. This is the Milwaukee's Harbor Island connection and is also used by the Pacific Coast to switch the Olympic Portland Cement plant adjacent to the East Waterway of the Duwamish River. A telephone box next to the crossing connects with the Spokane St. operator and is used for permission to block the NP tracks with the hand-operated gate.

The lower arm of the CMStP&P signal raises and the transfer run, horn blaring, crosses Spokane St. and halts opposite the tower. A switchman walks across the other two tracks and extracts clearance and orders from the small wood box that moves on a pair of wooden runners between the second-story operator portion of the tower and track level. In reality not much more than a vertical clothes line rope, the system allows the delivery of orders to trains without the necessity of the operator leaving his aerie.

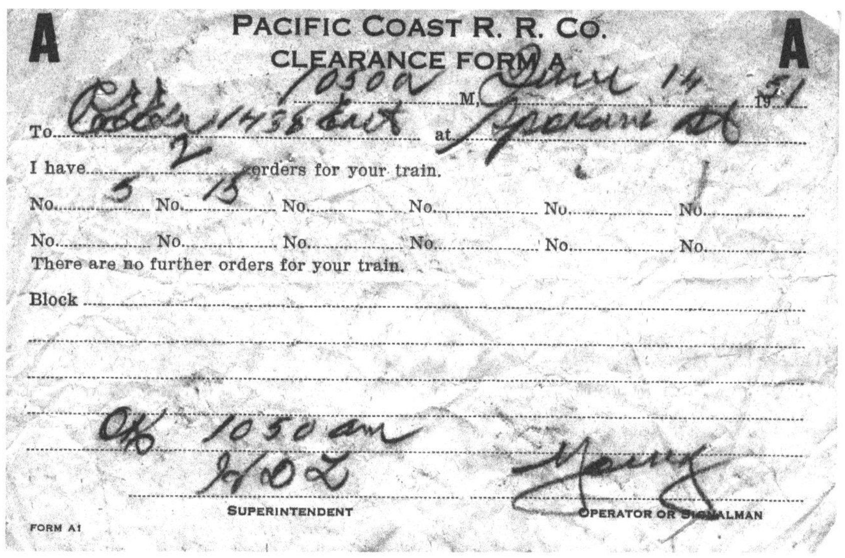
A PACIFIC COAST R. R. CO. A
CLEARANCE FORM A
1050 A M. June 14 1951
To C&E Eng 1438 East at Spokane St
I have 2 orders for your train.
No. 5 No. 15 No. No. No. No.
No. No. No. No. No. No.
There are no further orders for your train.
Block
OK 1050 am
HDL
SUPERINTENDENT
Young
OPERATOR OR SIGNALMAN
FORM A1

Pacific Coast R. R. Co.
Clearance Form A
1050 AM June 14, 1951

To C&E Eng 1438 East At Spokane St.

I have 2 orders for your train. No. 5, No. 15

OK 1050 AM
HDL Supt. Young, Opr.

Form 19 Pacific Coast R. R. Co.
Train Order No. 5 June 14, 1951
To: C&E Eastward Trains At: Spokane Street
No. 15 wait at
Maple Valley until 1055 AM
Black River 1115 AM
No. 28 wait at Argo until 1155 AM

HDL

Made: COM Time: 531 AM Williams. Opr.’

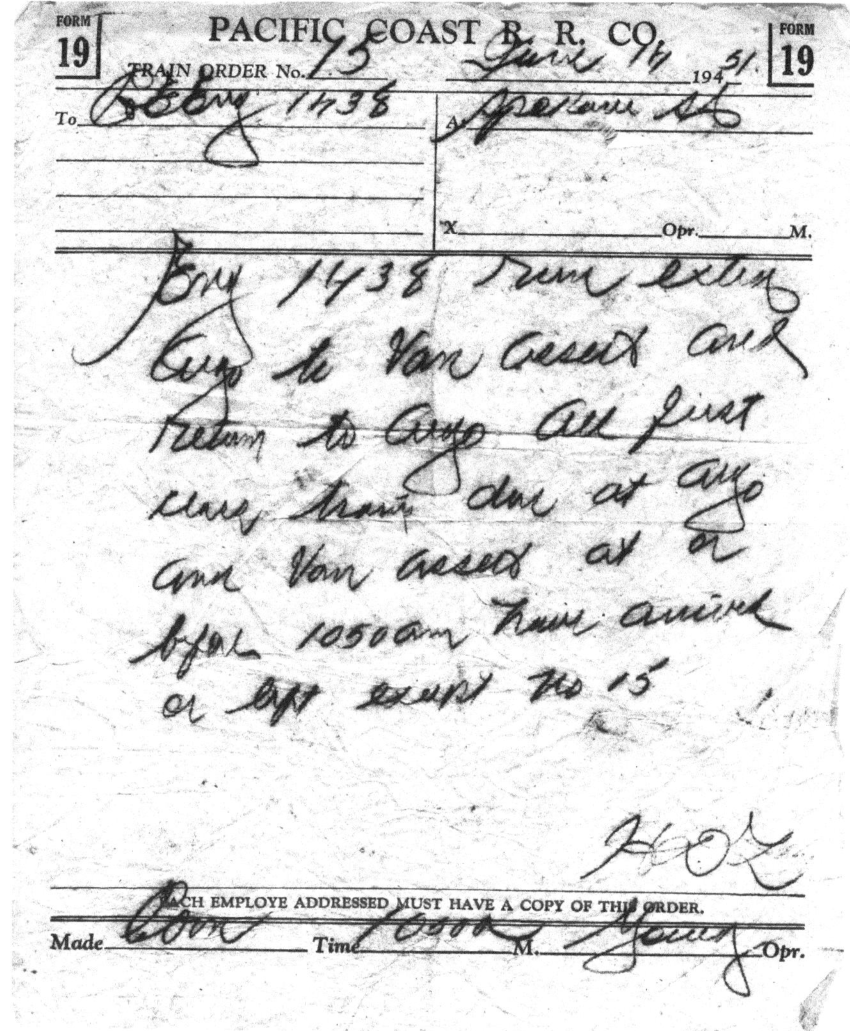

FORM 19 PACIFIC COAST R. R. CO. FORM 19

TRAIN ORDER No. 15 June 14 1951

To C&E Eng 1438 At Spokane St

X Opr. M.

Eng 1438 run extra Argo to Van Asselt and return to Argo All first class trains due at Argo and Van Asselt at or before 1050am have arrived or left except No 15

HDL

EACH EMPLOYE ADDRESSED MUST HAVE A COPY OF THIS ORDER.

Made Com Time 1050a M. Young Opr.

Form 19 Pacific Coast R. R. Co.
Train Order No. 15 June 14, 1951
To: C&E Eng 1438 At: Spokane St.
Eng 1438 run extra Argo to Van Asselt and return to Argo. All first class trains due at Argo and Van Asselt at or before 1050 AM have arrived or left except No. 15

HDL

Made: COM Time: 1050 AM Young, Opr.

Orders in hand, the 1438 accelerates through the crossover onto the eastbound main. As the train curves left towards Argo, the rear car of a passenger train is backing down the tail track next to the PC's westbound. Another mainline consist is being wyed on the "diagonal wye" located between the confluence of the PC/NP lines and the NP/(GN) mains. Now five tracks wide, and with the UP yard on the right, the various lines converge on the Argo interlocking. The Milwaukee crew observes a stop aspect and slows their transfer cut. A three-unit Great Northern engine moves past on the left and bangs through the plant, a long string of freight cars trailing behind. The pneumatic switch machines wheeze and whack their switch points into place, allowing the transfer to cross the NP mains. Before the interlocking plant is cleared, the headlight on a bi-polar appears on the westbound track and No. 15, the Olympian Hiawatha, diverges from the PC main line and onto the UP tracks leading to Union Station.

EASTWARD						
SECOND CLASS				FIRST CLASS		
78 FREIGHT Except Sunday	264 Time Freight Daily			18 PASSENGER Daily	16 PASSENGER Daily	28 PASSENGER Daily
	C.M.St.P.&P.			C.M.St.P.&P.	C.M.St.P.&P.	C.M.St.P.&P
L 8:30 AM						
8:50				From U. P.	From U. P.	From U. P.
8:55				L 10:40 PM	L 2:53 PM	L 10:53 A
9:00	From C.M.St.P.&P.			10:43	2:56	10:56
9:10	L 8:30 AM			10:49	3:01	A 11:01
A 15 9:20 L 11:10	8:43			10:54	TO 3:06	To C.M.St.P.&P
11:25	8:56					
11:30	9:03			11:03	3:14	
11:35	9:07					
A 11:50 AM	A 15 9:30 AM			A 11:12 PM	A 3:21 PM	
To Black Diamond Branch	To C.M.St.P.&P.			To C.M.St.P.&P.	To C.M.St.P.&P.	

The transfer moves past the ancient Georgetown area industrial buildings. Suddenly the old brick structures are left behind and the five tracks of the NP/PC/UP parallel Boeing Field. Now the UP swings east and the north crossover to Van Asselt is approached. Stop, line the switches, wait the obligatory five minutes; the crew checking their watches as the time in the wait order for No. 28 approaches. Finally, they cross over and enter the yard. The small train pulls down the track previously assigned by the yardmaster, stops, and the engine cuts off. Before they can line the lead switch, the 4-lamp headlight of a "pelican" box cab heaves into view, heralding the arrival of the mainline connection, an extra west. In turn pulling into an empty track, the electrics cut off their Seattle block. Simultaneously, the bi-polar on No. 28 accelerates past coupled to the Sky Top observation of what had been No. 15 inbound to Seattle. The Hiawatha is on the last leg of its journey from Chicago to Tacoma. Working together, the road and yard crews switch the transfer caboose from one end of the yard to the other. The road engine lines out of the south end of the yard, crosses over to the eastbound and returns light to Black River. The transfer pumps up the air and lines out of the north end of the yard.

The 1438 pulls north to Argo and halts beneath the Albro Place street bridge. A UP 4-8-2 is pulling out of their yard and across the trackage of the other railroads. The Portland-bound freight accelerates and as the caboose lurches through the crossings, the Milwaukee yard crew prepares to move. However, the home signal remains stubbornly at red. Whistle signals are ignored, but before the switch foreman can walk to the phone, a Northern Pacific 4-8-4 on No. 408, a Portland pool train, bangs through the plant and picks up speed. Whoosh-whack, the switches are lined and the signal clears. The little EMD trundles down the PC track and at the diagonal wye passes yet another "Hill road" passenger being wyed by an NP 0-6-0 before washing, cleaning, and stocking at the King Street coach yards.

				MAIN LINE	WESTWARD							
						FIRST CLASS				SECOND CLASS		
26 PASSENGER Daily	Car Capacity Sidings	Car Capacity Com'l. Tracks	Miles from Seattle	Time Table No. 11 July 31, 1949 Stations and Railroad Crossings	Symbols Rule 6(A)	17 PASSENGER Daily	15 PASSENGER Daily	27 PASSENGER Daily	25 PASSENGER Daily		263 TIME FREIGHT Daily	79 FREIGHT Except Sunday
C.M.St.P.&P.						C.M.St.P.&P.	C.M.St.P.&P.	C.M.St.P.&P.	C.M.St.P.&P.		C.M.St.P.&P.	
	Yard		0.	D-P Seattle (Dearborn St.) N.P.—U.P.—C.M.St. P. & P. Crossings, Atlantic St. 2.0 SO	BCRTVWZ							A 5:10 PM
From U. P.			2.0	DN-P Spokane St. Tower N.P. Crossing 1.5	IJV	To U. P.	To U. P.	To U. P.	To U. P.			4:55
L 7:59 AM			3.5	DN-P Argo Tower N.P.—U.P. Crossings and Slip Crossing 1.9 G	IJV	A 7:05 AM	A 10:13 AM	A 2:17 PM	A 9:39 PM			4:50
8:02	C.M.St.P.&P. Yard		5.4	P Van Asselt 4.3	X	7:00	10:08	2:14	9:36		To C.M.St.P.&P.	4:45
A 8:10 AM	Yard		9.7	DN-P Black River Tower U.P. Crossing 2.4 BI	BIJRVX	6:50	9:58	L 2:07 PM	L 9:29 PM		A 3:01 PM	4:25
To C.M.St.P.&P.	70	Yard	12.1	D-P Renton N. P. Crossing 3.4 RN	BRWXYZ	S 6:45	S 78 9:53	From C.M.St.P.&P.	From C.M.St.P.&P.		2:30	L 16 4:15 A 2:45
			15.5	P Elliott 1.5							1:44	2:30
	96		17.0	P Indian 1.5		6:37	9:38				1:41	2:25
		5	18.5	P Cedar Mountain 3.8							1:38	2:20
	Yard		22.3	DN-P Maple Valley DS	BJKRVWX	L 6:30 AM	L 264 9:30 AM				L 1:30 PM	L 2:05 PM
						From C.M.St.P.&P.	From C.M.St.P.&P.				From C.M.St.P.&P.	From Black Diamond Branch

DOUBLE TRACK — SEATTLE YARD — AUTOMATIC BLOCK SIGNALS

EASTWARD TRAINS ARE SUPERIOR TO WESTWARD TRAINS OF THE SAME CLASS

EASTWARD				BLACK DIAMOND BRANCH	WESTWARD	
SECOND CLASS					SECOND CLASS	
Car Capacity Sidings	Car Capacity Com'l. Tracks	78 FREIGHT Except Sunday	Miles from Maple Valley	TIME TABLE No. 11 July 31, 1949 STATIONS Railroad Crossings	79 FREIGHT Except Sunday	Symbols Rule 6(A)
	Yard	L 11:50 AM	0.	P-DN Maple Valley 4.2 DS	A 2:05 PM	BJKRVWX
	7	12:05 PM	4.2	P Danville 1.1	1:50	
	25	12:10	5.3	Henrys 2.0	1:45	Y
	Yard	A 12:20 PM	7.3	P Black Diamond	L 1:35 PM	XY

EASTWARD TRAINS ARE SUPERIOR TO WESTWARD TRAINS OF THE SAME CLASS

MAXIMUM SPEED PERMISSIBLE: Between Maple Valley and Black Diamond.........20 M.P.H.

Westward trains on Black Diamond Branch will come to a full stop just east of Bridge 13 before pulling down to C.M.St.P. & P. Junction switch. If necessary to stop for this switch to be lined, trains will stop to clear west switch of P.C.R.R. siding.

This time the Spokane St. plant is lined through and the run returns to CMStP&P rails for the short trip into the yard. A Northern Pacific class W 2-8-2, with its distinctive, sloping inboard-valve-gear cylinders pulls out of the NP yard with a transfer run to Auburn, whistling for the street crossings. The transfer cut from Van Asselt is yarded and the crew backs down to the tiny yard office. In spite of the delays in their run back from "Van," the crew discovers that the YM has them scheduled to switch the freight house next to First Avenue South north of the yard. The crew groans, knowing that they will have to assemble a cut of cars in the proper order and at the freight house, switch them in on the three tracks at the proper doors, simultaneously pulling some cars and re-spotting others. Finally, all cars must be spotted so that the car doors are in line with the building doors to allow access to each car. Yet spotting and pulling can't start until shift change at the freight house at 3 pm. The hoped-for early quit has suddenly become a much longer day, only partially compensated for by overtime.

Appendix

I started riding CMStP&P switch engines about 1949 when I was in junior high school, and they were the first of many on roads from coast to coast. Most of the time it was just yard switching, incessant back and forth moves on the lead, but I was happy as hell riding on an oil-fired 0-6-0 in the beginning, followed by SW1's and NW2's. I even had a genuine blue-and-white-striped engineer's cap EXACTLY like the engine crews – they bought theirs at Sears also. A sharp eye was kept out for the Trainmaster, and when he appeared I bailed off the opposite side of the engine and disappeared, only to return when the coast was clear. Hindsight tells me he knew I was there – it always took him a LONG time to reach the engine after he became visible.

I rode just about all the jobs at one time or another. Argo transfers, car barge loading and unloading, water front piers, Harbor Island, switch the freight house, interchanges, but I never rode a switch engine into Union Station. They rarely ran there, only a very occasional head-end car to put on or cut off a passenger run. I did get one trip out of the depot on an engine - an unbelievable ride on a bi-polar towing its train backward to Tacoma on a miserably rainy day. I remember the cab being extremely cramped, the ride extremely smooth, the visibility extremely poor – I guess the Northwest equivalent of a trip on a GG-1. We arrived at the old Milwaukee depot on D Street, I did my usual disappearing act off the "other" side, and I probably sloshed down to the "Union Station" to catch a pool train back. The return paled into insignificance after that centipede ride! Today, I can't remember many specific details, but the impact on an early teenager of that ride in the rain is undiminished. Dammit, why, to paraphrase somebody or other, is youth's experience experienced before it can possibly be fully appreciated?!

Switching barges was a kick – figuratively, NOT literally. Despite many published statements to the contrary, cars were not pulled/placed one or two at a time from/on opposite sides to "balance" the barge. Rather, the idler cars (again, contrary to popular opinion NOT required because of engine weight. Many loads outweighed an SW1, but to keep the stresses of engine acceleration and braking off the apron. Hey, how else were engines transferred to those barge-only-served branch lines if they couldn't cross the apron?) were coupled - gently - to an outside cut on the barge which in turn was still coupled to the deck house at the stern. After the air was cut in, the whole damn track was pulled and the barge listed heavily to the opposite side, while the apron adjusted accordingly. Usually, the unloaded cut was reversed back onto the barge to the opposite track (the barges were all three-track), causing an even MORE alarming list. Couple, pull; now the barge is level, but much higher in the water. Grab the cut off the center track, pull back blocking Alaskan Way, and either push into the barge yard tracks or onto the transfer tracks parallel to the street. Loading was just the opposite, except that it was mostly empties so that vessel stability was much less affected. But by God you better have the cut under control when you made the joint with the coupler on the face of the deck house!

Back and forth, on steam engines or diesels, it was great. One afternoon, we all walked over to the adjoining Pacific Coast yard, sat on a pile of coal, and watched them re-rail ol' 17, an Alco 0-6-0 that'd stubbed its toe on a switch. 'Course, the PC guys might've rather not had our "advice." C'est la vie!

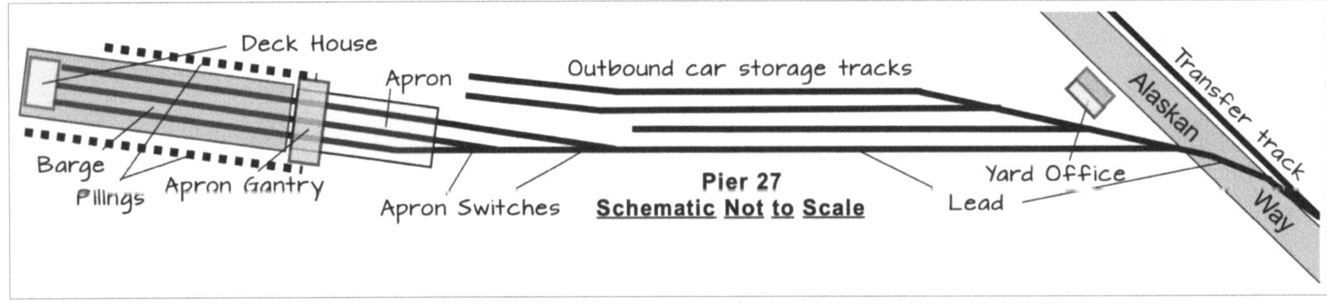

Pier 27 track arrangement. Schematic by David R. Clemens.

Wash the Builder, Pull the Shop, and Wye the Pool Train

A necessary adjunct to any passenger terminal worthy of the name is the "coach yard." Here the trains are cleaned, consists switched, water tanks filled, diners/lounges stocked, repairs from nearly insignificant to routine to major component change-outs made, and the whole consist run through the washer before spotting in the assigned station track for passenger boarding.

The joint Great Northern/Northern Pacific King Street Station coach yard in Seattle fulfills all of the required tasks in a compact facility branching off the station lead tracks and terminating in a stub-end tail track just south of Horton Street. On the east side, the classic Northern Pacific commissary building (shorn of its "Route of the Great Big Baked Potato" sign) is a provisionary beyond compare, supplying dining cars with not only potatoes, but all the required comestibles plus such mundane supplies as linen, china, silver, and flowers for the tables serving cuisine equaling that of any four-star hotel en route.

Northern Pacific commissary in Seattle, March 1970, with its "Route of the Great Big Baked Potato" sign. *Photograph by Dan Perkins, DRP065-004, PNRArchive collection at Burien, WA.*

Other buildings contain a myriad of supplies required for both passenger comfort and the mechanical integrity of their conveyances. A two-track shop building diverges from the tail track and though the walls don't reach the ground, is fully equipped with light overhead cranes, a drop pit for changing out wheel and axle assemblies, and even the required hues of paint to touch up such minor scrapes as occur in transcontinental travel.

Coach yard routine is both flexible and repetitive. Most passenger trains consist of the "same" cars, X number of coaches, Y Pullmans, diner, baggage, possibly an observation car, and maybe Railway Post Office, mail storage, and Railway Express Agency cars for the head end. As repairs or heavy shopping are a required, a specific car may be switched out and a twin, differing only in name/number replaces it. But normally, the train is wyed, serviced, washed, and spotted for loading in typical day-to-day repetition. At King Street, a pair of Great Northern diesel switchers perform the required tasks at the north (station) end of the yard, while an NP 0-6-0 holds down the tail track duties.

An arriving train pulls into its assigned station track and the road engine cuts off (unless it's a local tucked into a stub track) and heads for the roundhouse. Passengers and baggage are unloaded, and the coach yard switchers take over. Full mail storage cars are cut off and switched to the terminal annex. Mail from the RPO has already been placed on the ubiquitous baggage wagons for transfer. A switcher couples into the south end of the passenger consist

The Empire Builder, Seattle King Street Station, on a typical rainy Seattle day. Sacks of mail move to and from an RPO car... *Photograph by Philip R. Hastings, Philip Ross Hastings, MD, collection, California State Railroad Museum.*

and the air is cut in. If time is short before the scheduled departure, car cleaners are already aboard, removing the detritus accumulated on the inbound run. The train pulls slowly out of the track in response to the switchtender's signal, accelerates on the double-track main line, then slows to negotiate the puzzle switches at Holgate Street at the required 10 mph. Crossing watchmen activate their signals and hold their stop signs as the movement crosses city streets. Past the NP roundhouse and across Spokane Street, the line curves left and adjoins the freight lines from the Pacific Coast/Milwaukee/NP yards on the waterfront.

This is the site of the "diagonal wye" that forms a triangle between the two sets of tracks. The train slows, stops, and backs down the leg of the wye next to the freight lines. Stopping at the curved leg switch, a long consist will extend nearly to the Spokane Street interlocking tower. Now moving forward, the train crosses an industrial spur and approaches the mainline once again. A switchman lines the wye switch and the crossover to the westbound main, the engine pulls the cars forward, and stops to allow the switches to be lined back normal. The train returns to King Street, backs into the coach yard, and activity accelerates.

Any car requiring major repairs is switched out to the shop by the 0-6-0 at the south end and a substitute pulled from a storage track and inserted in the proper position. The consist is pulled back across Horton Street, reverses, and is slowly pushed forward through the washer on the far west track next to the mainline. Automobile drivers held back by the crossing watchman for this movement fume impatiently, most ignoring the aesthetics of an 0-6-0 chuffing slowly forward as the whirling brushes scrub away the accumulated grime of the inbound journey. Now sparkling on the exterior, the passenger train is pulled back and then spotted on a yard track.

BN (ex-GN) switcher turning an Amtrak passenger train on the "diagonal wye," February 1972.
Photograph by Dan Perkins, DRP019-083, PNRArchive collection at Burien, WA.

On August 30, 1948, Ron Nixon photographed the two-year-old Spokane Club, NP 393, as it was pulled through the car washer in Seattle, bringing up the rear of the Northern Pacific's North Coast Limited. Amazingly, this round-end observation car has been preserved after some 70 years of active service and is now at the Northern Pacific Railway Museum in Toppenish, Washington. In the distance, an NP 0-6-0 with its tender full of coal "holds down the tail track duties." *Museum of the Rockies, Ron V. Nixon collection.*

The car cleaners already on board are assisted by additional laborers, who help with the window cleaning, vacuuming, and dusting. Bags of debris are thrown into wire-sided wagons pulled by small tractors. More wagons of supplies from the commissary are spotted alongside the diner and lounge. *More* wagons, carrying linens, ice, pillows, and blankets; Cushman scooters with car knockers, electricians, and supervisors converge on the train. Brake shoes are changed out, an air hose replaced, air conditioning examined, light bulbs - the multitude of details necessary to preserve the ambiance of an Empire Builder or North Coast Limited, International or Portland pool train are checked, rechecked, and okayed. The dining car crew is busy stowing everything from cuts of beef to fresh-baked pastries, crates of vegetables to silverware, fresh carnations to dish soap, presto logs for the stove to salmon scarcely off the fishing boats docked less than a mile away. The lounge car attendants are stocking liquor, peanuts, beer, swizzle sticks, linen, and more fresh flowers.

As departure time approaches, final checks are made, crews don their uniforms, and the train is pulled back into the station. The switcher cuts off, negotiates the slip switches into the tunnel at the north end of the station, and is then cleared out by the South Portal operator. As the train crew registers in and picks up clearances and orders, another switcher adds mail and express cars, and perhaps an REAX reefer loaded with fresh fish switched only a short time before from the waterfront pier track of Washington Fish & Oyster Co. The road engine arrives, couples on, an air test made, and the Station Master announces another departure from Seattle.

Meanwhile, its shift change on the King Street Terminal Railroad. One GN switcher ties up next to the yard office on the station lead, while the other swaps crews and goes on working. The 0-6-0 clanks up from the south end and onto the main, only to reverse and run back down to the NP engine facilities to take on coal. Other days, it will merely replenish the water supply and have its grates shaken down by the fireman on the appointed track next to the yard office. Today, coal, a little overtime, another pair of moves across the city streets to the irritation of the motorists, and the crew ties up. But the activity in the coach yard continues around the clock as trains ranging from the 16-car Western Star to the 3-car Grays Harbor Local are prepared for their next run.

March 1971: GN's morning International has covered 155 miles since leaving Seattle's King Street Station at 8:00 am. One more will put it into CN's Vancouver, BC, terminal station. Even a "lesser" train like the International could rate a round-end observation! *Photograph by Mike Chandler.*

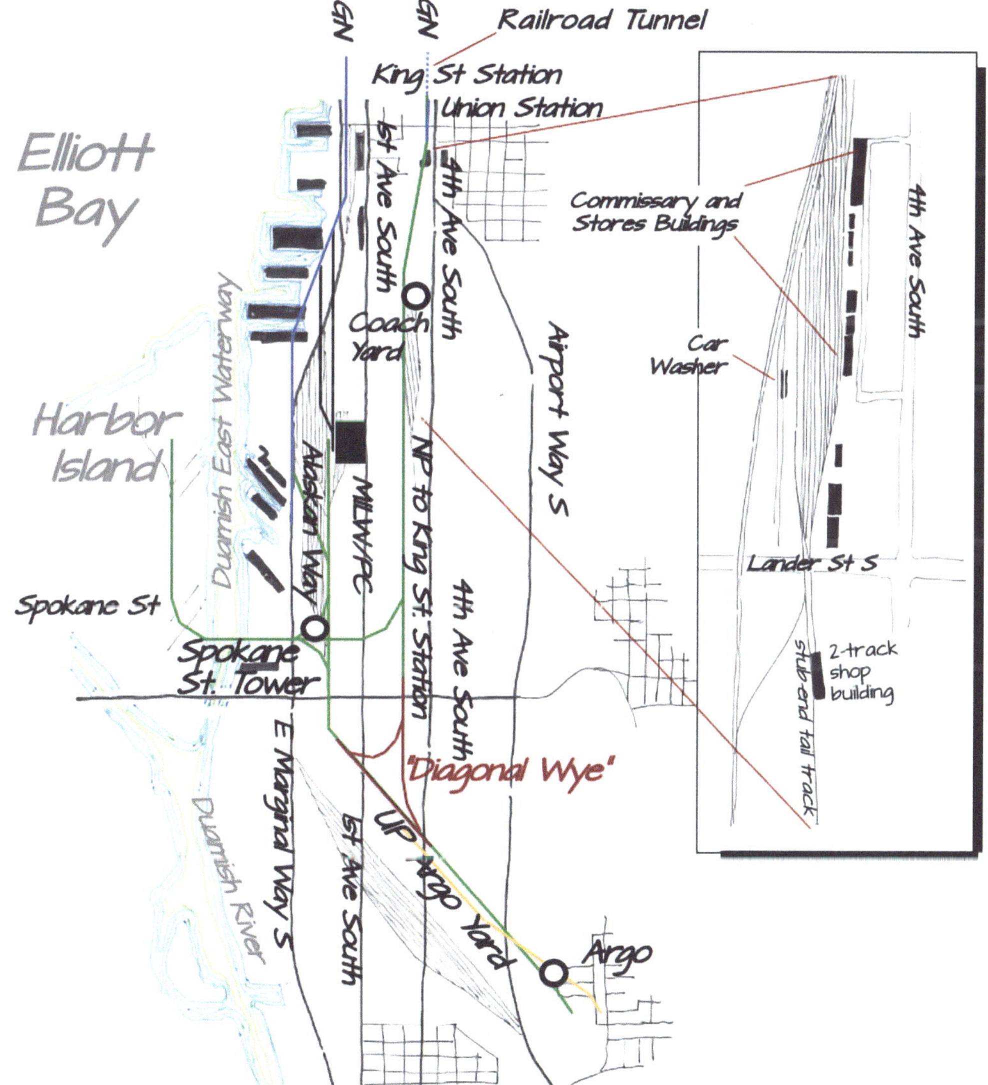

Stations, coach yard, and the "diagonal wye"—servicing passenger equipment in Seattle. *Map by David R. Clemens..*

Addendum

While in high school, I rode with the 0-6-0 crew at least once or twice a week. Andy Anderson was the engineer and Lionel Coleman the fireman. My first duties were merely to operate the bell and wave at the motorists at street crossings (in retrospect, I'm SURE they loved the attention!!). Before long I was hand firing, taking on coal and water, passing signals, and my injector responded to the water level in the boiler gauges. The ultimate was when Lionel got married and I was the fireman for that Saturday – no relief fireman was called (unofficial, illegal, but he didn't lose a day's pay) and it really was my engine.

Mike McLaughlin wrote about his experiences firing Northern Pacific 0-6-0s in the Seattle area. The engines he worked on would most certainly have been in the L-9 class like the 1070 pictured. NP had a lot of them (90 in total) and I believe they were the only class of 0-6-0s still in service during the post-war era on NP. The 1070 was assigned to the Tacoma Division for several decades prior to being retired in 1958. Therefore, it's quite likely that Mike would have fired this locomotive at least once during his adventures as an unofficial fireman. The 1070 is believed to have been the last locomotive under steam anywhere on the NP system when it was retired. When I photographed it, the engine was working for a tourist railroad running over the old NP branch into Bellingham.
—Mike Chandler. *Photograph by Mike Chandler.*

As time went by, we switched the shops, changed out cars, washed, wyed, and occasionally ran for coal. Immediately adjacent to the tail track was a pond (swamp) slowly being filled in with the debris from the trains. Several ducks nested here, so Andy kept a bag of corn in the seat box and religiously fed "his" birds. Rather large rats also inhabited the area and attempted to feed on eggs and ducklings. Andy's .22 pistol, also kept in the seat box, somewhat evened the odds. In retrospect, how many rules can you break? No fireman, a kid taking his place, and a gun in the cab!

Rain or shine (and in Seattle, you damn well know which predominated), l bailed in coal. I learned how to place my scoops, fill the corners, spray the whole grate by bouncing the heel of the shovel on the fire box door lip. Scoop, swing around, step on the butterfly door pedal, and into the firebox RIGHT where it's needed, all in one motion. Even on a "main line" trip to the wye at a *very* rocking, pitching 20 mph.

Not all of the time was spent on the engine – I rode the cars through the washers, watched the cleaners vacuum as we turned on the wye, carried linen and flowers, and lined switches when the switchman was at the other end. But if only for an hour or so after school, I generally shoveled, waved, and returned home very gritty, trying to convince my mother l hadn't been messing around in the railroad yards. The time I unloaded at "speed" at Spokane Street to catch the bus home and twisted my ankle on a "round" rock - not ballast - and went ass over teakettle, ripping my pants and carving a rather large gash in my hand, the fiction was rather difficult to maintain. I wonder what my peers were doing? Probably occupied with such mundane pursuits as cars and girls.

Today, on one of my great NP audio tapes by Elwin Purington, there is a cut with the slow chuff-chuff-chuff of an 0-6-0 pushing a train through the washer. Who knows, maybe I was firing that day!

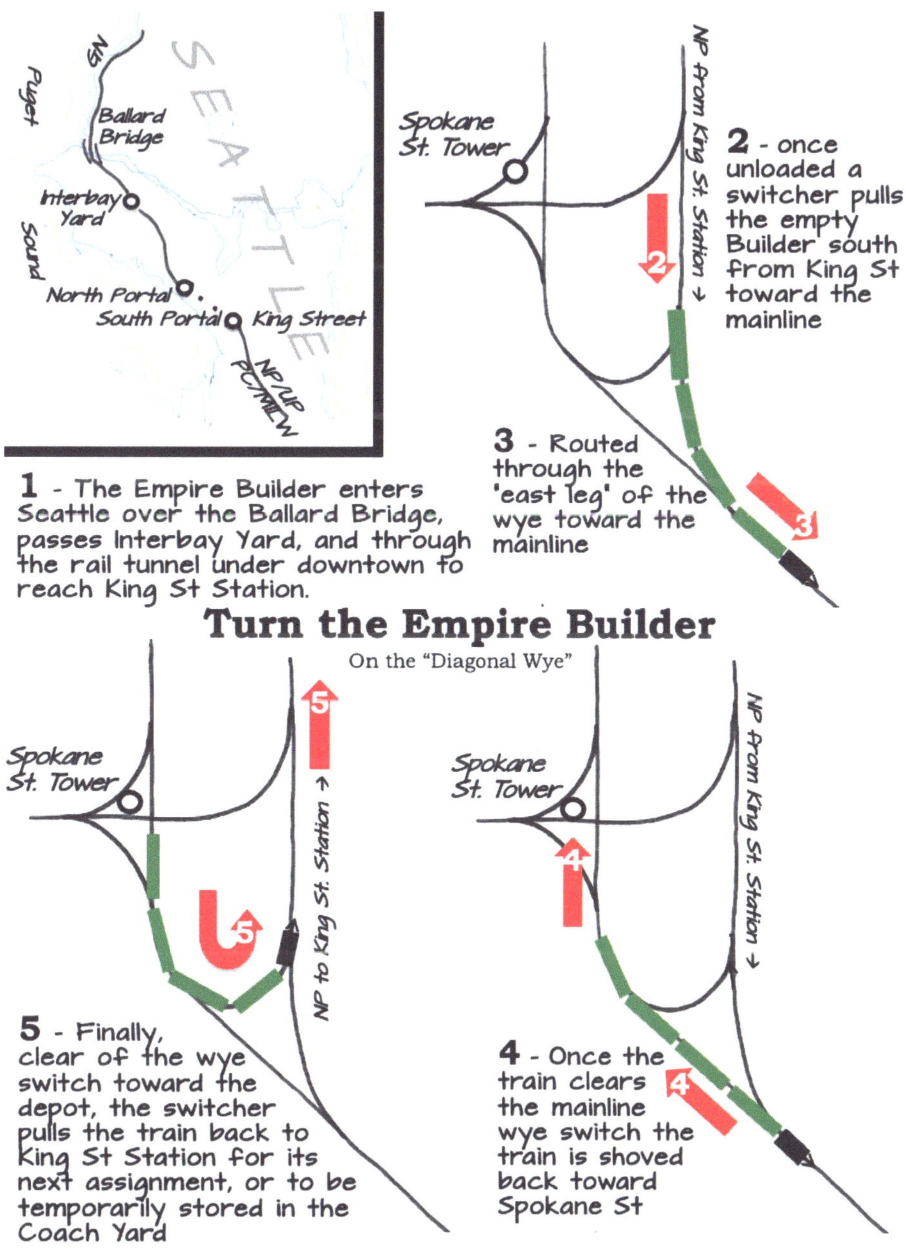

Turning the Builder on the Diagonal Wye. *Illustration by David R. Clemens.*

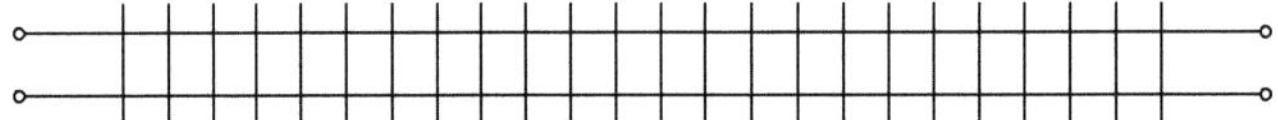

Seattle Engine Terminals (1950s)

Pacific Coast Railroad engineer Fritz Soderback (right) reports for his run to Black Diamond on December 31, 1947. On duty at 8:30 am, he will have 2-8-0 No. 14. Hostler Tommy Wieltschnig (left) watches shop foreman Charles Newman (center) marking Soderback up on the call board. Predecessor Columbia & Puget Sound call board is just visible behind the PC board. *Photographer unknown, photo MVHS_PC0079, PNRArchive at Burien, WA.*

Railroad engine terminals are ideally located alongside the freight yards and passenger terminals they support. However, in real life, they're frequently located "down the line" from one or the other of those facilities, and occasionally at a site not near either. The result is a complication for the yardmaster, possibly money for the engine crew if a hostler isn't employed, and fascination for the observer.

July 29, 1973: This is a photo of GN SW1 #83 at the Interbay roundhouse, but the interesting thing about it is the box car red F7 just catching the light in the open doorway. At the time BN had a handful of F units which were used to power their rotary snowplows. Not long after I took this photo, traffic levels on BN surged and the railroad found itself short of motive power. Consequently, these units had their traction motors reinstalled and were spotted roaming the BN system while still painted box car red.
—Mike Chandler. *Photograph by Mike Chandler.*

In Seattle, King Street Station is properly located "downtown." However, the Great Northern roundhouse is at Interbay, some five miles north of the station. While alongside the freight yard, the location requires that passenger engines pull out of the ready tracks onto the single-track main line through the power switch controlled by the operator in the big white yard office on the hill overlooking the leads, main, and roundhouse. They then back down the main, across an NP industrial track and through the spring switch indicating the beginning of double track, and continue a substantial distance down the waterfront and through a one-mile tunnel to the depot to pick up their trains. Conversely, engines off inbound trains must back to the Interbay engine terminal in the reverse direction. Only the power for the south-end Portland pool trains begin and end their journeys properly oriented moving to and from the roundhouse.

In their movements, the engines have negotiated a single power switch (from roundhouse to main), an automatic interlocking (NP Pier 91 lead across the south end of Interbay yard), a mechanical interlocking (North Portal on the waterfront, a classic two-story wooden tower), the tunnel, and an electric interlocking (South Portal, at King Street Station, a tiny single-story brick building located beneath the Jackson St. viaduct).

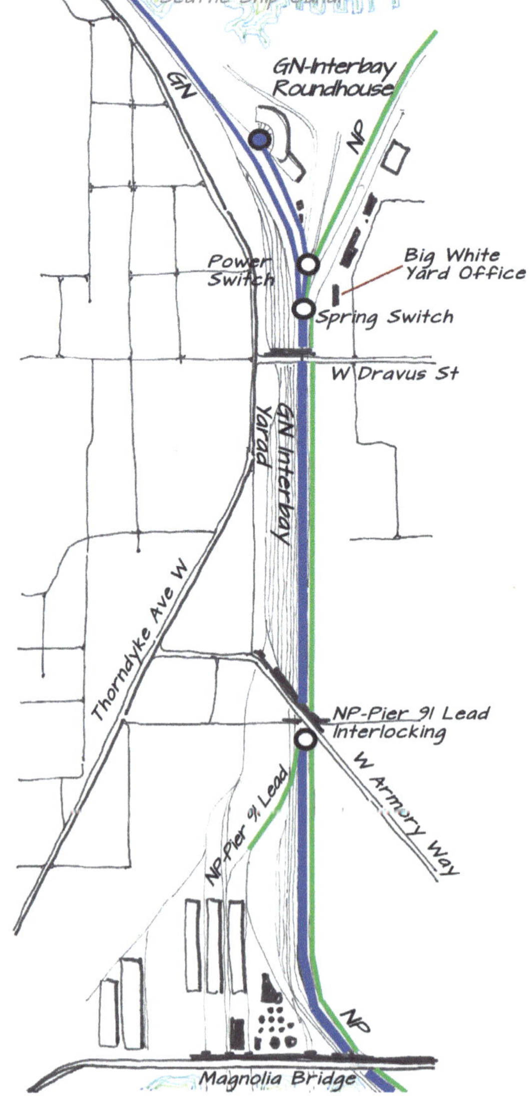

Great Northern Interbay to Magnolia Bridge.
Map by David R. Clemens.

The south portal of GN's tunnel under downtown Seattle, with its single-story brick tower with electric interlocking—in the shadow of the Jackson Street viaduct. The left-hand tracks lead to King Street Station, which is just out of view on the lower left. *Photograph by Ralph Wehlitz, R. Wehlitz Collection, photo 2023.010.12-030, Lake States Railroad Historical Association, Baraboo, WI.*

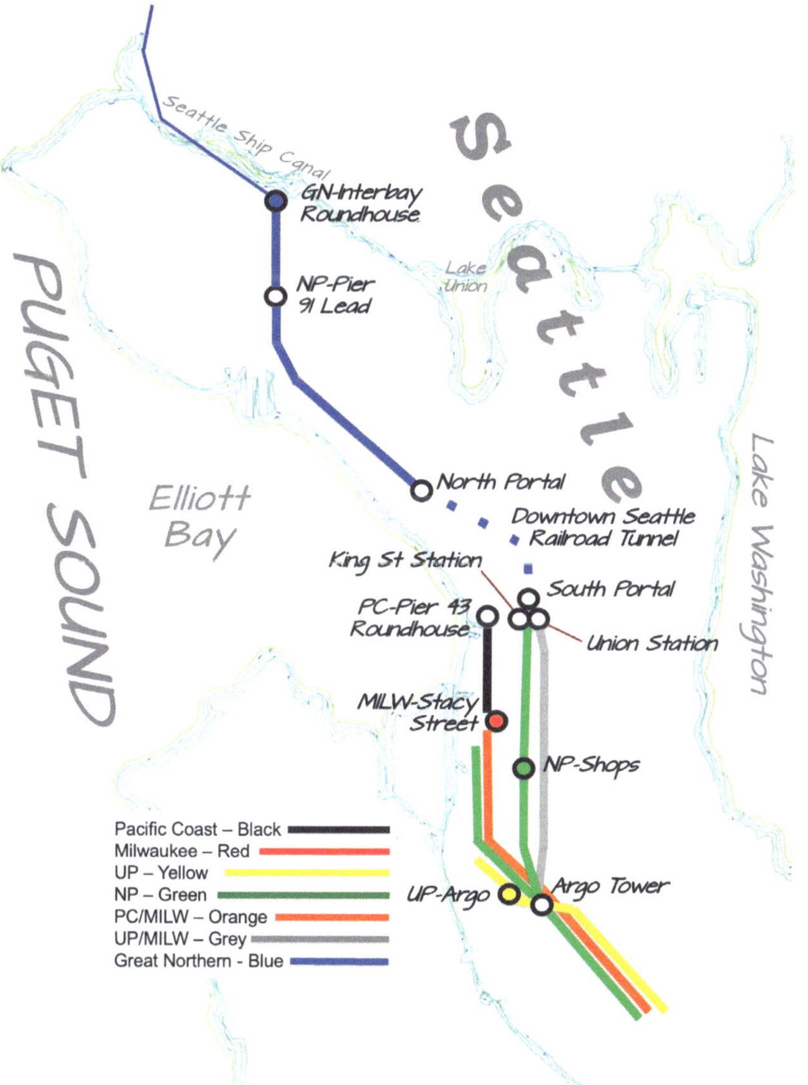

Seattle Engine Terminals—a bird's eye view. Map by David R. Clemens.

The Northern Pacific managed to locate their engine terminal remote from both passenger station and freight yard. It's about 1½ miles south of King Street adjacent to the passenger (and GN freight by trackage rights) main. This is a relatively easy backing move to and from the station for out- and in-bound passenger engines, but the freight hogs face a more complicated procedure. Outbound power heads south across, and then west parallel to, Spokane Street. After crossing the Pacific Coast (CMStP&P) double-track freight main and the NP's single freight line at Spokane Street tower, the engines back around the connecting curve between what has become the Harbor Island/West Seattle industrial branch, onto the "Colorado Avenue" freight main previously crossed, and continue reversing to the south end of the freight yard to pick up their trains.

NP 1098, a class L-9 built by Alco-Dickson in 1907, at the NP Seattle Roundhouse in 1934. *Photograph by James M. Fredrickson, JMF00-00349.2, PNRArchive collection at Burien, WA.*

Inbound power usually follows a different route. After cutting off at the north end of the yard, the Atlantic Street crossing flagman waves ("NP: one motion with green flag or light") them across the multiple crossings of the UP, CMStP&P, GN and PC railroads and they proceed down the waterfront alongside Alaskan Way to King Street, four blocks due west of the King Street Station. Here, the engines reverse onto Railroad Way, a narrow thoroughfare cutting diagonally southeastward from the waterfront across lower downtown and into the industrial/freight house district south of downtown. Once the site of the "Ram's Horn War," a turf battle between the PC predecessor Columbia & Puget Sound, the City of Seattle, and a saloon, it now provides right-of-way for both NP and GN engine and freight transfer movements. Moving backwards down the center of the street between ancient brick buildings containing facilities ranging from warehouses to taverns, the engines squeeze past parked cars, cross First Avenue South and parallel the NP freight house/team tracks to the "puzzle switches" at Holgate Street. Here they enter a running track parallel to the passenger main, ending at the engine terminal three-quarters of a mile south.

Outbound engines have had main- industrial- and freight-line running while crossing through a mechanical interlocking controlled from a small two-story brick tower. Inbound power has negotiated a flagged crossing of other railroads, street running, and waterfront and industrial areas.

The Union Pacific in Seattle copies the Great Northern in its concept of engine terminal placement. The facilities are immediately adjacent to the Argo freight yards, but 3½ miles south of the joint UP-Milwaukee Union Station located across Fourth Avenue South, east of King Street Station. Outbound passenger engines pull out of the yard through the UP's Argo interlocking, an electro-pneumatic plant controlling a maze of tracks where the NP Colorado Avenue freight line joins the NP/(GN) passenger line; the double-track (PC/CMStP&P) freight line joins the double-track passenger line (UP/CMStP&P); the UP double-track freight leads from the yard cross the above trackage and a connecting line provides a route between the freight and passenger mains; and, finally, the NP "Shore Line" (or "Lake Shore Line," a remnant of the old Seattle, Lake Shore & Eastern connection) crosses *ALL* of the above to meander down through its industrial area.

After negotiating the intricate trackage, and most likely being delayed by the trains of the other roads in the process, the UP engines have a straight shot backwards to Union Station under the catenary providing power for the Milwaukee Road's bi-polar electrics. Inbound engines follow the reverse route through the industrial area, certainly far less scenic than the GN's waterfront approach.

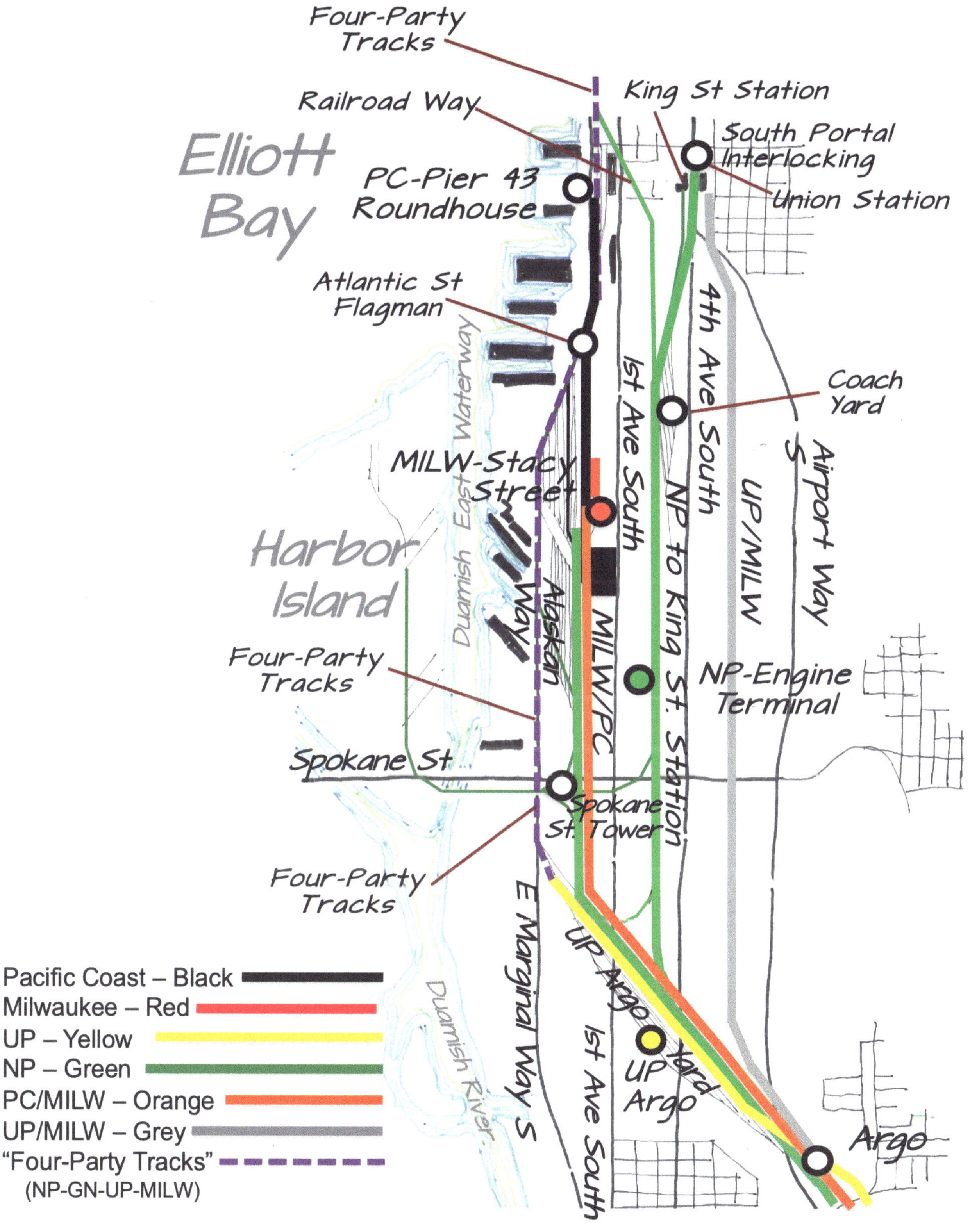

South Seattle, showing MILW, NP, PC, and UP engine facilities in relation to King Street (GN and NP) and Union (UP and MILW) stations. *Map by David R Clemens.*

The Milwaukee has the only "pure" engine terminal placement in Seattle. Its compact four-track roundhouse, turntable, and service facilities are merely a few feet from the yard lead. It supports only the yard engines and the power of the daily local from Tacoma, a turn arriving about noon and immediately returning south. Mainline freights set out their Seattle blocks at Van Asselt, retreat to Black River, and continue to Tide Flats yard in Tacoma. Passenger trains arrive in Union Station, pause while the bi-polar runs around the train to couple to the Sky-Top observation, and then are hauled ignominiously backward the 38 miles to Tacoma.

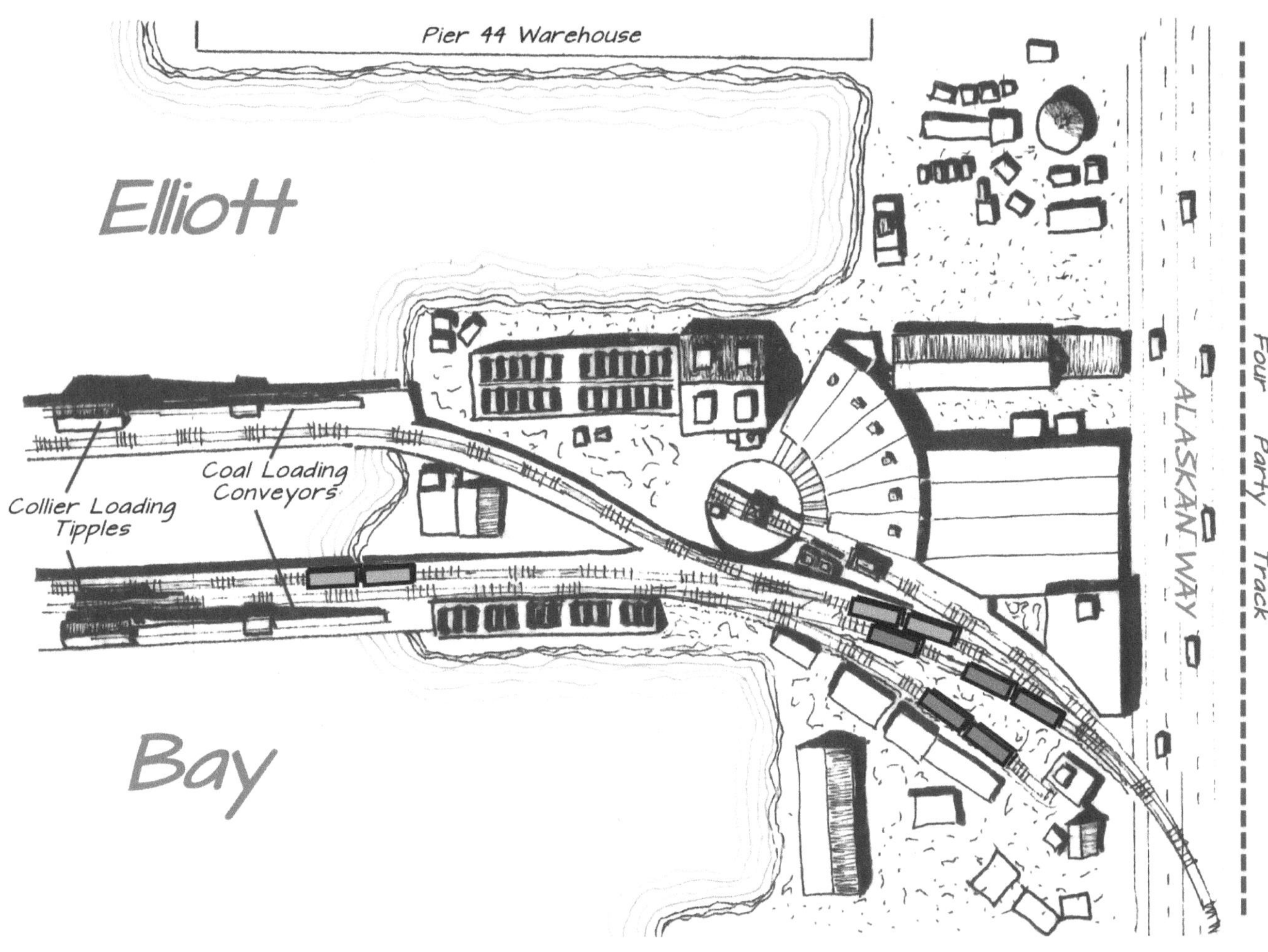

Pacific Coast shops and coal dock at Pier 43. *Map by David R. Clemens.*

One would think that the 30-mile Pacific Coast Railroad would also have a "pure" terminal. But time and circumstance have given the short line a remote roundhouse that's simultaneously both the most unusual and the most scenic in Seattle. The PC's roundhouse has its rear wall right next to the sidewalk along Alaskan Way at the base of PC's Pier 43 collier loading docks. The turntable is farther out on the pier, mirroring, to a certain extent, its Seattle & Walla Walla Railroad predecessor which had ALL of its yard, turntable, engine house, and shops on trestles over the tide flats. Coal pier tracks curve around the roundhouse and turntable while increasing their elevation over the water and also allowing a dump for filling tenders with the product the engines haul down from the coal fields.

But this scenic location requires the motive power to emerge from the engine tracks and cross Alaskan Way, cross the "four-party track" next to the street and proceed to Atlantic St., be flagged across the multiple crossings of the other roads ("PC: three motions with green flag or lantern"), and thread their way past the shop and through the yards to the yard office at Lander Street, a distance of just over a mile. The inbound 2-8-0's travel a reverse route only slightly shorter by virtue of their departure from the north end of the yard.

Pacific Coast #11 on the turntable at the Pacific Coast's Seattle roundhouse. The photo was taken from the PC's elevated track leading to its coal dock at Pier 43, circa 1940. Cars can be seen parked on Alaskan Way above the roundhouse rear wall. *Photographer unknown, photo WWAPC0309, PNRArchive collection at Burien, WA.*

One or several of the above elements could be utilized in selecting model engine terminal locations. The result is an increase in operation, interest, and the potential for urban scenery of a more unusual sort.

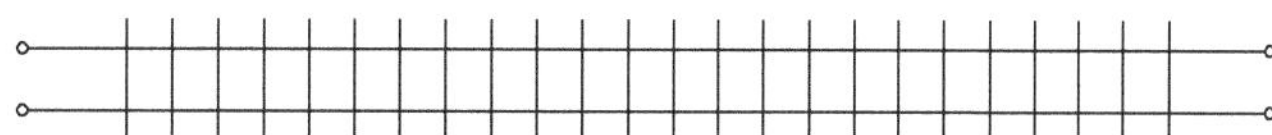

Chicago, Milwaukee & St. Paul Railway Bellingham Division

I had just graduated from West Seattle High School, was spending the summer of 1955 on Great Northern Railways signal gang #17, looking forward to my freshman year at the University of Washington, and contemplating the various tasks that had the gang wandering up and down the GN coast line between Seattle and Vancouver, BC when one July day our outfit was moved to Bellingham and I discovered a Chicago, Milwaukee, St. Paul & Pacific operation that has fascinated me ever since.

Great Northern outfit car, GN Bellingham yard. "One July day our outfit was moved to Bellingham..." *Photograph by T. R. Wahl, TRWahl0784, PNRArchive collection at Burien, WA.*

I was no stranger to the Milwaukee - my first cab rides at about age 11 were in MILW yard goats behind Sears & Roebuck in Seattle's central rail yards. I had ridden engines switching cars onto barges for Port Townsend and Bellingham, however I had never observed the up-Sound destinations of these marine operations. Suddenly, from the side-door of a kitchen car, I saw the CMStP&P's barge slip, numerous crossings of the GN main, a vest-pocket yard, and only hints of wonders to come - and smelled the rank odors of the Georgia-Pacific pulp/paper mill.

This highly picturesque branch was originally constructed as the Bellingham Bay & British Columbia RR in 1884 and reached Sumas in 1891 where it connected with the Canadian Pacific and British Columbia Electric railroads. The line was extended up the Nooksack River to Glacier in 1900/01 and although the projected destination was Spokane, this was to be its furthest penetration of the Cascade mountains. A branch from Hampton to Lyndon was built in 1903 and there was also a branch from Goshen Jct. to Kulshan. The CMStP&P acquired the BB&BC in 1911/12 and, as everywhere in the northwest, found itself tripping over the Northern Pacific - an overhead crossing close to Lake Whatcom and at grade at Sumas and near Deming. The Kulshan branch was eventually abandoned, but the rest of the "Bellingham Division" soldiered on with gradual cutbacks from Glacier to Maple Falls to Limestone Junction and reduction in status to a "subdivision."

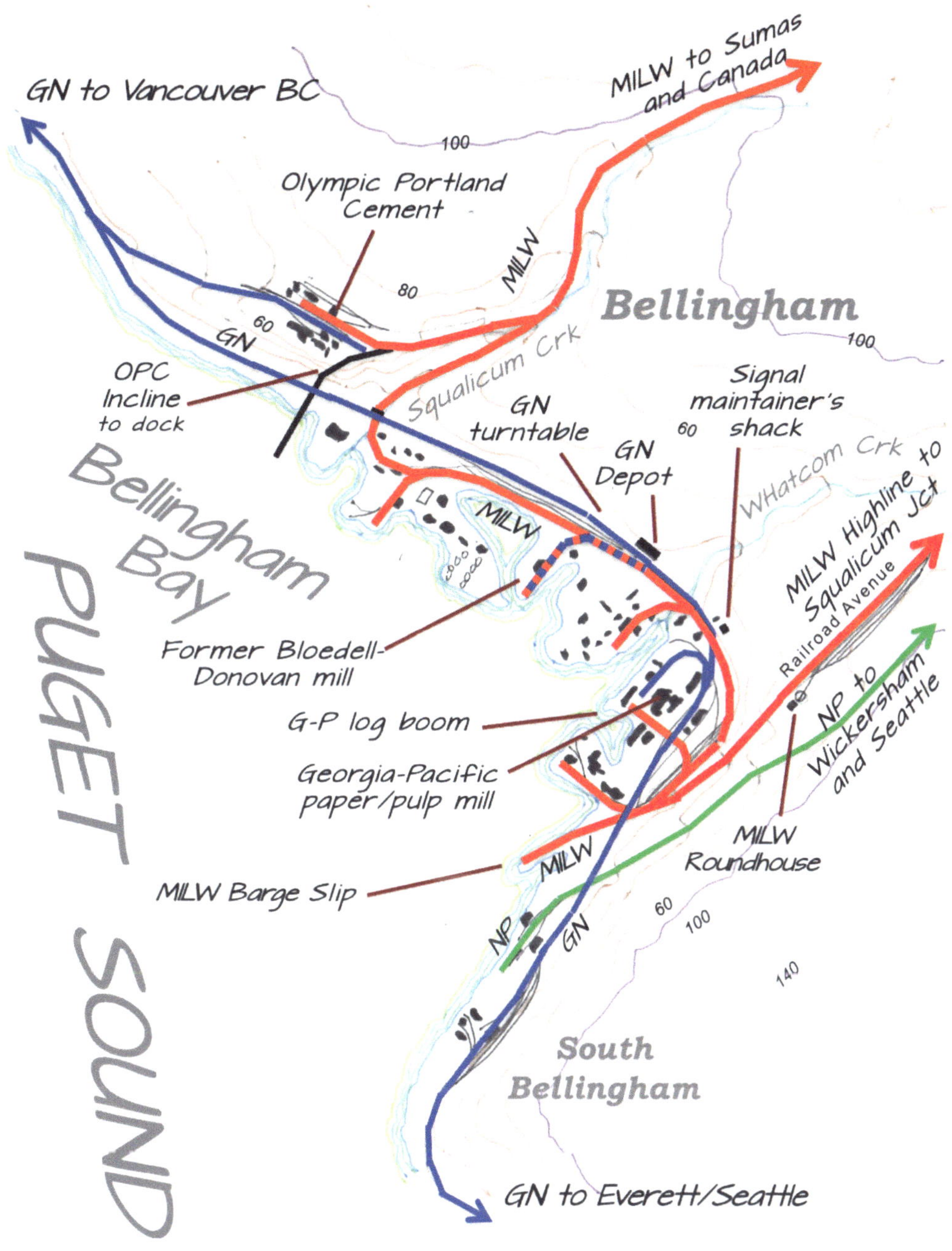

The Bellingham spaghetti bowl, mid-1950s. *Map by David R. Clemens.*

As a condition to the Burlington Northern merger, the MILW received trackage rights to Bellingham, but only over a very circuitous route on branch lines via Renton, Woodenville, Everett, and finally on the ex-3 foot mainline to Bellingham. The route would probably have been on the old NP Fifth Subdivision through Sedro Wooley to Wickersham and then down the NP Bellingham Branch, but the BN intended to abandon chunks of the former and all of the latter. This sounded the death-knell for the barge operation from Seattle to Whatcom Bay [Bellingham Bay], but also resulted in such incongruities as U36C's gingerly treading the spindly rail of the Lynden branch. Ultimately unable to compete with the Burlington Northern, the Milwaukee retrenched to its pre-Pacific Coast extension format and the 21st sub of the Coast Division was up for grabs along with the rest of the railroad west of Minnesota. The BN purchased the viable industrial trackage in Bellingham plus the Sumas-Lynden branch and the rest became history.

CMStP&P Bellingham barge slip. *Photograph by T. R. Wahl, TRWahl0661, PNRArchive collection at Burien, WA.*

However, the Bellingham Branch remains an eminently fascinating prototype, whatever periods/trackage layouts: 4-4-0's of the turn of the century, 2-8-0's and 0-6-0's pre-diesel, or the SW's and Geeps following. My personal preference is the line as I knew it in the mid-fifties/early sixties, but retaining such features as the "high-line" running through the center of town still connecting with the "main" at Squalicum Jct., the Goshen Branch to Kulshan, and at least one logging incline feeding skeleton flats of Douglas fir to be transported to the salt chuck for delivery to a mill at Bellingham. I have no problem with going back in time some ten years to accommodate typical MILW steam power such as 0-6-0's and 2-8-0's. The more I think about it...

The CM&StP originated at a barge slip of typical wooden construction located alongside the steep bluffs characterizing the city. The lead crossed the Great Northern mainline and entered a six-track yard. Immediately adjacent, a second crossing of the GN began the climb up to the engine terminal and the street trackage through the city center.

The yard was on a fill over the tide flats at the base of the bluff and included a scale track. A spur at mid-yard crossed the GN again and served the Georgia-Pacific paper/pulp mill complex. At the north end, the yard narrowed down to a single track, passed under a street overpass, and crossed the Great Northern for the fourth time, with the GN signal maintainers' shack located in the convergence of the lines. The branch connection continued north paralleling the GN on trestle and fill past the GN depot. A large Bloedell-Donovan mill was once located here and the Big G also had access to the B-D mill via a crossover to the MILW.

GN turntable at Bellingham. Unlike the Milwaukee Armstrong-style turntable, this one was powered. *Photograph by Mike Chandler, May 1972.*

North of F Street there was a small GN yard and rudimentary engine service facilities including a short turntable. Here the GN line started climbing up from the bay. The MILW stayed on the shore, serving a variety of industries including a fish processor, an oil dealer, a plywood mill, and a log dump, and then swung east under the GN up Squalicum Creek.

Climbing up the waterway, the line first encountered the lead to the Olympic Portland Cement (OPC) plant. This was a major industry and received/shipped a large volume of car loads. Inbound limestone arrived via the MILW and outbound traffic was routed both MILW and GN. There was also an incline down from the plant, elevation 80 feet, to a dock on the bay for water shipments to various points on Puget Sound. A little further up the canyon, a coal mine contributed tonnage to the branch. Just above this point the line through town joined the primary line at Squalicum Jct., elevation 120', although the junction was long abandoned in the 1950s.

Olympic Portland Cement critter with two covered hoppers of cement, heading down the incline to their dock on Bellingham Bay. *Photograph by T. R. Wahl, TRWahl0553, PNRArchive collection at Burien, WA.*

Returning to the Bellingham yard, the "high-line" diverged from the yard lead/barge lead, crossed the GN main, and climbed up the bluff (there was also a lumber mill spur south of the crossing which was joint with the bigger road). At about the midpoint of the yard and some 55 feet above it, there was a small engine terminal with a turntable and a five-stall roundhouse.

On the other side of the line was a freight house with an open - but roofed - platform, end-loading ramp, and an interminable flight of stairs descending to the yard below. As the line continued to climb in the center of Railroad Avenue into town, industrial spurs branched off on the east side, became level, and sometimes were on trestles to serve the various companies. Another spur on the bay side also served various warehouses. On the hillside behind and above the engine terminal there was an NP line that crossed the draw above them. This was a steep spur from the NP's mid-town yard through alley ways and down to an interchange with the GN and a crossing of that road to a log dump. A fifth gate-protected crossing of the dominant road within city limits!

May 26, 1972: A pair of SD9s lay over at Milwaukee's Bellingham engine terminal. This is the five-track roundhouse and short turntable Mike McLaughlin referred to and I think it's safe to write, judging by the age and deteriorated condition of the structure, that it was the original Bellingham Bay and British Columbia shop facility. —Mike Chandler.
Photograph by Mike Chandler.

One of the five gate-protected level crossings in Bellingham. The headframe of the CMStP&P barge slip is just visible to the rear of the left gate and below the group of electrical transformers. *Photograph by T. R. Wahl, TRWahl0306, PNRArchive collection at Burien, WA.*

The "St. Paul" continued through town, passed the NP yard, and then wandered up to Squalicum Jct. at MP 5.9 (MP 3.1 via the high line). A branch diverged near Sunset Drive to run east to the lumber mills at Larson on Lake Whatcom. To get there this branch crossed over the NP Bellingham -Wickersham line just north of downtown Bellingham. From Squalicum Jct. the main line continued to climb up to a "summit" at Wahl (250', MP 11.4) and then dropped to the "Sumas Prairie," elev. 90', and meandered northeast toward the town of the same name.

There were occasional spurs in the small farm towns along the route and at Hampton the Lynden branch diverged to run some 5.5 miles west to serve the local market area. Before reaching Hampton, the old "Goshen Branch" left the line at Goshen Jct. (MP 12.7, elev. 200'), with a terminus at Kulshan (MP 11.5 from Goshen Jct., elev. 300'). This was primarily a forest products line and reached into the southwest foothills of Mt. Baker and crossed the NP just before Deming (MP 6.1, elev. 180'), where there was an armstrong interlocking operated by the train crews.

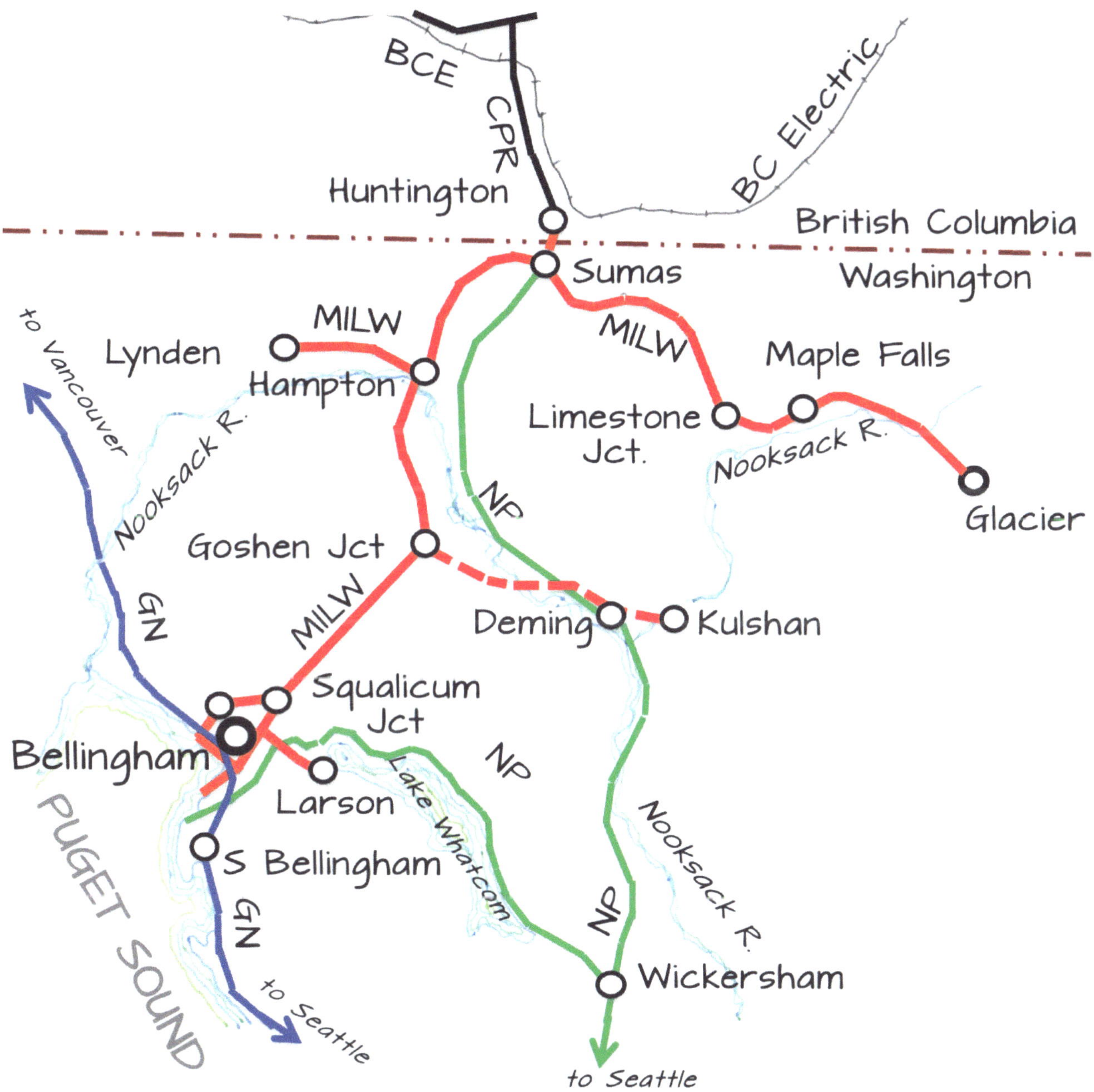

Railroading in and around Bellingham. *Map by David R. Clemens.*

Sumas, MP 25.1, was an important interchange with the CP-BCE that was shared with the Norn Pacific. The Canadian roads came into the "twin" town of Huntingdon on the north, while the two US roads entered Sumas from the south. The MILW directly approached the CP interchange, then swung south via a wye and crossed the line continuing on toward Glacier while a loop connection branched off and circled around the east side of Sumas to the BCE interchange. The line began climbing east of Sumas (elev. 40') and reached Limestone Jct. at MP 33.4, elev. 500'. At this point the incline descended from the limestone quarry (elev. 1700') to the end of the OPC-owned spur which was about one mile from the junction.

The branch then dropped slightly to Kendall (MP 36.3, elev. 440') and then climbed again through the Cascade foothills to Maple Falls (MP 39.5, elev. 610'), Warner, and Glacier (MP 46.8, elev. 900'). At one end or the other, some 21 logging lines were tributary to the MILW branch according to Kramer Adams' book *Logging Railroads of the West*. Two of the lines, headquartered in Glacier, had inclines: both Hogg-Houghton Logging and Wamick/Glacier Lumber featured 60-70% grades reaching up into the timber areas. All of the lines together rostered a wide variety of rod and geared locomotives and ranged in size from 1 to 58 miles in length. There was even a "pole" road, the Lyle-McNeil show at Deming.

Motive power on the division was most likely 0-6-0's and 2-8-0's in the late steam era. Dieselization brought the various classes of switchers, Geeps, and SD units. 1960-era timetables noted that "1750 hp, 4-axle units" were prohibited, and that "1000 and 1200 hp switchers" were restricted to 10 mph. Apparently, only SW1's and SD7/9's were allowed to attain the branches' 25 mph speed limit. It's interesting to note that Geeps were prohibited, but after the trackage rights over the BN were established, U36C's and SD40's were used on the line, even on the 65-lb rail of the Lynden branch.

MILW GE U36C locomotives 5800 and 5803 with a train of "refugee ore cars" on lightweight rail at the limestone quarry near Limestone Junction, Washington, on a typically soggy August 27, 1975. *Photograph by Dan Perkins, DRP051-073, PNRArchive collection at Burien, WA.*

Equipment. Obviously, era-dependent, but in the fifties we're looking at SD7/9's and any of the NW's/SW's from 1 up to 9 (I don't remember any of the FM's, Alco's, etc. being operated on the Bellingham Sub, but they certainly could have been). Freight equipment was typically a mix of wood and steel box cars, composite gons, hoppers, standard or skeleton logging flats (and composite gons for this service too), and tank cars bringing in petroleum products or chemicals for the pulp mills. An occasional Hooker chlorine car, flats of farm equipment, generally whatever was moving on the 1950 rail system.

Oh yeah, and a whole bunch'a ore car refugees from Minnesota/Wisconsin used for the lime rock traffic. There were both cupola and bay-window crummies, a gondola-mounted snowplow, and a coupl'a idler flats used while switching the car barges. Barges were the instantly-identifiable "horizontal rib" crafts with rear deckhouses that the MILW used on Puget Sound. A typical green-and-white tug would be tied up to the slip dolphins while waiting for unloading / loading to be completed.

May 26, 1972: A gondola mounting a homemade snowplow waits for winter in Milwaukee's small Bellingham freight yard. Even though this photo was taken nearly two decades after Mike McLaughlin wrote of seeing such a plow in Bellingham, I feel certain that it's the same one. There were always several of the ore cars lying around in the yard as well. —Mike Chandler. *Photograph by Mike Chandler.*

Seagulls wheel overhead, fishing boats and small freighters ply the waters of Whatcom Bay, and a Puget Sound Tug & Barge tug brings a log boom into the G-P mill. The deck crew places jacks and tie-down chains in the incessant drizzle at the barge slip while in the yard office the Yardmaster and clerks prepare for the next moves on the Bellingham Sub.

May 26, 1972: A Milwaukee SW1200 competes with traffic on Railroad Avenue as it serves numerous shippers along Bellingham's waterfront. *Photograph by Mike Chandler.*

Ballard Bridge—Redux

One day a "For Sale" sign appears in the front yard of the duplex overlooking the Washington Ship Canal and the Ballard Bridge: the absentee landlord has decided to dispose of his investment. A steady stream of potential buyers passes through the larger side of the building, commenting on the desirability of living there after the renters are moved out. Strangely enough, the property doesn't sell. Dismayed at the prospect of leaving their home along the railroad and waterway, the occupants mention the "sleep-destroying" nocturnal railroad operations; the "incessant clamor" of canal traffic; and the "nerve- wracking" sounds of the bridge. Inevitably, one or more of the described conditions occurs during the showing with the added comment, "and you should hear how loud it is at night!" Much to the owner's puzzlement, the duplex remains unsold until the renters move to Denver, a new railroad job, and life along other tracks.

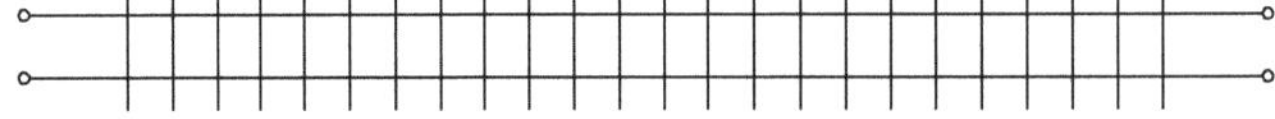

3

WORKING ON THE RAILROAD

1955–1961

Section crew and their motor car at Siskiyou Summit on the SP Siskiyou line, circa 1979. The outfit car Dick Steinheimer photographed 20 years earlier is long gone—but the work, and waiting on trains, remains the same. *Photograph by Jim Providenza.*

The Clock

A signal maintainer's shack resides underneath the viaduct on the Bellingham waterfront, at the crossing of the Great Northern mainline and a Milwaukee Road branch line/yard lead. The atmosphere is a combination of sulfur emanating from the Georgia Pacific mill, salt water drifting up from Bellingham Bay, and diesel fumes spewed out by the GN road engines and the yard goats of both roads.

The GN shack is aligned so that the Milwaukee headlights shine in the windows from the north, as do those of the GN trains. It is maybe fifteen feet from the mainline, and only a similar number of yards from the crossing. The shack itself is GN standard: a metal building, small office at the north end and a combination motor car shed/work shop at the other end. The office sports a wooden desk, roller chair, and several filing cabinets. However, the piece de resistance is a railroad Standard Clock, obtained from some unknown source. Octagonal face, pendulum extension, emblazoned with the inscription "Standard Time," the clock dominates the office.

The tick-tock of the mechanism may be momentarily drowned out by the noise of the passing trains or the fog horns from the harbor, but it continues relentlessly, metering the one constant of a railroader's life: time. A signal helper has been assigned to work with the Bellingham maintainer, and as this is "headquarters," no lodging expense will be paid. Therefore, the helper camps on a cot in the office, using an enameled basin to wash and other outdoor locations for other necessities. The erratic racket of the passing trains, yard cuts, and the somewhat more distant harbor noises are merely occasional outbursts that temporarily override the dominant sound inside the shack: the tick-tock, tick-tock, TICK-TOCK of the clock.

Standard Clock at the California State Railroad Museum. *Photograph by Jim Providenza.*

The railroad may be different but the work is the same: a Canadian National sectionman painting a switchstand at Sarcee Yard in Alberta, Canada. *Photograph by Mike Chandler.*

The signal helper arises each morning, washes and dresses, and wanders to a nearby cafe for breakfast. He returns to the maintainers shack, waiting for the boss to outline the day's work. His blankets are rolled at the foot of the cot and he watches as the clock ticks off the minutes to 7:30. The maintainer enters with his usual cheerful greeting in a strong Scandinavian accent. A brief phone conversation with the Signal Supervisor in Seattle eliminates any unusual projects, so the helper collects his normal equipment: paint, brushes, thinner, rags, and a certain amount of anticipated boredom.

The helper works his way slowly down the Bellingham waterfront, painting switch circuit controllers, battery boxes, signals, the gates at both the Milwaukee Road diamonds, and the more important highway grade crossings. Plus relay cases, spring switch mechanisms, and—it seems—anything else within sight of the right-of-way. Mainline trains pass, as do local freights, industry jobs, and the various transfers between the MILW, GN, and NP, arrayed in layers on the bluffs along Puget Sound. A manual crossing gate protects a Milwaukee lead into the Georgia Pacific paper plant where it crosses the Great Northern mainline. The breeze off the bay meanders through the buildings and the rank smells hit the painter with full force as he attempts to finish this one location and move down the line toward the MILW car barge slip. Quitting time produces a near-sprint back to the shack and escape from the sulfite odors that are so much a part of Bellingham's economic well-being.

The clock indicates that time is no longer a company imperative, but a commodity to be squandered "uptown." Dinner, maybe a movie, a couple of beers, and back to the quarters alongside the railroad. Inside the shack, lights out, it seems that the clock assumes ever-larger proportions until the tick-tock, tick-tock, TICK-TOCK shake the building with every swing of the pendulum. A third 711 freight moving south over the Milwaukee crossing with the attendant racket of wheels on the frogs has little effect on the helper. Headlights shine through the end windows from both GN and MILW engines, illuminating the interior of the building. None of those occurrences bother the sleeper, but as soon as the waterfront returns to a nominal decibel level, the tick-tock, tick-tock, TICK-TOCK assumes awesome proportions.

Another day, more paint, passing trains, ships and barges along the waterfront, and cliché of clichés, thank God it's Friday… not a respite from labor, but from an incessant tick-tock, tick-tock, TICK-TOCK, until Monday renews what seems to be endless repetition all out of proportion to the task at hand.

Great Northern Railroad Wheel Stops

Approximately 55 years ago, while working as a welder's helper on the GN, we built a pair of wheel stops for the end of an industrial spur using old rail. The description below and the attached drawings should make it possible to duplicate these.

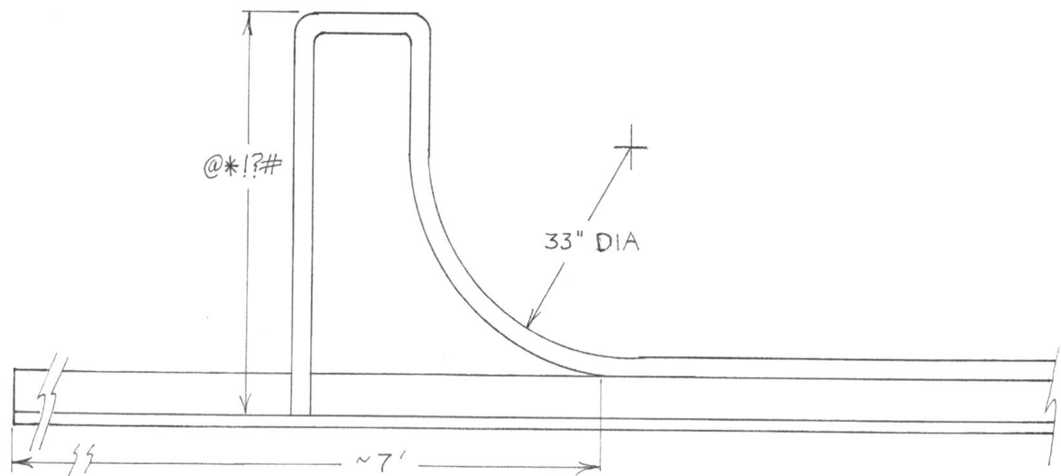

GN Wheel Stop. *Illustration by Kimberly Hoverter Morris based on drawing by Mike McLaughlin.*

1. Draw a 33" diameter circle on a piece of scrap plywood and cut out.
2. Take about a 15' length of scrap 80-90 lb rail and cut the ball of the rail loose from the web with an acetylene torch for a distance of approximately 7'.
3. Spike the rail to the ties in the middle of the track and using the torch, heat about 26" of the ball of the rail red hot from the end of the cut toward the rail end.
4. Using the plywood circle as a pattern and employing large hammers, bend the heated portion of the rail into a 90-degree quarter circle, reheating as required. A large amount of swearing will accompany this step.
6. Heat the ball red hot about 4" beyond the end of the quarter circle for a distance of about 9" and make an abrupt 90 degree bend so that the ball is parallel to the base.
7. Around 8 or 9" from this bend, heat the ball red hot for 9" and bend 90 degrees so that it meets the base of the rail at a right angle. Note that these two steps also require a great deal of hammering and @*!?# swearing.
8. Cut the ball of the rail off where it meets the rail base and cut a vertical slot in the web of the rail that is equal to the thickness of the ball.
9. Heating as necessary, twist and force the end of the rail into the slot in the web so that the ball is centered in the web, hammering and swearing as required.

10. Weld the ball to the web and base.
11. Unspike the wheel stop, and move to one side, select another piece of rail, and repeat the above steps.
12. Upon completion of the two wheel stops, cut them to length, cut bolt holes in the rail web, and fasten to the end of the spur with angle bars. If the stops are correctly placed, a wheel set will contact both curved surfaces simultaneously as it's rolled to the end of the track.
13. Cut off the web and base of the rails beyond the vertical member of the wheel stops so that the "tail" extends over about three ties. Spike the whole damn thing in place.
14. By now, it should be quitting time. Put away all tools and equipment and gather at the Triangle Tavern at the corner of Railroad Avenue and First Avenue South for a post mortem of the day's project. This also tends to result in additional swearing as more and more cold beer is consumed. Many suggestions are offered to streamline the next installation, but as nothing is written down, it'll all be forgotten in the nine or so months before the next pair of wheel stops is constructed.

There are so many good stories in this work (Fatha Hines!) but this is my favorite. It's so funny.

I am honored to be the artist of a few of these stories' illustrations. But I'm also an engineer and a machinist. I worked for my father building the machines he designed and everything was to strict tolerance. Even the items we had to torch and bend. We always worked with a jig. We knew what to expect. My father would have shuddered at what is described here! But what fun.

Just think. They did this in the field...how the heck did they manage to get that big, chunky piece of "ball" over the web? It's huge! He says he bent it at 90 degrees, but it had to be all skewed and then they had to guesstimate to cut it. And bending the ball? Holy mother of iron, that's a lot of metal to bend around a piece of wood at 33" diameter, let alone to 90 degrees in a smaller diameter. (I notice he doesn't say what that diameter was!) And the cutting by acetylene isn't pretty either, so the nice clean lines shown in the drawing are a complete fantasy. Kudos to these hard-working, hard-swearing railroad men (maybe some women?).

—Kimberly Hoverter Morris

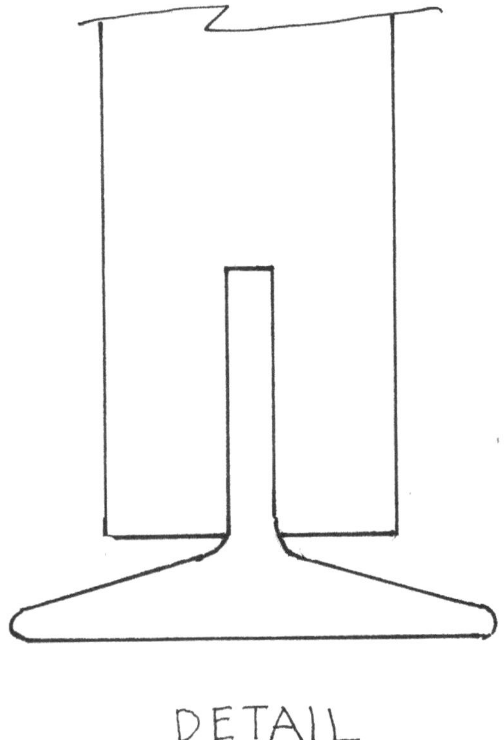

End-on view. *Illustration by Kimberly Hoverter Morris based on drawing by Mike McLaughlin.*

Cascadian (No 6) Train Order

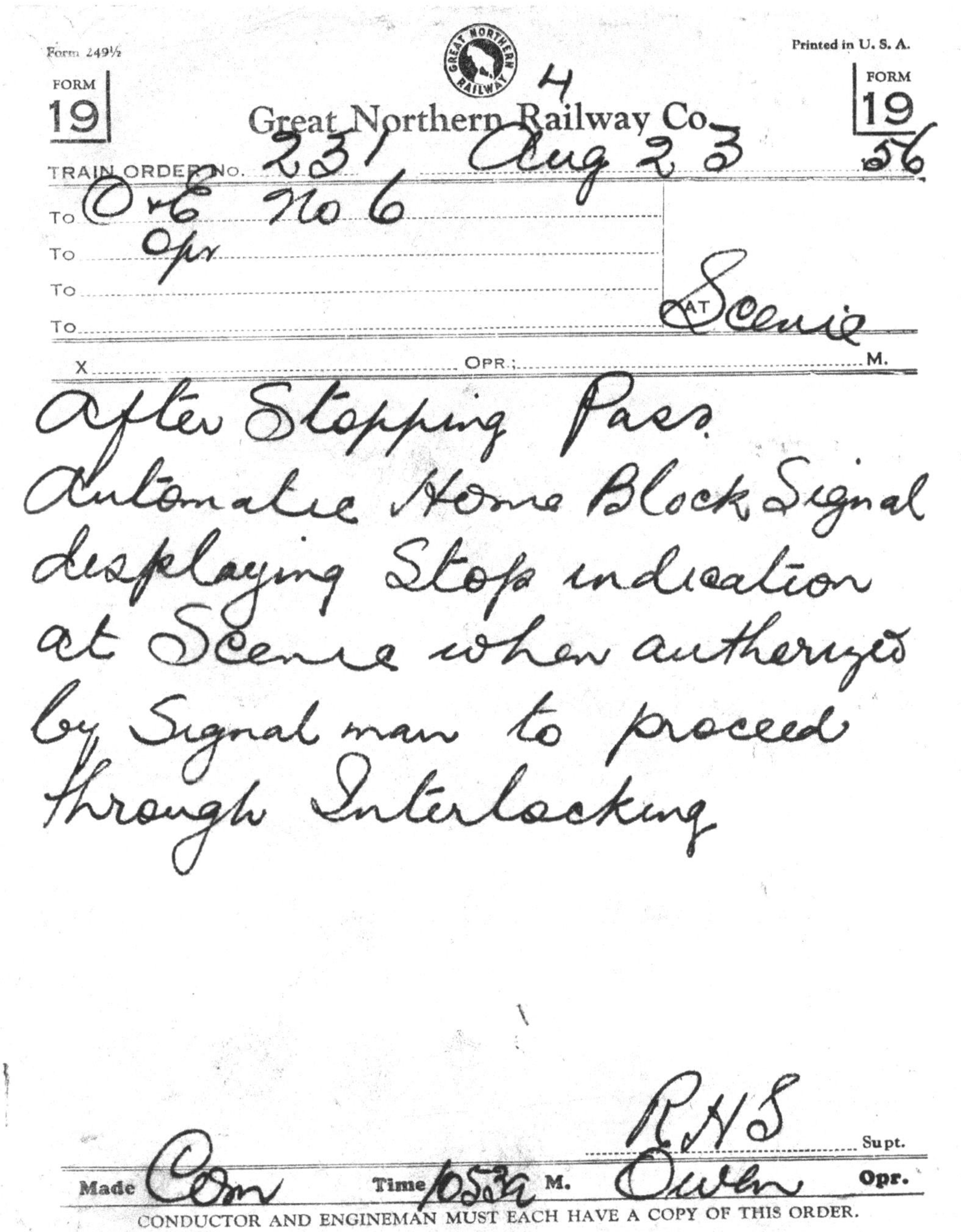

Form 249½

Printed in U. S. A.

FORM 19 — Great Northern Railway Co. — FORM 19

TRAIN ORDER No. 231 Aug 23 4 56

To O&E No 6

To Opr

To

To

AT Scenic

X .... OPR.: .... M.

After Stopping Pass
Automatic Home Block Signal
displaying Stop indication
at Scenic when authorized
by Signal man to proceed
through Interlocking

RHS Supt.

Made Com Time 1053a M. Owen Opr.

CONDUCTOR AND ENGINEMAN MUST EACH HAVE A COPY OF THIS ORDER.

GN Order 231 of August 23, 1956, a Form U Train Order. *Collection of D. T. Sprau.*

If you look in the July 2010 "Dispatcher's Office" magazine [of the Operations Special Interest Group] at Dave Sprau's train order article, you'll see a copy of a Great Norn order issued at Scenic authorizing No. 6 (the Cascadian) to pass an absolute signal. Yeah, I was there...

The order date is very close to the cut-over date when we dropped the electrification from Skykomish to Wenatchee. Don't know the exact date, but on August 23, we were either finishing up all the little bits and pieces and/or testing the new system, or the cutover had just occurred and we were monitoring the new system under traffic.

My guess is that it's not the actual cutover day as the 23rd was a Thursday and you wanna cut over early in the week so you got a few days to watch operations before the week-end. Regardless, whatever we were doing prevented the Scenic op from lining the train through the tunnel, hence the order allowing a signal dept. guy to flag the train through the hole.

I was either in the tunnel working at one location or another, or I was at Berne where there was always a bunch'a GN and Morrison Knudsen guys working on the door, the fans, the signals, or... Yep, and a ton of officials in the way, offering idiot advice, getting their pictures taken, and generally being really important before heading back to St. Paul. At least the Seattle brass knew what the hell was going on and what had to be done to complete the job.

Jezuss, fifty-four years ago???

June 1, 1972: This helper set for a westbound train is passing the station site of Scenic, some 16 years after the cutover. NP F9 810 leads three GN F7's, one in Empire Builder colors and two in the Big Sky Blue paint scheme. The F units, mainline power a decade and a half earlier, are still earning their keep. They will continue downgrade as far as Skykomish.
—Mike Chandler.
Photograph by Mike Chandler.

But before the wire came down, when EMD cab units were the newest thing in head end power… On February 17, 1947, Ron Nixon was riding in the rear cab of electric helper engine 5012. He took this picture as the train exited Cascade Tunnel, approaching the station at Scenic. *Museum of the Rockies, Ron V. Nixon collection.*

A Steel Gang Isn't All Gandies

Most people familiar with the railroad scene instantly categorize a steel gang as nothing but glorified section hands—gandy dancers if you will. Not true. If the gang is working on a signaled main or branch-line, there is a tag-along member of the Brotherhood of Railroad Signalmen.

Even on remote routes, highway grade crossings and/or crossings of other railroads may require his presence. When relaying rail on the high iron, the signal department is charged with maintaining the continuity of operations at a speed somewhat over 10 mph. Therefore, the signals will operate, crossings will be protected, and hazards such as broken rails, misaligned switches, and all the other impedimenta resisting normal train movements will be reduced to the nonexistent.

If passersby observe the scene at all, the most they will notice is a long, strung-out group of men and machines. Men knocking off rail anchors, men manning bolt-machines releasing the angle bars at each joint, a welder to cut bolts with frozen nuts, spike pullers looking like gigantic mechanized praying mantises as they rip the square-cut spikes loose from the rail base.

A funny-looking, homebuilt "donkey" crane removes the rail and deposits it on the shoulders as following laborers hook off the tie plates, drive down headless spikes, and clean the tie cribs. An adzer, creosote machine, men placing tie plates, and a burro crane setting the new rail pass in rapid succession. More men setting spikes, pneumatic spike drivers, more men placing and driving rail anchors, a steel gang is an orchestrated production with one goal in mind: from the laborer placing fiber shims between rail ends to allow for expansion during hot weather, to the Roadmaster hollering for more speed, the ultimate challenge is to lay more damn rail than any other gang on the system. So, what of the aforementioned signalman (in reality, probably not even an assistant signalman, but an experienced helper)?

He has a dichotomous existence. The steel gang can't begin production until the temporary track circuit jumpers are removed from the joints between the old steel and the new rail, and replaced as shunts across the track to reinforce the flagman's prohibition against trains entering the work territory. But once these preliminary duties are accomplished, the signalman coasts until a signal or battery box location is reached. Insulated joints are installed

D&RGW steel gang, Schramm compressor, and hammers, Monument, Colorado, July 21, 1987.
Photograph by Chuck Conway.

primarily with gang labor and only perfunctory supervision. Temporary track wires connect the old cables from the signal cases to the new joints, and with a few holes drilled and the new wires pounded in place, the signal system continues to function.

So, what does this junior functionary of the signal department do the rest of the work day? Well, the steel gang organization dictates part of the day's activities. A "soup cook" is provided by Addison-Miller who contracts to the Great Northern to provide "clean, comfortable" accommodations and "nourishing, tasty" food. The soup cook generally warms both soup and sandwiches on iron sheets held on temporary foundations of rocks, ties, or whatever over the ever-present fire. The signal helper, with few urgent duties, scrounges for firewood, helps prepare ("stir") the noon meal, and generally makes himself useful to the soup-cook. His reward is a break in tedium, proximity to the fire, unlimited hot coffee, and a free meal to be reported otherwise on the miserly expense allowance provided by the company.

Burro crane at work, D&RGW milepost 0.0, Denver Union Terminal, Denver, Colorado, June 1, 1988.
Photograph by Chuck Conway.

To contradict the abuse from the more active railroad employees, the signal helper does point out that nobody can begin work until he removes the bonds and shunts the track; conversely, he is "the last to leave" because he must remove the shunts and reapply the bonds. Occasionally, a mishandled rail dangling from the tongs at the end of the boom of the donkey or burro crane will damage a signal or other equipment, and repairs will have to be made. A battery box full of caustic-soda primary batteries shattered by a carelessly handled piece of track material is no picnic to clean up.

But for the majority of the day, the signalman bribes the soup-cook, rides with the donkey and burro crane operators, learns how to run various pieces of track machinery, and deliberately blocks out the knowledge that in the days ahead, each and every rail joint will have to be bonded with cad-weld bonds welded to ground-clean rail ends, all of the track wires will have to be replaced with new cables buried from signal case to insulated joint, and a variety of other "clean-up" tasks imposed. Today, he will ride back to Blaine on the old beat-up school bus, clean up in his solitary box-car-cum-bunk-car-abode, wander downtown for dinner, and engage in a futile conversation with a waitress regarding his expectations for the evening vs. hers.

No, not everybody on a steel gang is a gandy...

June 13, 1992: A maintenance-of-way gang has finished work for the time being and cleared the main line at Castle Gate, Utah, as an eastbound drifts downgrade.
Photograph by Mike Chandler.

Desert

I am more than a little amazed that Mike went from growing up, going to school, and working in the almost year-round cool, damp drizzle of Seattle to the subzero winters and 120+ degree summers of the Rio Grande in the Utah-Colorado desert. From seemingly endless rows of mountains clothed in a Douglas fir rain forest to a land naked under the sun with nary a tree in sight. But he did, and grew to love Utah and Colorado, and the Rio Grande, with a passion. This next group of stories picks up the thread of "Moving Day–D&RGW"—a signal gang in the desert.
—Jim Providenza.
Map by David R. Clemens.

The sun beats down out of a burnished blue sky, baking the already parched land. This is desert. The high, rolling desert of eastern Utah. To the south, the great bulk of the LaSalle Mountains is visible, patches of snow still remaining in the high valleys. Shimmering in the sun, the red rock walls of the Colorado River canyon drop away to the east. Elsewhere, the land is brown, dry, endless.

Across this land, rolling with it, runs the railroad. Curving, climbing, falling, picking out the best grade, it appears from and disappears into the distance. On the downgrade between Cottonwood hill and the undulating climb to Cisco, a siding with the ends marked by signals and silver relay bungalows breaks the monotony. A small rabbit rests in the shade of the west bungalow. At the east end, an extension of the siding is under construction. New rails snake back and forth, the ties like gaunt ribs in the blowing sand on the new fill. Barrels of spikes lie scattered about, and half-built signals stand where they will guard the new switch.

Two young men are high on a pole near the yet-to-be-completed east end, sun-b1ackened, sweat-streaked backs bare to the waist. Working together, they bolt a small transformer to the crossarm. One of the linemen moves his feet up the pole a few inches, leans back and holds a brace-and-bit at the end of the arm. His partner reaches out and twists the bit into the wood, boring holes for mounting the lightning arresters and "cat-heads"—fused cut-outs—that are an integral part of a signal location installation.

From far to the west comes the discordant honk of an air horn. Soon black-and-gold diesels storm down the grade, negotiating the curves along the green-tinted cliffs approaching Agate. The linemen shift their weight on their hooks, easing sore muscles, and relax in the wide leather safety belts. The engine reaches the west end of the siding and blares a raucous warning that sends the conejo leaping away in sudden panic. The enginemen raise their hands in reply to the waves from the pole, the track on the fill placing them at eye level with the men perched far above the ground.

The hot-shot crashes past, eighty-three loads of fresh fruit in cars bearing the reporting marks of PFE and ART and FGEX and MDT. The crummy whips by and the noise of the eastbound fades into the distance.

"Two young men are high up on a pole... his partner reaches out and twists the bit into the wood." *Illustration by Kimberly Hoverter Morris.*

D&RGW Train CHOAT westbound at Agate. The crew of the hot-shot pig train has "the track on the fill placing them at eye level with the men perched far above the ground." *Photograph by R. C. Farewell, 1990.*

Reluctantly, the men return to their labor, wiring the new location into the existing signal system. Suddenly, from the east comes the sharp exhaust of a motor car. Through at last, the linemen drop their equipment to the ground, unsnap their belts, and climb down. Once off the pole, they take off their hooks and gather their tools beside the track. The bright orange motor car stops and five more young men jump off. They shout ribald greetings to the two linemen and load the line tools on an already laden push car. The foreman waits at the telephone, requesting an extension of his block from the dispatcher. Clearance received, the gang begins the climb to the west, heading home to Cisco.

Exhausts racketing in the afternoon sun, the motor car works its way up-grade. The men sit silently, staring sleepily into the desert, abruptly rallying to snatch back a gang member who—lulled by the heat, sound, and motion—slowly falls forward off the seat.

The small procession halts for a highway crossing, then walks the cars through the power switch into the passing track. Stopping in front of the maintainers shack, the signal gang unloads tools and supplies, swings the motor car off the pass onto a setoff and chains the wheels. The push car is man-handled onto the ground alongside, and the foreman calls the dispatcher to clear his block.

Slowly the men walk down the tracks in small groups, one of them stopping to get some ice out of the ice-house made from old ties covered with earth. The rest of the gang enters the silver bunk car that rests on a spur next to the sheep pens across from the boarded-up station. Inside, the men collapse on the bunks, waiting for their turn in the shower. The signalman with the ice fills the galvanized water can from the gray tank car that supplies Cisco with its potable water, and then enters the bunk car. Music from a portable radio fills the air intermingled with the chatter of the gang. Finished with their showers, the men head for the adjacent highway, the small cafe/service station and dinner.

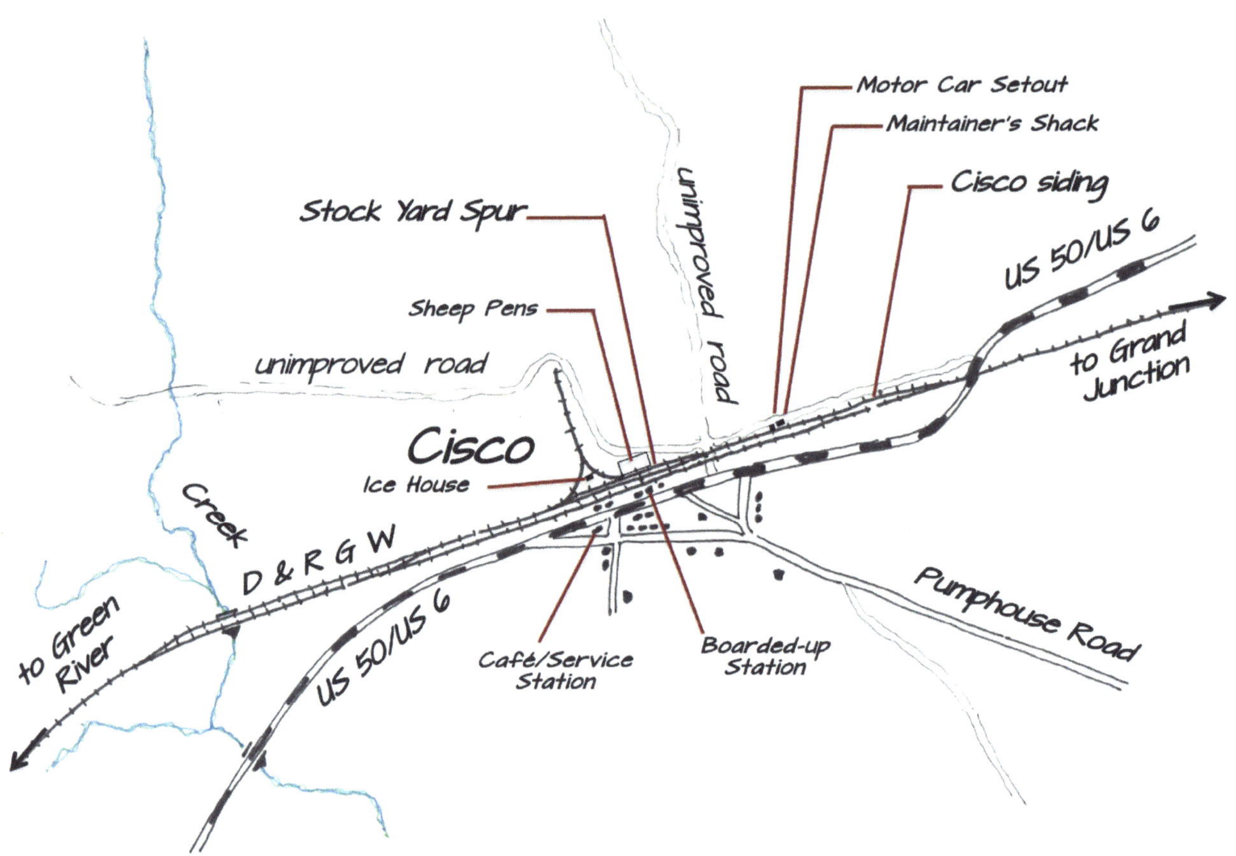

The D&RGW at Cisco, Utah. *Map by David R. Clemens.*

The sky becomes a blazing red, the parched hills glowing in the sunset. A small rabbit hops across the right-of-way, and the low rumble of a hurrying freight can be heard in the distance as night comes to the desert.

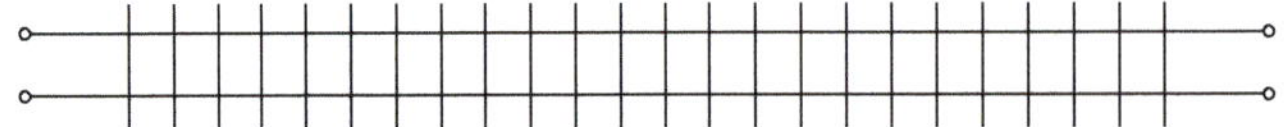

OS Soldier Summit

The small brick station sits close to the eastbound main line, the sharp night air carrying the click of the telegraph, amplified by the traditional Prince Albert tobacco can behind the sounder. Light from the operator's window spills out across the rails. Overhead, the order board glows red. Waiting...

From the east comes the muted sound of an airhorn. Inside the station, the operator glances at the local CTC panel, yawns, stretches, and pulls orders and blank clearance forms towards himself on the counter. Now a distant rumble can be felt more than heard.

Operator copying an order, Soldier Summit, July 28, 1964. The indicator lights on the local CTC panel are visible behind the candlestick telephone. As is the norm, a Prince Albert tobacco can is being used as a resonator behind the telegraph sounder seen in the upper right. *Photograph by John B. Charles.*

"Hello, dispatcher, Summit. He's in the block now. Anything else? Okay, we'll clear him up. Soldier Summit clear extra 5774, five-seven-seven-four west, w-e-s-t, with two orders, numbers 25, two-five, and 26, two-six. GA." "Okay at 3:15, three-one-five AM, GHH."

Down at the east end of the yard, a headlight suddenly swings into view around the curve and over the hump into the broad pass of Soldier Summit. A four-unit diesel clatters over the switches, trailing a seemingly endless line of GS gondolas and triple hoppers, loaded with Carbon County coal, fifty tons to the car. Slowly the drag pulls past until eight more units clear the crossover, exhausts muting from run-eight to idle. With a harsh, clanking crash the train comes to a halt. The helper engine backs down the last third of the train past the switch, then—clank of pin lifter—uncouples from the train with a pop of parting air hoses and pulls into the adjacent track.

June 12, 1992: The late evening sun reflects off the sides of three SD40T-2 "tunnel motors" as they head their loaded coal train to the crest of Soldier Summit. *Photograph by Mike Chandler.*

A lantern makes a quick circle in the night. Far ahead, three blasts of the air horn answer and the roar of the road engine drowns out the wheel clicks as the black cars slowly creep back to meet the rear end. The joint is made, air hoses coupled, and a hissing sigh is heard as the brakes release, take hold, and release again in the all-important air test. The lantern of the swing brakeman approaches, pauses at each car, then moves on as he turns up the retainers to the twenty-pound position. A moment of insults exchanged with the helper crew, then on down the long line of dirty black cars.

Two sharp blasts from the road engine in response to the highball relayed from the caboose, and the sound of EMD exhaust again resounds in the mountain air. Slack rolls out; Extra 5774 pulls over the hump, and moves down the hill accompanied again by the inevitable crash of slack slamming in against the head-end dynamic brakes.

In front of the station, the operator stands in a pool of light as he extends the train order hoop toward the approaching caboose. The brakeman on the platform thrusts his arm through the string held on the fork and the green tissues are delivered to the rear end crew. The operator returns to his office as the red eyes of the markers drop down grade past the west end safety switch.

The helper engine pulls up to the station and idles quietly as the engineer and fireman go in to pick up their orders for the return trip to Helper. Coffee; and with a low rumble, the engine drifts back down the hill, so recently the scene of a titanic struggle to lift 9000 tons up through the twisting canyon that reverberated with the furious clamor of 18,000 brute horsepower.

"OS Soldier Summit. Extra 5774, five-seven-seven-four west, w-e-s-t arrived at 3:36, three-three-six AM, departed 4:17, four-one-seven AM. Extra 5424, five-four-two-four east, e-a-s-t departed 4:29, four-two-nine AM."

Once again, the Wasatch summit night is still, with only an occasional outburst from the telegraph. The ka-lunk, ka-lunk, ka-lunk-a-lunk-a-lunk of the dispatcher phone selector sounds at random intervals to summon operators at various train order offices across the division. The order board, now a verdant green, shines in the high, thin air. Waiting...

Train Order signal showing green, "No Orders." *Photograph by Philip R. Hastings, Philip Ross Hastings, MD, collection, California State Railroad Museum.*

The Railroad Selective Calling System allowed a dispatcher to ring any station on a division train line. It did this with small gear-driven contacts controlled by pulses (similar to rotary dial phone pulses) which drove a ratchet-like mechanism. The first pulse starts a fast relay which pulses the solenoid of the ratchet mechanism; a second, slow-release relay operates and stays up a predetermined time, then releases ("clunk!"). This causes the selector to advance to the next digit. Another relay notes the second digit has been received ("clunk"). The final digit is followed by another clunk for the relay controlling a bell. After working around this, you quickly note which patterns of clicks and clunks may be for you. —Seth Neumann.
Photograph by Seth Neumann.

Night Call

"Hawley? Trouble at West Ruby. The slide fence is down. Yeah, okay... Luck." Half an hour ago, the dispatcher had called the signal maintainer and now he and his helper—after driving to Mack where the truck was traded for a motor car—continue down the valley.

Following the rails as they abruptly turn to the left and thread their way between the high hills, the motor car scurries along, headlight shining in the darkness. Now the track clings to a narrow shelf between the Colorado River and the high rock walls of Ruby Canyon. The moonlight casts dark shadows on the red rock, highlighting the wind-and-water-carved pinnacles. Exhaust racketing off the sheer walls, the small orange car crosses a dry wash, cut deep into the soft sandstone. Occasionally, traces of the old right-of-way are visible, faint cinder-strewn reminders of the line that had replaced the original narrow gauge railroad that fought its way across the desert. Twisting and turning up the canyon, the motor car stops at the end of a siding, the signal a crimson eye in the night.

Ruby Canyon night ride. *Illustration by Kimberly Hoverter Morris.*

The two signalmen, armed with lanterns and climbing gear, mount the high poles that support the slide fence. As they string new wire, a faint rumble overhead signals a new slide. The men listen to the click of rocks on the face of the cliff, then tense in the sudden silence as the rocks fall free through the darkness. Relaxing in their safety belts as the boulders thump clear of the track, they resume work. The broken wires spliced, the signal blinks out.

DRGW 5314 leads a westbound at the west switch at Shale on March 4, 1984. The slide fence is visible between the cars trailing the 5314 and the rock cliff. *Photograph by R. C. Farewell.*

Checking with the dispatcher, the maintainer is told that two trains are approaching. He walks back to the motor car and waits beneath the towering rocks. From far up-river comes the muted rumble of a train, the sound almost lost in the river's chuckle. Gradually the sound gets louder, until a headlight reflects off the sheer walls as the passenger train comes into view. At the other end of the siding, a long freight pulls into the clear, guided by the dispatcher from his panel in Grand Junction. The varnish rolls by, the switch points throw with a low whir, and—exhausts thundering off canyon walls—the freight pulls back onto the main line.

The signalmen flip a friendly greeting to the crew in the caboose, then roll their motor car back onto the track. The breeze off the river has cooled considerably, causing the men to shiver as the little car picks up speed. Wheels singing, exhaust echoing across the water, the speeder quickly retraces its path through the canyon. The eyes of a deer are momentarily reflected as the headlight sweeps the willows along the river. Suddenly the canyon right-of-way ends at a curving tunnel and the track emerges into the broad, moonlit expanse of Grand Valley. The motor car disappears into the distance, and the night is again quiet.

Dotsero

The early morning air is bitterly cold; the snow squeaks beneath the feet of the men as they leave the warmth of the long gray bunk car.

Half of the signal gang walks along the outfit, past the kitchen car with its still-lingering odors of breakfast, and forces open the side door of the battered tool car. The rest of the men cross over to the maintainer's shack near the main line. Gradually a pile of equipment grows on the frozen ground as picks, shovels, ropes, climbing gear, and the other supplies needed for the day's work are gathered from the cars. Two signalmen walk to the small yellow motor car on the set-off and kick the frozen brakes to free them from the wheels. The light dusting of snow stirred up by passing trains is brushed from the seat and the heavy hoarfrost is scraped from the windshield. Although the sun shines from a brilliant blue sky, the temperature at Dotsero has yet to climb above -20 degrees.

While waiting for an eastbound freight, the men gather around the ever-present fire that is built wherever the gang stops for a few minutes. Soon a muted rumble is heard down the river and becomes louder as the orange-and-b1ack-striped diesels come into view near the stock pen. A westbound freight idles on the Minturn main, waiting for the eastbound hot-shot to sway through the crossover and swing up the Dotsero cutoff. With exhausts thundering, the train clatters past the men standing by the fire.

The RODVM is approaching Dotsero on January 16, 1997, the last year Rio Grande power was frequently seen. I'm standing next to the maintainer's shack... It wasn't too cold that day, as I recall, between 10 and 20 degrees. But it could get miserably cold there, as Mike indicates.—Chuck Conway. *Photograph by Chuck Conway.*

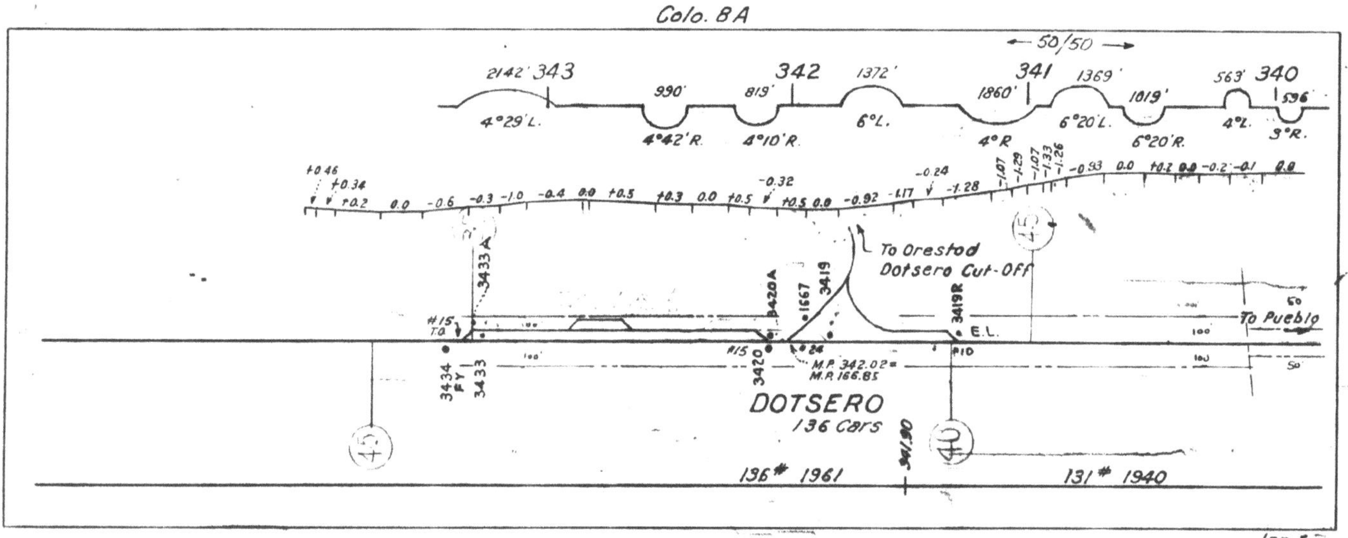

D&RGW track chart, Dotsero, Colorado, January 1967. *Michael J. McLaughlin collection.*

As soon as the caboose clears in a swirl of snow, the motor car and push car are put on the track and loaded with tools. The lunches, which will be frozen before noon, are put on the motor car while the men labor over the crank in a futile effort to start the engine. Finally, after thawing the carburetor with a fusee, the motor coughs into life. The small car moves up the cutoff, the men muffled in their heavy clothing. The cruel wind of their passage numbs hands and feet as first Niche, then Sweetwater are passed. The mighty Colorado River is frozen from bank to bank wherever the current slackens. A bald eagle wheels lazily and deer are seen on the steep sides of the canyon. At Range, the small procession stops while the riders hover over the section gang's fire in a vain attempt to thaw out. Then on up the canyon past Red Dirt, Sylvan, Burns, to the new switch at the east end of Dell.

The gang sets off the cars and starts to work. A new pole line must be built and the old poles taken down. Holes are blasted in the frozen ground and the new poles are man-handled into place.

Lunch time, and the signalmen gather around the fire to thaw their lunches and rest. Midway through the meal, the plush California Zephyr glides past. A brief glimpse of a pretty girl in a dome, envious glances at passengers dining in steam-heated comfort, and the workers resume eating. All too soon it is time to return to work.

Phil Hastings took this shot from the dome car on the Yampa Valley Mail, train No. 9, as it passed Finger Rock south of Yampa, Colorado. Riding "in steam-heated comfort..." *Photograph by Philip R. Hastings, Philip Ross Hastings, MD, collection, California State Railroad Museum.*

Loathe to leave the warmth of the fire, the men straggle back to their labors. Three linemen set about transferring the wires amid a flurry of profanity directed at the hard surface of the new poles. The sun has raised the temperature to ten above and heavy jackets lie where they have been shed. Slowly the afternoon passes, punctuated only by the passing trains.

At last, it is time to gather up the tools and put the motor car on the rails for the long ride back down the canyon. The pale light of the setting sun adds to the bleakness of the countryside. The cars racket over the bridge at Red Dirt and, flanges singing on the curves, drop down to the tunnel at Sweetwater where a fusee is used as a substitute for the malfunctioning headlight. At Niche, they head into the clear to wait for an eastbound drag. Cursing, their breath white plumes in the cold, the men stamp their feet in an attempt to restore circulation. One of them recalls the previous summer when the gang worked beneath the blistering sun on the high desert and had looked forward to the relief of winter. A hurled snowball his reward, he resumes watch for the tardy freight.

After an interminable wait, the drag grinds past and the motor car drops down-grade through the gathering twilight to Dotsero. Wearily the men put away their equipment and enter the outfit. Hot showers, a dinner of fresh venison cooked on the glowing coal stove in the kitchen car, and the lights are turned out, leaving a warm darkness tinged with coal smoke.

Outside, the moon glitters on the snow; the rails stretching down the valley sparkle with frost. A coyote's call echoes, then fades, as the mountain valley lies in the grip of the winter night.

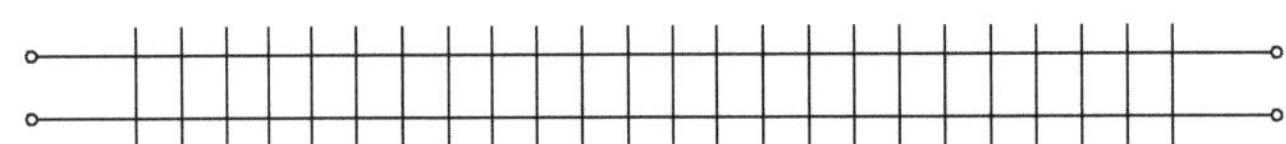

Train Crews Shouldn't Sleep

There is nothing that irritates those members of the railroad fraternity who really work for a living more than to observe a passing freight with the rear-end crew sound asleep in their chariot tacked regally on the train's posterior.

After all, the Book commands in the various sections of Rule 111 that "employees are required...to observe passing trains for defects." Further, "two or more employees must...be on each side of the track" and "will signal crew...if any such defect or condition is observed." This responsibility is not one-sided, for "crews of trains must be on the alert to receive signals from employees when passing any location where employees are near the track." Thus, countless section men, signal maintainers, members of B&B gangs, and other railroad employees who are required to prepare the way for the all-important trains peruse the passing equipment, vigilant in their inspection, alert to prevent incidents varying from the trivial to the catastrophic.

Dutifully splitting on both sides of the right-of-way, examining running gear, listening for flat wheels, watching for open car doors and shifted loads, both contract and salaried personnel prepare to offer the rear-end crew signals ranging from a high-ball to an easy stop to a washout. But is this dedication reciprocated by the members of the ORC, BRT, or the UTU? Night or day, winter or summer, the crummies roll by with neither observance or acknowledgement of the wayside employees and the information they may wish—or urgently need—to convey.

Imagine a section hand, called out to clean switches during a blizzard at Soldier Summit. Remember that at one time each switch had a switch broom prominently displayed—and which was utilized by train crew members—to clear the turnouts so that the traffic could move. No longer. If a switch has the slightest dusting of snow, a plaintive call to the dispatcher requests assistance in the form of the afore-mentioned gandy, else the entire railroad be shut down. The long-suffering section man arrives, attacks the snow in the switch points in a nearly futile exercise where each shovel full/broom stroke is replaced by twice the volume of snow borne by the unceasing wind blowing across the broad summit. Finally, the switch is cleared, the signal blinks green, and the train moves on. As the consist rolls by, the nearly-frozen man on the ground follows the dictates of Rule 111 and watches for those defects, nearly invisible, that might cause even more unendurable labors down line. The intended recipients of this intelligence—vital even to their own safety—are eagerly observing the switch location, ready to halt the train at any indication that all might not be well with the 5000 tons of rolling equipment in their charge. Wrong! The caboose rolls by and the interior lights illuminate two bodies sound asleep in the warmth generated by the coal stove, oblivious to all about them.

It is the high desert of eastern Utah, and the summer sun bakes the right-of-way with temperatures of 110°+ in the shade, and shade is non-existent. Employees in this area live for the end of the day and, hopefully, relief from the blistering heat. Passing trains provide only interruptions—not respite—in the day's labor. Metal tools become too hot to handle when left in the sun, and even the water can with its iced contents provides only transitory relief from the heat. A train approaches, the section men split to both sides of the tracks, and a roll-by is performed. The employees highball the rear end, but all that is visible through the open cupola windows of the caboose are recumbent bodies, feet up, arms folded, heads down, cooled by the wind of their passage.

A Rio Grande short and fast freight, near Thompson, Utah, July 1984. "As the caboose advances… Two hours later a twin dust plume on the railroad access road…" *Photograph by Mike Danneman.*

A signal gang works out on the desert, laboring in the sun, accepting the hardships but resenting the injustice of the sleeping train crews. Finally, one gang member exclaims "I'm gonna wake up the next goddam crew that's sleeping, and to hell with 'em!" When a train approaches, he mounts a signal ladder and waits on the platform with a can of ice water. As the caboose advances, he observes the usual feet up/head down attitude of a sleeping crew. Carefully he times his movements and throws the contents of the container through the crummy window. The ice water ricocheting around the cupola is mirrored by the disjointed movements of the rear-end crew as they are violently roused from their slumber. The signalman descends from the signal and joins the rest of the gang, who are nearly hysterical from the results of their escapade. The men resume work in the heat of a desert afternoon, chuckling occasionally as they perform their various tasks.

"Besides, if they hadn'ta been asleep, nobody would'a thrown water on 'em." *Illustration by Kimberly Hoverter Morris.*

Some two hours later, they observe a twin dust plume descending upon them along the railroad access road following the right-of-way. As the small caravan approaches, it becomes apparent that it is comprised of a signal supervisor's truck and a company automobile. The vehicles come to a halt and the signal gang is confronted by an Assistant Signal Supervisor, a Trainmaster, and a Special Agent. The officials immediately begin interrogating the gang members about the "assault" on the rear-end crew. Accusations, denials, and general rhetoric increase the desert temperature. The train crew had reported an unprovoked attack upon themselves while diligently pursuing train observation duties across the division. The signal gang responds that whatever happened must have been perpetrated at another, distant location and that furthermore, if the train crew had truly been awake as required by the Book, it would be easy for them to identify both location and the guilty individual.

Pressure from the brass is met with veiled threats to "get the General Chairman out here" until it becomes obvious that nothing further can he accomplished in the line of discipline. The Signal/Train/Police supervisors return to their vehicles amid "if it ever happens again" and "we know what really happened" and "don't think you can get away with this" utterances. The only intelligent remark, which earns him dirty looks from his associates, is by the Signal Supervisor: "I don't give a damn, you're not hired to keep train crews awake."

As the vehicles prepare to return up the access road to Cisco, a not too muffled voice proclaims to nobody in particular, "Besides, if they hadn'ta been asleep, nobody would'a thrown water on 'em."

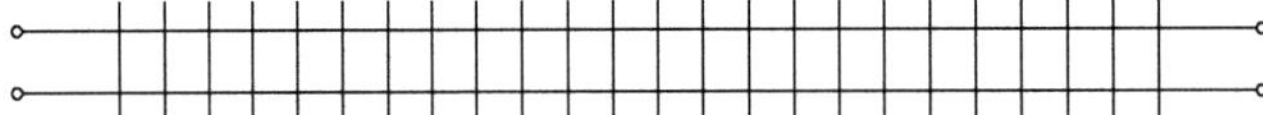

4

THE ROCK ISLAND

1961

Photograph by Philip R. Hastings, Philip Ross Hastings, MD, collection, California State Railroad Museum.

CHICAGO, ROCK ISLAND AND PACIFIC RAILROAD COMPANY

PERSONNEL AND LABOR RELATIONS DEPARTMENT

LASALLE STREET STATION

CHICAGO 5

TELEPHONE WABASH 2-3200

G. E. MALLERY,
VICE PRESIDENT - PERSONNEL

F. J. MEYER,
DIRECTOR OF PERSONNEL &
LABOR RELATIONS

M. E. PARKS,
MANAGER OF LABOR RELATIONS

G. T. GILLULY,
MANAGER OF PERSONNEL

U. E. WIDMAN.
E. E. MARGASON,
W. B. JONES.
LABOR RELATIONS OFFICERS

R. A. LESOVSKY.
LABOR RELATIONS ASSISTANT

R. J. MCGARRY,
PERSONNEL OFFICER

May 22, 1961
File: S. E.

Mr. Michael J. McLaughlin
4523-51 Pl, SW
Seattle 16, Wash,

Dear Mr. McLaughlin:

Officers in the Signal Department have reviewed your letter of April 28th with considerable interest. You have had training and experience that would fit in well with work that will be undertaken by the Signal Department this summer. However, the greatest problem is that we cannot make a firm commitment to you until such time as you have undergone physical examination and other employment processing. There is little chance that you would fail to meet our employment requirements but there is this slight risk to you.

We do not know where your home is but assume that it is some place North and, West of Denver. Will you please complete the enclosed biographical summary and return it to this office. Also, in your letter of transmittal, indicate the date that you would be available for work and, any restrictions that you might have regarding your placement. The chances are that you would be placed in the Chicago area. We are enclosing a brochure which explains the training programs that are available with this company which I am sure will be of interest to you.

Very truly yours,

G. T. Gilluly

DTD:nr
Encls.
Cc: Mr. W. Johnson

Yeah, I Worked for the Rock Island

How come you wear that Rock Island belt buckle?
I used to work for the Rock Island.
You must'a liked it if you're still wearing that belt buckle.
Oh I dunno, it was kind'a screwed up. Well... Yeah, I guess...

Unh huh, we were working on a signal job in Belleville, Kansas and we didn't have hardly any tools, or material, or... But somehow, we got the job done. Some shovels - can you believe it, a signal gang without enough shovels? And some track wire showed up tagged for some government job up in Chicago. That's the fastest ditch job ever. Can you imagine a gang being happy because they got some shovels?

We had kind'a ratty old bunk cars, but hell, no railroad I ever worked for put gangs up in really first-class equipment. But they were comfortable, sort of. You knew they'd been around, we bitched 'cause they were hot in the summer, but they were okay in the cold. A coal stove not only felt good, but it smelled good. 'Course, the smell of drying socks, wet jackets, and other odors sort'a vied for attention.

Man, they ran their trains! I'd started out in the northwest on the Big G, and was used to heavy steel, deep ballast, and - for the most part - slower speeds because of the curves in the mountains and along the shoreline. The Rock Island just screamed across Iowa! I looked at the track - chat ballast, beat up rail - and decided it was sort'a like riding a bicycle - the faster you go, the easier it is to keep your balance.

Rock Island "screamin' across Iowa": former EMD demonstrator 952—now Rock Island 643—leads two sisters on the eastbound Golden State at Fairfield, Iowa, January 25, 1968. *Photograph by Philip R. Hastings, Philip Ross Hastings, MD, collection, California State Railroad Museum.*

The first time I climbed into the bunk cars at Belleville, some jerk pointed a .22 at me. Said he was worried about getting robbed—the average South Chicago citizen would've contributed to us, looking at our living quarters. But you know, looking back on those days, and other days in other bunk cars in other locations, if we hadn't a liked it, we wouldn't have been there. There was an attraction in being good at what we did, in being able to "cut it" no matter how miserable the conditions, and even though we never really discussed it, damn it, we were railroaders!

I got transferred to become one-half of a two-man crew following a communications gang. They were rebuilding the pole line: poles, cross-arms, stubs, or whatever was required. Talk about crude quarters: we had a little dinky trailer about 12 feet long - I mean my folks had a more spacious camping trailer! This "accommodation" was parked alongside whatever station happened to be our base of operations - red brick or frame depots at the foot of "Railroad Avenue," next to the mainline. Hey, that thing shook when we rolled over, never mind when a train went by. But that was a fun job.

Watching a train pass late at night has its own special delight—the complete lack of distraction from the world, the moody and uneven illumination of the giant mostly black beast slowly rolling along, a hyper-sensitivity to the sounds of the steel wheel rolling on steel rail. But perhaps mostly it's the realization that, come morning, this train will be hundreds of miles away, continuing its journey into the great American dream. The Iowa City depot watches the nocturnal passing of Rock Island westbound, the shadow of the operator showing up on the slowly exposed negative.—Phil Monat. *Photograph by Phil Monat.*

The communications gang was also mostly young, college guys and they formed a baseball team. Now, you probably think a ball game's a ball game—no way! In Iowa, every one of those little towns, strung out like beads along the Rock Island, had a baseball team. And I tell you, they took it serious. The whole town turned out when Adair played Anita or Casey. The teams sported bruises more like football players than baseball players, but after the game everybody retired to the bar—one of the players was always a bartender/owner—and the game was replayed into the wee hours. The great thing about the Rock Island team playing the "townies" was we already lived there—sort of—and the food and beer were, if not free, drastically reduced in price.

That was the damnedest job. Two of us following a whole gang and trying to keep up. We had this reject motor car without even a windshield, let alone a roof. We went out early, came back late, spending the day stomping through the weeds from pole to pole, accompanied by chiggers, flies, sweat bees, and every other thing that flew, crawled, hopped, bit or burrowed. Those chiggers homed in wherever anything that was tight: boot tops, hooks, safety belts, underwear. The only relief we found was alcohol - external on the affected areas and internal as required. It worked, we survived. I used to go back to Colorado for long weekends, and more than once missed the train back to wherever we were supposed to be headquartered but we got the job done. I guess that's the mark of a Rock Island employee.

I finally wangled my way to Chicago, which is where I wanted to go in the first place. I'd gone there to hire out and take my physical, got sent halfway back home to Belleville, and gradually worked east to where I'd started. We were working at Englewood where the Rock Island crossed the Pennsy and the Central split off east.

South part of Chicago. BAD area. Hey, the first day on the job, when we went to lunch, they stole our picks and shovels! Who the hell would want wore out old crap like that? But the traffic was amazing. Suburban trains on each other's blocks during rush hours, and pretty damn frequent the rest of the day. Mainline trains, transfers, hell of a place for a guy from Seattle.

But, man, this was the Rock Island in all its faded glory. We were moving and rearranging tracks and signals for the extension of the Dan Ryan expressway downtown. Any other railroad would'a replaced the whole damn thing, but we converted half of a mechanical interlocking to electric. Oh, well.

One time we'd been doing something, and a route across the Pennsylvania crossings wouldn't clear. It was pouring rain, and the tower operator went out to flag the "dummy" (Chicago Rock Island for commuter train) over the diamonds. Just as he got there, the pot cleared and the train whistled off. The op came screaming back in, dripping wet, hollering at us for making him go out and then clearing the dummy. We hadn't touched anything in that 120-lever plant, and the PRR operator and leverman hadn't either. The damned thing had cleared itself. We tore out *everything* we'd done that day. You don't mess with false clears.

The Pennsy ran a funny train about noon—I remember eating lunch in the tower and watching it stop at the Englewood station. As I recall, it had a bunch of head-end cars, coaches, diner, Pullmans, and a caboose (?). Never did figure that one out.

Rock Island "dummy," Joliet, Illinois. *Photograph by Philip R. Hastings, Philip Ross Hastings, MD, collection, California State Railroad Museum.*

Englewood Tower – "moving and rearranging..." Don Davis shot a Rock Island train crossing the Pennsy in 1969, about 8 years later. The Alco motive power included RS3 #487, built in 1951. *Photograph by Don Davis, Charles Stats collection, photo 2021.009.1.036, Lake States Railroad Historical Association at Baraboo, WI.*

I was the only out-a-towner on the gang, so I lived in the bunk cars belonging to a signal gang at Blue Island. They were alongside the suburban line next to the roundhouse. Big gang, putting in a new interlocking at Vermont Street. Another guy and I got caught up like a couple of moths in the night life of Chicago. Damn bars don't close until four! Lots of female companionship, entertainment, hey, I even survived a real Polish wedding! Sometimes we'd drive, sometimes take a dummy—I rode the most unbelievable collection of cars pulled by locomotives that existed only on the Rock Island. Everything from ratty old coaches behind BL2's to the Aerotrain. The Illinois Central suburban station was close to Vermont Street, so I also rode their electric trains. One night I went on a date driving the ugliest orange, terminally abused railroad line truck that ever plied the streets of Chicago.

A Sunday afternoon at Sieben's Brewery, a Friday night at the Bird House with the coolest jazz anywhere.

Hey, I still like to go to Chicago. A great town, and if you like railroading, there ain't none better! The railroad provided living quarters, a paycheck, and the chance to make mistakes I'd like to repeat.

Chicago and Belleville, Omaha and Adair. Rockets at 90 mph, freights ranging from reckless abandon to locals dying on the law. Stainless steel and maroon, or disreputable orange bunk cars. I was there, I saw it, I wouldn't a' missed it.

Damn right I worked for the Rock Island!

Earl "Fatha" Hines, legendary jazz pianist, during a gig at the Bird House, September 8, 1961. *Illustration by Kimberly Hoverter Morris from uncredited photo on Chris Albertson's Stomp Off blog.*

Rock Island's long and painful slide into dereliction is on view here, as a westbound freight, headed by three U25B's and a Geep, gently rocks its way past the Iowa City, Iowa, station on mainline track only good for 20 mph. Resurfacing and welded rail would never make it to this part of the Rock. Shortly the train will cross the Iowa River and then continue west to Denver and its connection with D&RGW.—Phil Monat. *Photograph by Phil Monat.*

Chicago

Brick Towers - Board Towers
Busy Towers - Dead Towers
Trains Slamming Past
Trains Creeping Past
Light Engines
Lost Engines
Crisscross
Chicago

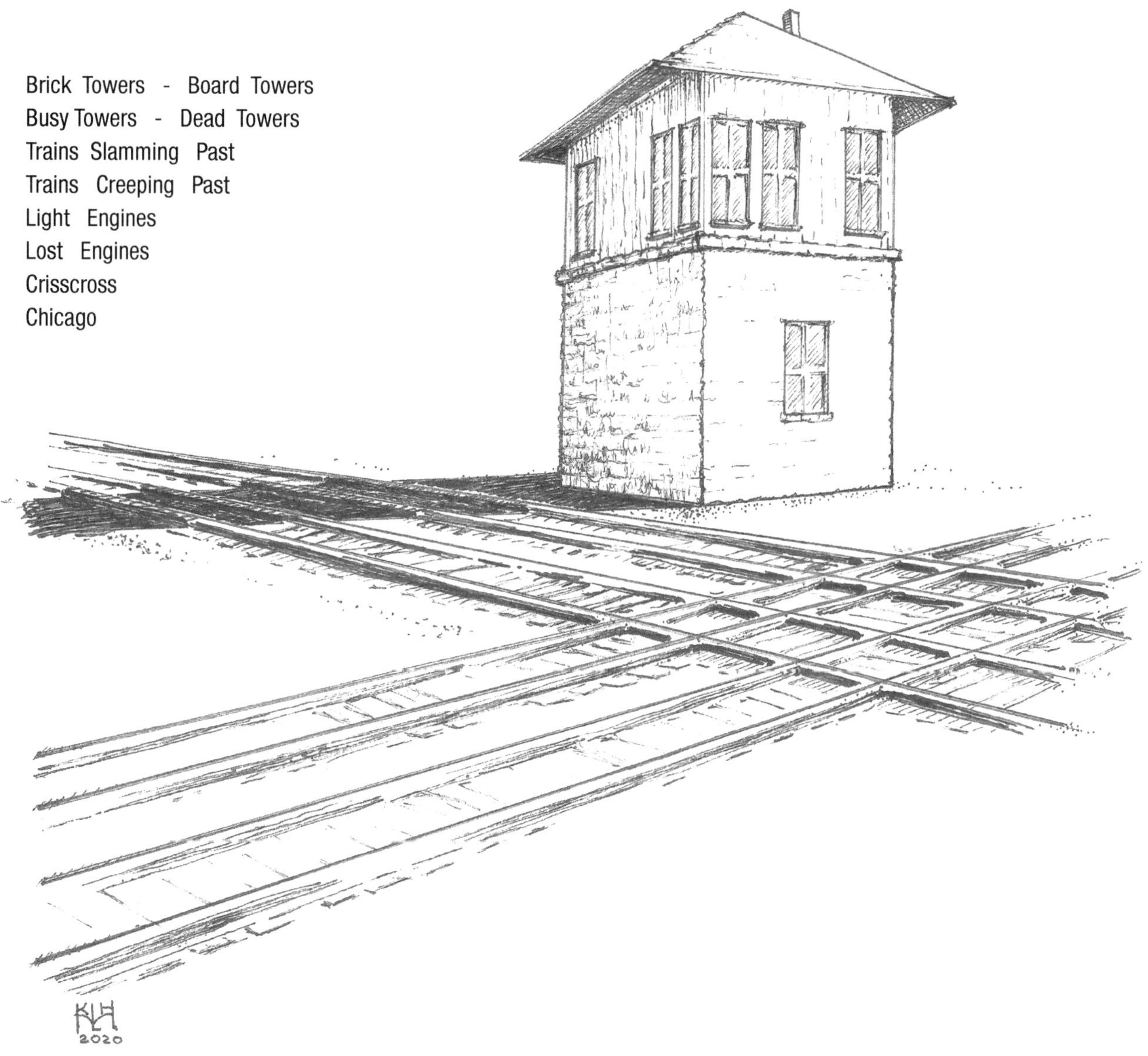

llustration by Kimberly Hoverter Morris based on drawing by Mike McLaughlin.

Email response to Dave Clemens, "As far as travel time from Chicago to Hinkle goes, I agree with your seven days to arrival, with the caveat that the cars picked up in Chicago are from an industry that's located on a railroad that has a direct connection with the UP in Omaha: C&NW, CMStP&P, IC, or CRI&P. If it's off one of the two major inner-city belt lines, BRC or IHB, probably the same or plus one day, if off another railroad add a day or two days, and if it's one of those odd-ball 'via' connections (fer example 'via B&OCT, CR&I, IN,' etc.), it could be anywhere from two to four days more. Oh yes, Chicago, the black hole of American railroading..."

The Faded Red Depots

On a September 1964 afternoon, the section crew prepares to put their motor car back on the track at Walker, Iowa, as train No. 104, its work at Walker complete, heads to Cedar Rapids to finish its day. The two-story wooden depot with agent's quarters upstairs is a standard design of Rock Island predecessor Burlington, Cedar Rapids & Northern. *Photograph by Philip R. Hastings, Philip Ross Hastings, MD, collection, California State Railroad Museum.*

The Rock Island goes across Iowa at speed. The mainline arrows through the fields, flat, straight, relentless.

The small towns are strung along the track at regular intervals. Each has its faded-red, two-story station flanked by grain elevators. Each has narrow red-brick streets leading up to the tree-shaded business district. Outside of the towns, the corn stands in endless fields, crackling with the urgency of its growth.

A dilapidated, roofless motor car sputters into one of the towns and stops on the set-off. The two men riding the car swing it around and off into the clear. Wearily, they wander into the station, out again, and into the tiny trailer parked in the shade of the building. An air horn, the discordant clamor of a crossing bell, and an eastbound freight slams past, disappearing in a swirl of dust.

The two signalmen emerge from the trailer and walk up the brick street that is almost the exact shade of the depot. Cold beer and vast quantities of good farm food wait in town, a meal which will be spiced with a procession of maroon diesels that slow not at all on their way across the land.

As evening falls, summer lightning flashes in the distance, but the night remains soft and warm. The station creaks gently, a sound almost lost in the chorus of crickets. The trailer lights are extinguished and the lamp in the operator's bay window shines in the darkness. The order board blinks its green light in a steady rhythm, beckoning to the hurrying trains.

An intolerably bright headlight appears in the west, the faded red depot harshly illuminated in its stark white light. Horn blaring, the Rocket smashes through town, vanishes, going across Iowa at speed.

Rock Island's Iowa City, Iowa, depot: train-order semaphore signal glowing green in the night, the maintainer's motor car tucked in under the canopy.—Phil Monat. *Photograph by Phil Monat.*

Bill Kuba caught Rock Island 635, an EMD E7A passenger locomotive, on the last Zephyr Rocket passenger train at Cedar Rapids, Iowa, the evening of April 8, 1967. The Zephyr Rocket was run by the Rock Island and the Chicago, Burlington & Quincy; the name combined the nicknames of the two railroads' passenger fleets. Yes, going across Iowa at speed! *Photograph by Bill Kuba, Bill Kuba Collection, photo 013.010.CRIP.AD.072, Lake States Railroad Historical Association.*

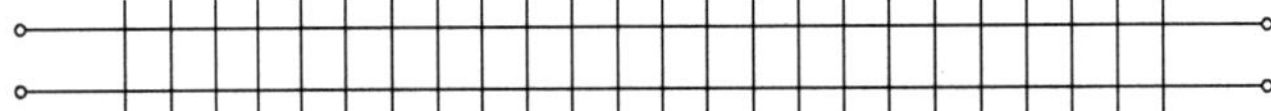

5

MANAGEMENT

1966–1970

Dave Clemens, Mike, and I had a shared view of management and its foibles (at least as perceived by those in blue collar ranks). We had all three worked our way up in our professions from line level worker bees to supervisors and eventually management. Hopefully you will understand why Dave and I fell in love with the "Nothing to Report Report" when Mike passed it on to us. It was just so, well, management think to require that "in all cases fill out and send this form in place of each and every report required from them whenever they have nothing to report."

—Jim Providenza

Form 229

MISSOURI-KANSAS-TEXAS RAILROAD COMPANY

NOTHING TO REPORT

Agent's Form No.________ Report of________
(Do Not Put More Than One Form in Above Space)

From________ Station. Period________ 19____

________ Agent.

Conductor's Form No.________ Report of________
(Do Not Put More Than One Form in Above Space)

Train No.________ Date________ From________

Conductor________ PUNCH

Station Agents and Conductors must in all cases fill out and send this form in place of each and every report required from them whenever they have nothing to report. Agents being particular to give the Form No. and Name of the report of which it becomes the substitute.

This Blank is issued and used for economy, as blanks wasted are a heavy expense, and all concerned are requested not to allow them to be used for figuring or other memoranda.

One little detail about 6 am reports: note they were mimeographed, not computer print-outs. Yep, an army of clerks to receive reports by phone or wire, type 'em up and run 'em off, then distribute to all and sundry. Oh yeah, and early enough to be useful for the day's business. Could always spot those clerks, they had mimeo ink clear to their elbows.

Maps for Four Stories…

Mike's stories and comments about his time in management on the Rio Grande often focused on when he was a track supervisor on Soldier Summit. These two Dave Clemens maps will help orient you as you read them.

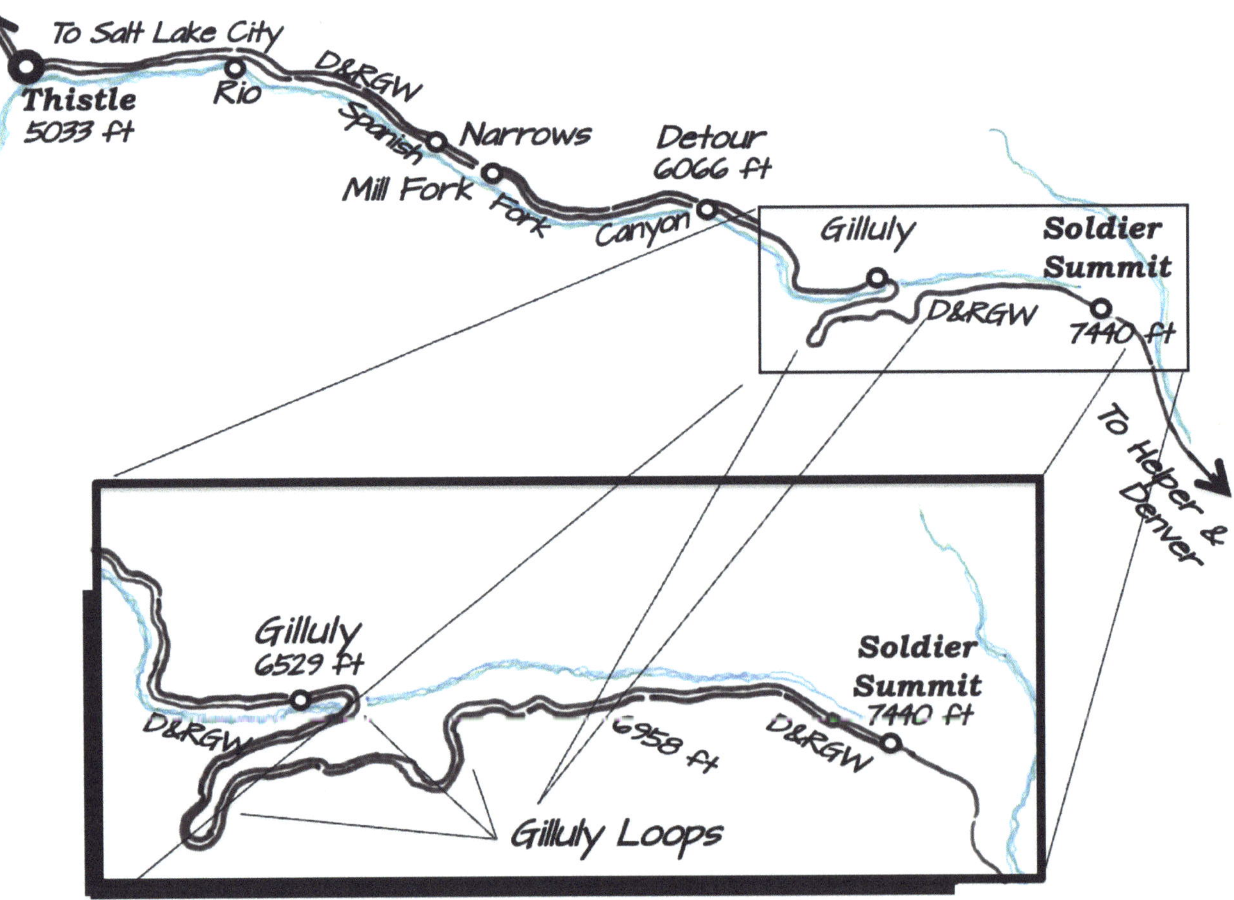

Denver & Rio Grande Western, Thistle to Soldier Summit including the Gilluly Loops. *Map by David R. Clemens.*

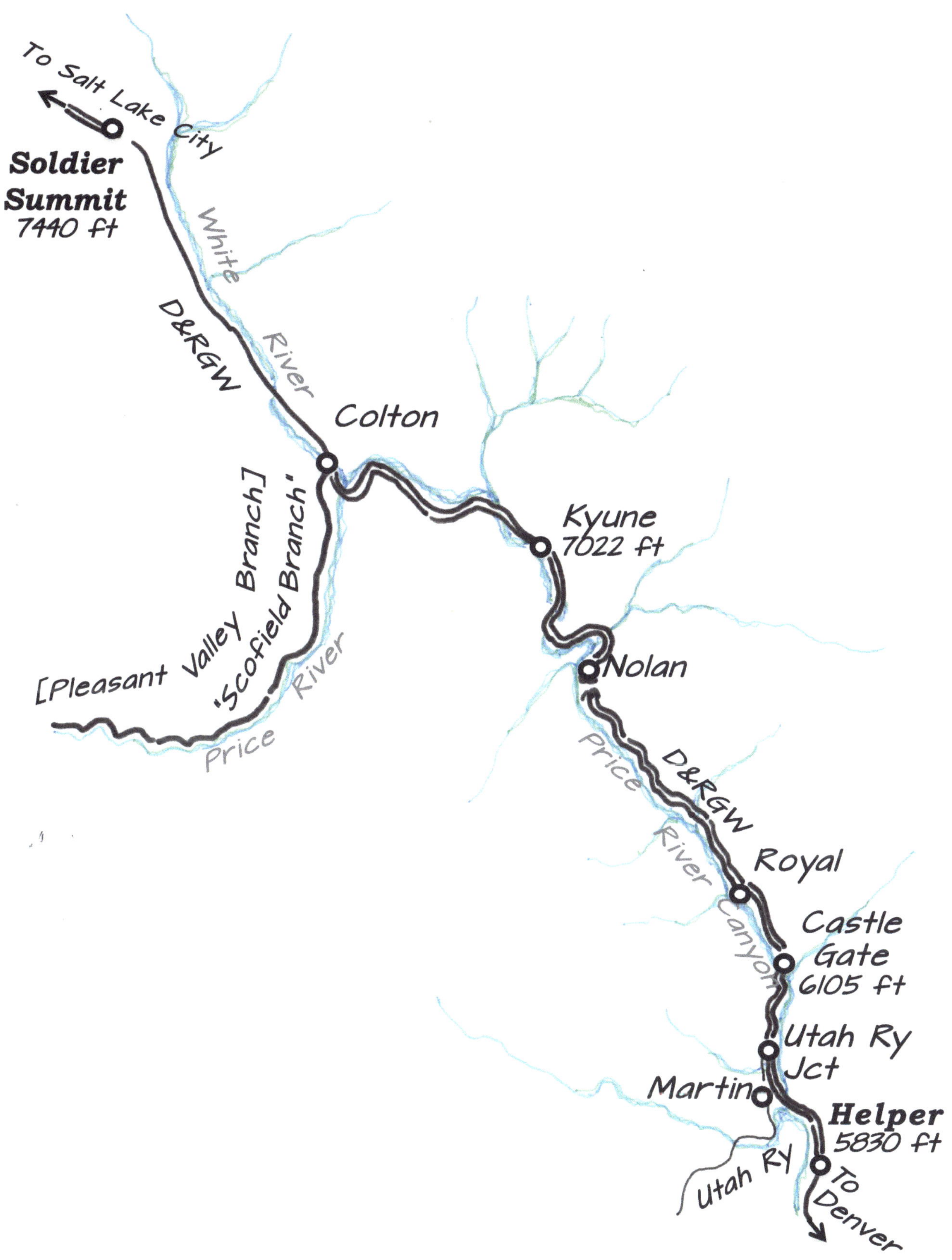

Denver & Rio Grande Western, Soldier Summit to Helper, Utah. *Map by David R. Clemens.*

Have You Ever Ridden A Motor Car?

Have you ever ridden a motor car? I mean really ridden one of those miserable, gut-busting, back-straining sons-of-bitches?

They go by, operator leaning back, feet up, the warm summer sun shining down on the idyllic scene. Sure, brother.

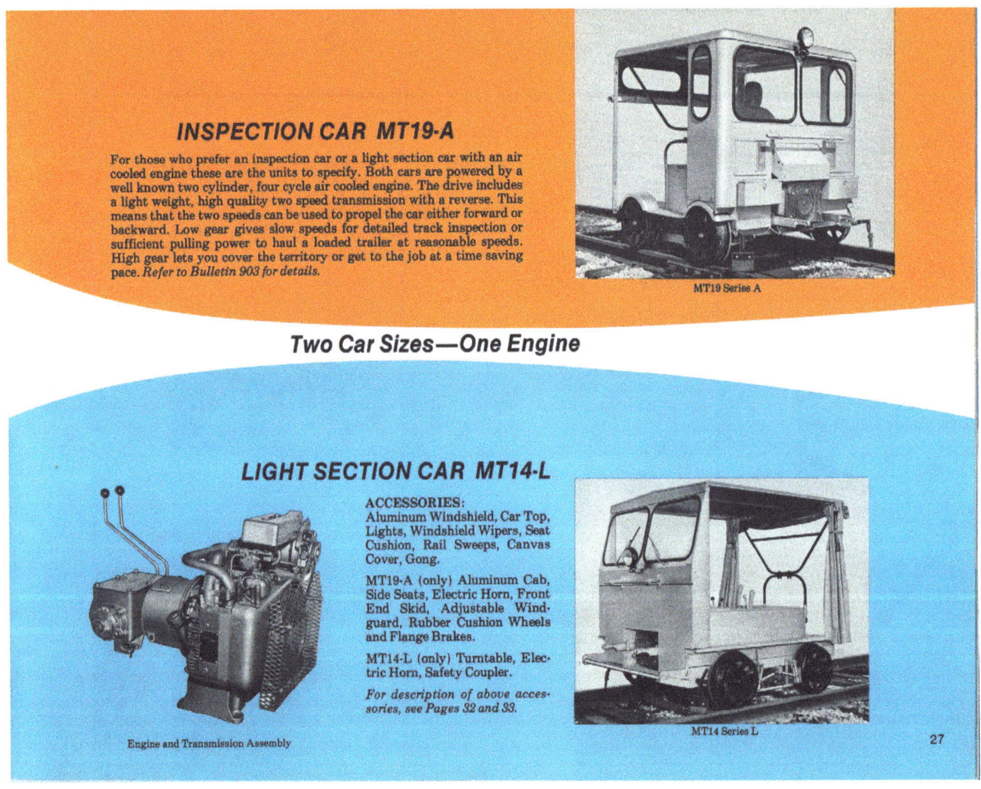

INSPECTION CAR MT19-A

For those who prefer an inspection car or a light section car with an air cooled engine these are the units to specify. Both cars are powered by a well known two cylinder, four cycle air cooled engine. The drive includes a light weight, high quality two speed transmission with a reverse. This means that the two speeds can be used to propel the car either forward or backward. Low gear gives slow speeds for detailed track inspection or sufficient pulling power to haul a loaded trailer at reasonable speeds. High gear lets you cover the territory or get to the job at a time saving pace. *Refer to Bulletin 903 for details.*

MT19 Series A

Two Car Sizes—One Engine

LIGHT SECTION CAR MT14-L

ACCESSORIES:
Aluminum Windshield, Car Top, Lights, Windshield Wipers, Seat Cushion, Rail Sweeps, Canvas Cover, Gong.

MT19-A (only) Aluminum Cab, Side Seats, Electric Horn, Front End Skid, Adjustable Wind-guard, Rubber Cushion Wheels and Flange Brakes.

MT14-L (only) Turntable, Electric Horn, Safety Coupler.

For description of above accessories, see Pages 32 and 33.

Engine and Transmission Assembly

MT14 Series L

27

Fairmont sales brochure. *Michael J. McLaughlin collection.*

Have you ever ridden one of those freezing, cantankerous, no-good bastards in a blizzard so thick that God Himself couldn't find His way?

Yeah, somebody in our insulated, isolated, air-conditioned headquarters has decreed that there is no other way to patrol track, maintain signals, and perform myriad other tasks along the endless miles of right-of-way. Have they ever cranked fruitlessly, to exhaustion, totally defeated in an effort to even start one of the damn things? Do they know a motor car is 600 pounds or more of dead weight that must be moved on or off the tracks by one person, yet is pathetically small when 10,000 tons of roaring, rocking, invincible dead freight comes slamming around a curve without warning?

You don't care? Then ride with me. Get up and have breakfast in the beanery at Thistle. Sarah will fix a breakfast doing justice to the ordeal ahead. Don't forget to order lunch and make sure you have a large thermos of coffee. Gather it all up and let's walk up to the set-off.

John Charles photographed D&RGW 5654 in front of the Rio Grande Café at Thistle, Utah, on August 1, 1964. The café was universally known to D&RGW employees as "the beanery." John was an operator at Thistle at the time and he rented a room above the café. *Photograph by John B. Charles.*

Okay, first task is to pump the mixed gas from the underground tank and fill the 2½ gallon can, a project that covers your arm with fuel sprayed through the leaking gasket. Fill the motor car tank and refill the can. Hey! Hurry up! Just because its 15° below doesn't mean you can drag it. Where's your line up... Right, walk back to the depot and find out what's coming at you, behind you, and for all you know, down on you.

First step: get the crank out, insert it in the bracket on the side of the car, and take a deep breath. Switch on, throttle advanced, spark retarded. Uh-hunh, you have to be retarded to be out here. Crank! No, no, that's a good way to break your thumb! But don't worry, it won't even sputter until you're worn out. Got it running? Fine, let's shove it out onto the mainline.

Yep, up over the rails, bang it across the pass and stop it before it goes off the set-off on the far side. See those handles? Pull them out, grasp them firmly and, hernia bulging, lift the rear end of the car, stumble over the timbers and ties, set it down on the rails. What do you mean the front wheels are on the ground? If you were lifting 200 pounds at the rear, 400 pounds is waiting up ahead.

Throttle open, spark advanced, tighten the drive belt. Listen to those wheels sing! Too bad all they're doing is spinning on the frosty rail. Slowly we move out. Oh, oh, a broken bolt in that joint. Why can't we stop when we want to? Brakes locked; we seem to slide forever. And if you think it's bad on this side, wait until we're going down the 2.4% below Kyune.

What time is it? That damn freight is on top of us! When you're running a snowplow, there's a set-off in the way every 100 yards, yet on a motor car they're five miles apart. Handles out, lift, strain, stumble as you swing around and set down. Grab the brake handle, there's no stop at the back of this set-off. Wait, wait, where the hell is that train? Finally, it drags past. Back on the track, slowly moving upgrade, checking the track as we go.

Past Gilluly, into CTC territory. Now we have block protection, and a head wind that slows us to a walk. Snow blowing, visibility zero, what the hell are we doing out here? Get out, shovel through the drifts, finally Soldier Summit. And 45 minutes late on the block. The dispatcher, in his infinite wisdom and from the warmth of his office in Salt Lake wants to know what delayed us. Go ahead, tell him...

Is there a more God-forsaken spot than the east switch at Soldier Summit? High on a fill, in an open pass, the wind screams around the man-made obstacles. The motor car is moving. Brakes locked? Better put a spike maul through a wheel and the tie crib. There wasn't a train all day when we were on double track, now we have to wait for an endless procession. Okay, we've got 12 minutes for the six miles to Colton—and it'll take six to get the damn engine restarted. The switch at Colton is lined for us—an ominous courtesy—and the call light is on. It probably has something to do with the train waiting on the westbound main...

Down grade, although in the snow it takes full throttle and a ready shovel. The four sandwiches and quarter of a gooseberry pie that Sarah packed for each of us in Thistle have long since disappeared. The back curtain on the motor car is eminently ineffectual against the snow. In North Dakota, the Great Northern has fully enclosed motor cars, but have you ever tried to bail out of one of them when a train suddenly approaches around a curve on your track?

Three of EMD's finest are in Run 8 as they blast up the 1.5% grade on the mainline at Winter Park, Colorado, passing a motor car sitting in the passing siding. The section man gets a break from the constant never-ending task of shoveling out switches... —Phil Monat. *Photograph by Phil Monat.*

Down through the Price River canyon the snow has stopped, although the wind is still bitterly cold. Rounding a curve, a drift is a couple of feet deep across one rail...

No, we're still okay. Pull yourself out from under the car and pick up the scattered tools. Now limp back to that goddam piece of machinery and figure out how we're going to get it back on the track. It's just possible, and finally we move -- slowly, jerking, a bent axle all but preventing forward progress -- down to Helper. Right, you get to call the dispatcher and tell him why you're late clearing your block - again

Hey, have you ever ridden a motor car up the Scofield to milepost five? Did you ever relax under the pines, line in the water? Did you ever drift back down to Colton with the rail joints pinging tinnily under the wheels...

D&RGW motor car, Tennessee Pass, Colorado, June 1980. *Photograph by Philip R. Hastings, Philip Ross Hastings, MD, collection, California State Railroad Museum.*

A Meet at Brendel

Train No. 783 approaching Brendel, Utah, June 18, 1981: "10,000 tons of roaring, rocking invincible freight..." *Photograph by R. C. Farewell.*

"Call the dispatcher. Go ahead, tell him why..." Track Inspector, Brendel, Utah, June 18, 1981. *Photograph by R. C. Farewell.*

Jumping the switch points to get from the branch to the siding, Brendel, Utah, June 18, 1981. *Photograph by R. C. Farewell.*

Is there a more God-forsaken spot than Soldier Summit in the winter? Maybe Brendel in the eastern Utah high desert in the summer? June 18, 1981. *Photograph by R. C. Farewell.*

Snowplow

No 17, the westbound Rio Grande Zephyr, makes its 7:05 pm station stop at Helper, Utah, on a snowy winter night, December 2, 1982. The tracks ahead over Soldier Summit are clear; the Zephyr's passage will be quick and uneventful. Most passengers will have no idea of the efforts made by maintenance-of-way employees to make that possible.
Photograph by R. C. Farewell.

"You awake? Hey, you awake?"

"Wha'timezit?"

"One-twenty. The crews say there's heavy snow from Gilluly all the way to Castle Gate. Matty thinks you better run the plow."

"Okay... Barry been called?"

"Yeah – I called his men for him about half an hour ago, they should be heading for the summit now."

"Right. Lemme talk to the crew caller."

"Hey, Jerry, I gotta call a plow. Who's first out?"

"Johnson, you want him?"

"Hell no! He's scared to death of a plow. Who's behind him?"

"Mac, he ought'a be okay."

"Good, how long do I have to wait until Johnson's called?"

"He'll get ninety-seven; about two forty-five."

"Okay, call the plow for three or whatever it works out."

The track supervisor, fully awake now, warms up the coffee and dresses for the long, cold job ahead. Three section men are called to go with the extra. By the time the train crew is on duty, the section hands will have the coal stoves in the plow hot and a huge pot of coffee perking.

The supervisor drives through the falling snow to the Helper depot where he goes in to talk to the dispatcher and plan his moves. An eastbound freight arrives, snow piled on the front of the engine. A brief conversation with the incoming engineer confirms the dispatcher's decision of calling for a plow.

The hostler moves the 3032, an orange-and-black GP35, from the ready track and couples into the plow. The section men connect the train line and the main reservoir hose that provides the air supply for the snowplow. After the tanks are filled, the men unchain the cage and wings and check their operation. Everything in working order, they walk over to the station to wait for the train crew.

In the depot, the crews for 97 and its helper sign in, then the helper crew goes out for their engine. Soon after, the plow crew wanders in and they good-naturedly bitch about being called for the plow and the fact that this will mean another night in Helper before returning to Salt Lake. The operator informs 97's crew that 97 is out of Maxwell and they walk out into the snow. After a short wait, 97's headlight shows at the east end of the yard and the train pulls in and stops with the engine just west of the depot. The helper is coupled on behind the caboose and an air test made.

"I'm ready when you are." "Let's go." The conversation between the helper engineer and the head end crackles from the radio in the yard office and, engines roaring, 97 accelerates out of town.

In the cab of the 3032, the track supervisor, engineer, and conductor hold a last-minute conference: "We'll plow the westbound to Kyune, drop back to the east end and get the pass, then go on to the summit." "Okay, how fast do you want to go?" "I'd like to go at least 30 or 35 to throw the snow over the other track, I guess as fast as you can go without putting us into the ditch." "Okay, and you'll have to call the signals on the radio 'cause all I can see back here most of the time is blowing snow."

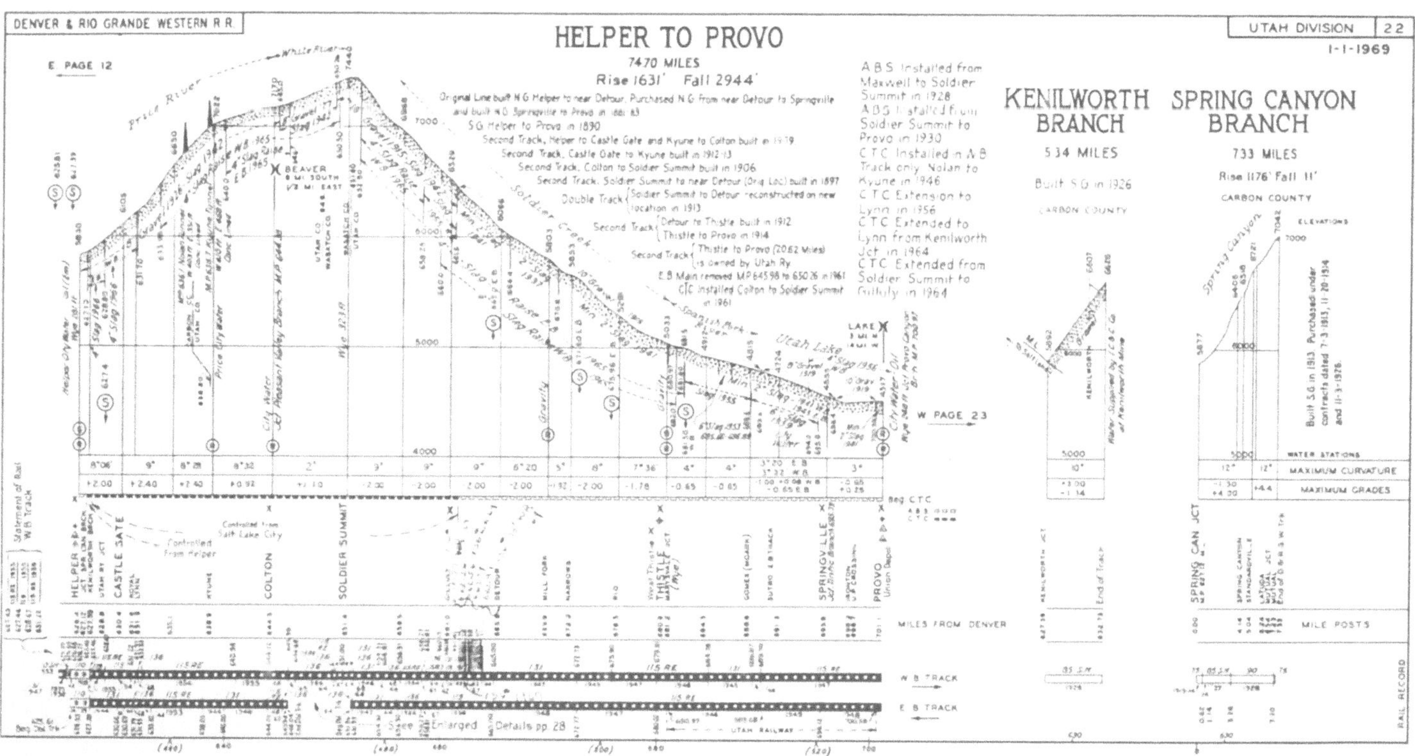

D&RGW Utah Division track chart, 1/1/1969, page 22. *Michael J. McLaughlin collection.*

"3032 to Helper Yard. Tell the man to line us out, we're leaving town." The plow train moves slowly down the lead and accelerates onto the main line at Kenilworth Junction. As they move out of Helper, the plow is primarily flanging the packed snow from between the rails. "Green, 3032." The supervisor and a section man at the plow controls lift the cage and wings briefly, then let them chunk down as they go through Utah Railway Junction. Lift and drop, lift again to clear the turnouts at Castle Gate.

"Green, 3032." The snow is deeper now and the wings are throwing a high, white arch as the short train rocks through Lynn. The line is one curve after another as the track climbs on a steady 2.4% grade. Periodically raising the plow cage to clear flange oilers, dragging equipment detectors and motor-car set-offs, the two men in the cab peer out at the blowing snow, steaming cups of coffee resting on the window sills. The head brakeman sits behind them, calling the signals as they appear in the darkness ahead. The other section men stoke the coal stoves and maintain the coffee supply.

Rio Grande plow train. *Photograph by Philip R. Hastings, Philip Ross Hastings, MD, collection, California State Railroad Museum.*

After clearing the west switch at Kyune, the train stops, waits for the dispatcher to clear the signal, then backs down to the east end. Moving slowly with wings raised to prevent filling the main line, the plow starts clearing the siding. A headlight appears and passes as the helper from 97 drops down grade on the eastbound main.

"Highball, 3032." Leaving Kyune, the train accelerates and once again the snow arches out from the plow blades. Speed is higher here and drifts explode as they are hit. The plow exhibits its characteristic nosing action and coffee slops from the cups.

Suddenly a headlight appears on the other main. "Eastbound, 3032. Stop and back down about a quarter of a mile. Soon's he gets by, we'll go again." The last time out, the plow crew had been following their usual practice of meeting opposing trains at speed when a chunk of ice flanged from between the rails broke a caboose window. While nobody shed any tears for the rear-end crew, considerable—and sobering—thought was given to the open tri-levels of new automobiles on the train.

The plow rocks through the switch at Colton and roars up the single track toward Soldier Summit. The wind is blowing hard across the open country and the track is alternately clear and then covered with deep drifts. "Easy at the east end, 3032, there'll be somebody cleaning switches." The train slows to a crawl and enters the siding. A figure muffled in heavy clothes stands in the clear, wind whipping around him as he dismally contemplates the snow being dragged into the turnout. In spite of electric switch heaters and plywood covers, the wind manages to plug the power switches at Soldier Summit and the railroad must resort to the age-old practice of clearing them with broom and shovel wielded by a 1ong-suffering section hand.

In the clear on the westward siding across from the brick depot, the train sits as the conductor and track supervisor call the dispatcher. An eastbound freight is climbing toward the summit while a westbound is passing through Kyune behind them, followed by the first Geneva turn.

"Let's eat." The train crew heads for the caboose with the exception of the head brakeman. He had been watching the preparations being made in the plow and now heads in that direction. In the cab, one of the section men has the stove covered with dishes and the smell of frying rabbit, venison chops, and eggs mingles with that of coal smoke and coffee. Homemade sourdough bread completes the meal. The brakeman had helped the section men clean switches and change flanger shoes and now claims his reward.

The first westbound rolls by and disappears into the storm. Shortly after, the eastbound freight crawls by on the eastward siding and grinds to a halt. The Geneva turn is out of Colton and climbing toward the summit in the gray light of dawn. Soon the turn is past, having cut off the helper on the fly at the east switch. The eastbound freight jerks into motion and the caboose rolls by in a swirl of snow. After a last-minute conference, the conductor waves a highball echoed by the track supervisor's "Any time, 3032" over the radio and the train tips over the summit and starts down grade on the eastward mainline. The sidings and wye at Soldier Summit are being cleaned by a rubber-tired dozer and the snowplow has work to do on the main.

"Green. 3032." The need now is for dynamic braking rather than brute horsepower as they wind down the hill. It is light now, as light as it will get until the storm is over. Everything is a featureless white without even the shadows cast by the headlight to provide contrast as had been the case during the night. At Gilluly the mainline is plowed and, after backing to the east switch, the siding. Because the west end of Gilluly marks the end of CTC, between that point and Thistle all operation is with the current of traffic and the train now works the westward main line.

Moving down grade past Detour, the snowfall is lighter, although there is still plenty of work to be done by the plow. Between Narrows and Rio where the tracks share the narrow canyon with the highway, the crew plays an old game. Without a word being spoken, the speed of the train is adjusted so that the snow being cleared from the track falls on the freshly plowed highway.

"Green, 3032." The train passes the east switch at Thistle and comes to a stop on the sharp curve in front of the brick station. After checking with the operator, the crew crosses over and spots the plow on the Marysvale branch behind the depot. They enter the building and sit down at the counter in the beanery. In the meantime, the operator gets a lineup and clearance from the dispatcher. Soon the men straggle back to the train and turn it on the wye. The snow has stopped, although the sky is still gray.

The siding at Rio is plowed, then the one at Narrows. As they finish at Narrows, a Utah Railway train of empties approaches. The brakeman sprints to the signal case and turns his switch key in the controller. The mainline signal turns red, halting the Utah drag and, after a brief wait, the leaving signal clears. The plow train pulls out through the spring switch and heads upgrade at better than twice the speed of the Utah train. At Detour, the siding is also plowed and as the empties approach, the brakeman again runs to let the plow out ahead.

Snowplow and section hands clearing snow at a switch, Tennessee Pass, Colorado, January 23, 1974. *Photograph by Philip R. Hastings, Philip Ross Hastings, MD, collection, California State Railroad Museum.*

"Green, 3032." The west end of Gilluly and back into CTC territory where they cross over to the westward main. The sky is starting to break up and patches of blue are visible. At milepost 654 the plow stops to meet a westbound train and then continues upgrade. As they approach the summit, the wind is still blowing and the section hands are still cleaning switches. Up here, they say, the snow never melts—the wind just wears it out blowing it back and forth.

The Kaiser unit train is waiting on the mainline as its eight unit helper is cut out into the eastward siding. The track supervisor walks to the phone and talks to the dispatcher. He decides to run to Colton behind the helper engine and plow the eastward main after the light engine gets far enough ahead to avoid running on their yellow block.

"Yellow, 3032." Out of the siding and onto the single track, the plow train moves east. Arriving at Colton, they wait for five minutes after the signal goes from yellow to green and then move onto the double track. As they pass the small yard, the supervisor makes a mental note that the Scofield Branch [Pleasant Valley Branch] will have to be plowed before the next train goes up to the Columbine mine. The sun is now shining and the white snow sparkles as it flies out from the plow and floats down into the icebound Price River.

Through the Nolan tunnel, past Lynn, Royal and Castle Gate, past Utah Railway Junction and Spring Canyon Junction, the plow train pulls into Helper, crosses over, and enters the yard. They stop across from the depot and the crew goes in to tie up. The section men and the track supervisor change the flanger shoes and then chain up the cage and wings. The main reservoir hose is disconnected and the plow closed up. The switch crew will turn the plow and put it away, ready for the next storm.

D&RGW plow 044, Helper, Utah, December 12, 1961. "Ready for the next storm." *Photograph by Jim Ozment, Western Rail Images*

Wearily, the men walk over to the station; snowplow extra 3032 now only an entry on the dispatcher's train sheet.

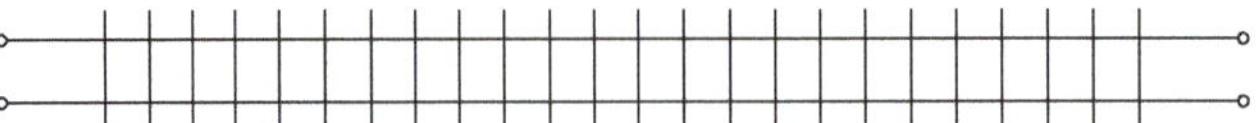

Rio Grande Men

Larry Parsons…

Naw, definitely not God, and not a genius in the commonly accepted definition of the word, but Larry Parsons is hell of a smart railroader who had/has a knack for getting his people to bust their butts for him and simultaneously knew/knows how a railroad should be run to maximize return over the long run. And don't forget his extreme talent for marketing.

Yeah, I/we knew Larry, used to play bridge with him and his wife, took weekend trips to various places in the mountains—our daughter even baby-sat for his kids. I first met him when I was at Coors and he was equipment manager or some silly thing like that for the railroad. Don't remember all his titles, etc., but he went up like a rocket and then over into operations. Remember some interesting stories when he was Utah Division Superintendent, finally ended up as Vice President Operations, where he accomplished such things as winning the gold Harriman medal year after year as well as running a hell of a railroad. He was Holtman's (W.J. Holtman, then president of the RR) heir apparent, and the Rio Grande was making money like they owned the mint. Which was a mistake: they had so much cash that some outfit tried to take them over and they had to get in bed with Anschutz to remain independent. Then Anschutz bought the SP (very good for him, terrible for the D&RG) and things started going downhill. It was decided to run the railroad from San Francisco and mostly with the old SP management. Larry went out there, looked around, and came back and told Anschutz it'd never work. Anschutz had his eye on a couple billion dollars' worth of real estate, which he grabbed, then sold the whole shootin' match to thc UP, which put another billion or so in his pocket, and not too long ago dumped another umpteen million in UP stock.

So, Parsons said adios. For a while, William N. Deramus IV had worked for the Rio Grande and was a close friend, and when WND III retired as CEO/Chairman from the KCS, IV took over as President and brought Parsons along as Vice President of Operations or something like that. Then Bill IV got crossways with the Board of Directors and got fired. Larry had been running the KCS like he had the Rio Grande, and them good ol' boys down there in the swamps didn't like it, so Larry got the boot also. Right about then the W&LE was on its last legs and they hired him to try to save the whole mess. Long story short, he did and ended up buying the railroad (and no, he didn't come from money at all—he was a U-Kansas product). So much for the background, there's also been other stuff in previous *Trains* magazine articles.

How good is he? I truly believe he could have done as well as Haverty on the KCS if he hadn't been dragged under by whatever it was that Deramus IV got involved in. I also don't believe he would have ever gotten involved with NS, Conrail, BN, etc. and he thought that the UP was from another planet. When he first took over the W&LE he offered me a job working for him back in Canton. That was a real tough decision, I would've loved being part of his management team, but I don't think I could have ever adjusted to central Ohio. Summed up? Great railroader and a hell of an individual. I consider myself extremely fortunate to have been able to call him a friend.

Hmmm, that got kinda outa control, didn't it?

John Norwood…

Letter to Brian Holtz, January 18, 1998

"I don't know if you get *Vintage Rails* magazine, but they had a great article about John Norwood, mostly his narrow gauge experiences, but also tossing in his culinary expertise. I wrote a letter to the editor… last night the phone rang. Carol answered, and then called down the stairs, "It's John Norwood."

"And what started out to be a brief 'thanks for the nice words' call became a solid hour of reminiscences about our membership in 'the family.' Sure, the remarks about Gus, Jack Ayer, etc. but more about the others such as Charlie Alberts (General Roadmaster), Ed Waring (Chief Engineer), Spud Eaton (Signal Engineer), and many, many others; for instance, Ed Moran who got promoted and busted on a regular basis (Rule G in the latter case) ranging from Division Superintendent to Assistant Trainmaster, depending on how pissed off Gus truly was. Talked about cooking, Jake's parties, what happened after 'marking off' in Helper, Salida, Grand Junction…

"John's 83, sharper than someone half his age, and doing great… As I said, a privilege to have known him when he was kicking ass and taking names. Yeah, and relaxing at Jake's with a large bourbon and telling us 'kids' what it was really like 'years ago and far away.'"

Hank Chappell…

Email to Dave Clemens and Jim Providenza, October 19, 2009

"Two more little stories about roadmaster Hank Chappell, then I'll let him rest in peace.

"The first, I'd only been a track supervisor for about 6 months or so when my boss went on vacation. The dust from his departure hadn't even settled yet when Hank and the Division Engineer showed up in Helper. They wanted me to load two cars with serviceable track material and send them to Hank at Salt Lake immediately, obviously figuring in John's absence I'd do what they said. Might'a been a new track supervisor, but a looong way from being a new railroader.

"Of course, we had material hidden away all over the mountain. Every employee, whether communications, B&B, water service, signal, or... hides stuff for "just in case," much as a squirrel hides nuts against the coming winter. After a few days, got a phone call asking where the cars were and I said I was loading it all as fast as I could. Friday before my boss returned, I billed two cars of "company material" to Hank at Salt Lake. When they showed up, they contained the damnedest collection of scrap; "Sperry" rail, tie plates for 75 lb rail, cracked angle bars, rail so curve-worn the ball was wore clear back to the web, terminal frogs, switch points that were new in USRA days; I was totally amazed at what I pulled out of the weeds with a little help from my section foremen. Of course, when he heard the story, John kept alternating between being pissed off that they'd tried to pull a fast one, and laughing every time he thought about Hank's face when he saw what was actually in the cars.

"During the winter, we frequently had to resort to gandies wielding picks, shovels, and switch brooms to keep the switches operating. Long, long hours, bitter cold winds, snow that won't quit, not your favorite evening's entertainment. We had standing instructions that they were to take breaks a couple of guys at a time, an hour's sleep in out of the cold. Also had permanent accounts at three all-night cafes across the territory where they could get a hot meal, steaks or whatever they wanted. Not to mention continuous overtime until the storm quit. And those gandies busted their butts for us.

"On the other hand, Hank had the nasty habit of sending his men home at 7 am, forcing them to return at 7:30 on straight time. Meals? Let 'em bring a bigger lunch... Well, came contract time and what to our wondering eyes did appear? A clause stating that not only did overtime continue until the men got eight hours rest and you couldn't lay them off on straight time to absorb overtime, and that meals were to be provided after X hours on duty. My, my, thought Mr. Chappell was gonna have a coronary. The sad thing was that we could never convince him that it was his actions, and those of a few other like supervisors, that finally forced the issue."

Walt Williams…

"Before the Grande sold the Silverton line to Bradshaw, we went down to ride it every year (this was in my traffic manager days) as guests of the railroad. Even when I was a consultant and not really 'eligible,' Walt Williams, the Regional Sales Manager, would always include me in his 'special' group. I brought books and answered questions about the line and railroading in general. We always had the private car Nomad and as we pulled out of the station, we stood on the rear platform and toasted the lesser mortals with our Bloody Marys. When I wasn't assisting the host, you could always find me on the platform pointing out features, explaining and mostly smelling the coal smoke. A warm summer day, a cold drink, feet up on the railing and good company (this was the one trip where Walt selected his guests by personality, not by carloads shipped), it don't get no better!

D&RGW narrow-gauge private car Nomad in 1959: "We stood on the rear platform and toasted the lesser mortals" …shades of Beebe and Clegg! *Photograph by John Buvinger, Colorado Railroad Museum collection.*

"After the Silverton was sold and Anschutz took over the Grande, we had similar trips on the Ski Train in his private cars. Usually the Kansas and Colorado, complete with a humungous breakfast going up and hors d'oeuvres coming back, and again the bar opened as we pulled out – "Salud! from the rear platform, Denver!" We usually went on Easter Sunday, when Walt again put together his 'special group' As usual, I had books, timetables, condensed profiles and grade and alignment charts, answering questions about everything from track maintenance to dynamic braking. A great tradition that disappeared when Walt retired a few years ago.

"Speaking of the Ski Train, my daughter Christine was a member of the Eskimo Ski Club and went up every Saturday for years. They were still honoring annual passes like my old one, so she carried it and rode for free. Once in a while somebody would ask her what her father did for the Rio Grande. "I'm not sure, but he works for Dee Butters (Chief Transportation Officer)." "Yes, MA"AM! Hope you have a good day." Later it became Larry Parsons (now president of the Wheeling & Lake Erie) and she could honestly add, "Matter of fact, I baby sit for Larry's kids." "Yes, MA'AM!"

D&RGW standard gauge business car Kansas at Denver Union Station, February 23, 1986. "Salud! from the rear platform, Denver!" *Photograph by Mike Danneman.*

6

CORRESPONDENCE

1992–2012

It was always with an unseeming amount of joy and anticipation, mixed with a bit of trepidation, that you opened one of Mike's "two pound packages"—a manila envelope with three or four typewritten pages followed by voluminous photocopies of items from his array of railroad documents, and almost certainly some hand drawn plans, maps and sketches… and not a few opinions.

—Jim Providenza

Lineups and Crutches

Having had some dandy experiences with lineups, believe I am qualified to comment on them. First, a lineup by its very nature is a projection of train movements already on line or expected to run in the next xx number of hours, based on traffic that's in yards, expected from connections, industry spotting and release notifications, etc. A lineup can't exist in a vacuum. Sure, there's a rather consistent ebb and flow of traffic (which's where they get the raw material for schedules), but lineups are much more specific and cover what's very much expected to run in the next four or so hours (copied a zillion 7:30 am and 12:30 pm lineups I have). And they're serious business; put a bunch'a "well, maybe" trains on 'em and nobody out on line gets anything done, leave something off and somebody's dead.

The D&RGW lineup for May 8, 1968, seems "over the top" until you realize how big a section of track you are talking about. 120 miles for the subdivision... basically 9 through trains each way. Still more than enough to keep you busy.

D&RGW Salt Lake City Sub.
Map by David R. Clemens.

D&RGW Form 3210
Section 8

TRAIN LINEUP

(Safety First)

To ALL CONCD At THISTLE Date MAY 8 19 68

At (time) 730 AM the following trains have passed or will leave the stations designated below:

ROPER TO HELPER

NO 18 BY THISTLE 646 AM
EX 3070 WEST 647 BY PROVO 657 AM
EX 5334 WEST 785 GENEVA TURN ARRIVED SOL SUMMIT 650 AM
EX 3067 WEST 195 BY SOL SUMMIT 703 AM
EX 3022 WEST 171 CALLED HELPER 700 AM
EX 3010 WEST 199 CALLED HELPER 715 AM
EX 5329 177 CALLED HELPER 725 AM
EX 5308 WEST 655 SCOFIELD CALLED HELPER 630 AM GOES TO SCOFIELD
MAY RUN EX WEST OUT HELPER ABOUT 11 AM
EX 3069 EAST 134 DEPARTED SOL SUMMIT 705 AM
EX 3080 EAST 772 CALLED ROPER 700 AM
EX EAST 142 BE CALLED ROPER ABOUT 930 AM
EX EAST BE CALLED ROPER ABOUT 1030 AM
EX EAST BE CALLED ROPER ABOUT 1115 AM
EX 5332 EAST 650 HELPER ENG LEAVE SOL SUMMT ANY TIME
EX 3041 EAST 650 HELPER ENG LEAVE KYUNE OR SOL SUMMIT ON ARR EX 3010 WEST
EX 3059 EAST 650 HELPER ENG LEAVE KYUNE OR SOL SUMMIT ON ARR EX 5329 WEST
5923-5306 684 MIDVALE TRAMP CALLED ROPER 900 AM
5921 688 PINGPONG CALLED ROPER 915 AM
SALINA TURN 662 BE CALLED ROPER 1230 PM
EX 5304 EAST 982 WORK TRAIN BY AMERICAN FORK 704AM
5914 EAST 668 TINTIC CALLED PROVO 900AM
5301 673 GENVA CALLED PROVO 800 AM
5931 673 PIPEMILL TURN CALLE PROVO 715 AM

ARJ
Chief Dispatcher

738.

Received at (time) 711.15AM by WIELAND
Operator

Acknowledgment:

I understand that this is not a train order, does not confer any right over any train, or waive any rules and is subject to change without notice after 45 minutes from time of transmittal.

Signature

The Lineup was issued almost exactly 42 years ago (5-8-68) at Thistle at 7:11 am. Oh, yeah! Forty-two years ago today—probably mid-forties for a high, mid-twenties for a low, and the wind blowing. A month later, green, flowers, great time to check the track on the Scofield branch up Fish Crik, and by then the wind had wore out all that snow blowing it back and forth. The third trick operator was Al Wieland and the Chief Dispatcher was Arnie Johnson. Number 18, the Zephyr, was running 23 minutes late at that point.

#647 was a dead freight extra, kind'a a long-distance local from Grand Jct to Roper.

#785 was one of the small Geneva Steel unit trains, cutting out his help at Summit.

#195 was the hottest westbound freight from Denver.

#171 was from Pueblo.

#199 was a real dog outa Denver and eventually made its way to Roper.

#177 was another train from Pueblo.

#655 normally just worked the Mine and power plant at Castle Gate, but about once a week went "high" to the Scofield branch outa Colton on the main line.

The "ex west" from Helper was probably a long-distance local to Roper.

#134 to Denver was the hottest eastbound at that time.

#772 was an ore train to CF&I at Pueblo.

#142 was an intermediate train that split at Grand Jct. for both Denver and Pueblo.

The two "ex east" trains are probably 2nd and 3rd 142, they usually ran extra sections.

#650 is returning helper engines from Soldier Summit, the 5332 being two SD45's cut off the 785 Geneva train.

#662 the Salina Turn runs Roper to Thistle then down the Marysvale branch to Salina.

#982 work train working between Roper and Lehi.

The remaining trains are locals that ran all over the Salt Lake valley and on the various branches:

Midvale Tramp works the branches to the Bingham Mine and smelter.

Ping Pong works Sugar House branch and north end of the valley.

Tintic works that branch outa Provo.

Geneva works Provo to the Geneva steel mill.

Pipemill works outa Provo to the industries surrounding the Geneva mill.

So there you are, a real-world working lineup and I managed to avoid everything and get back to Helper in one piece. Helper and Thistle had 24-hour operators, so they copied the lineups for section foremen, signal maintainers, track supervisors, et al. Nope, didn't sign anything, just picked up a copy and got on that goddam motor car.

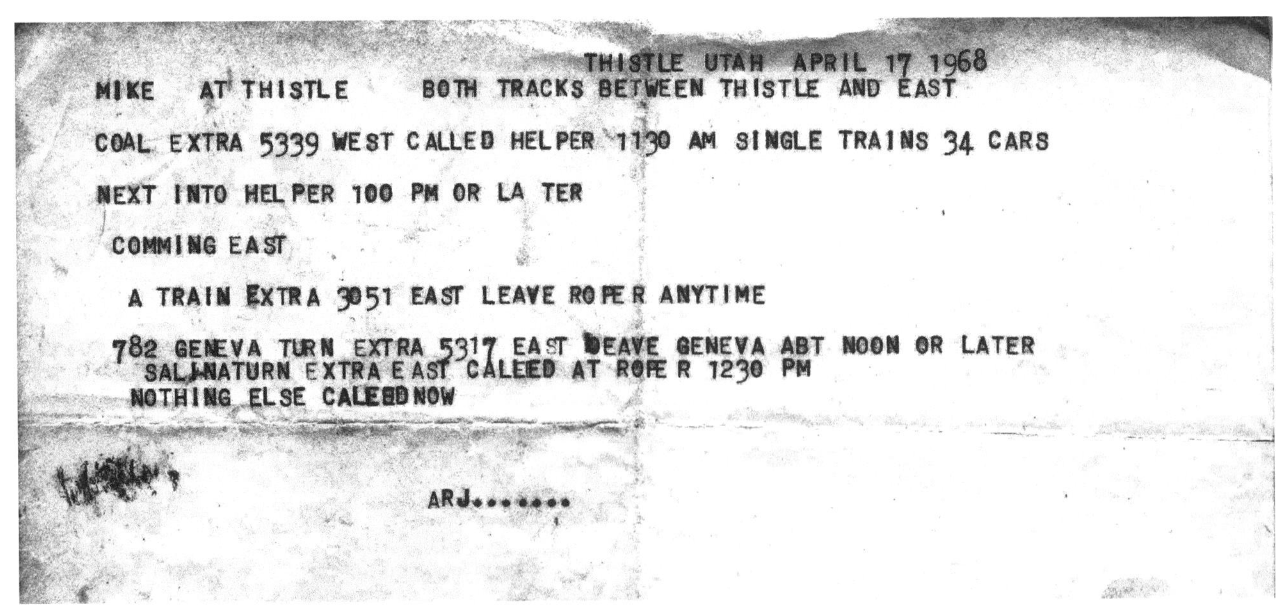

THISTLE UTAH APRIL 17 1968

MIKE AT THISTLE BOTH TRACKS BETWEEN THISTLE AND EAST

COAL EXTRA 5339 WEST CALLED HELPER 1130 AM SINGLE TRAINS 34 CARS

NEXT INTO HELPER 100 PM OR LA TER

COMMING EAST

A TRAIN EXTRA 3051 EAST LEAVE ROPER ANYTIME

782 GENEVA TURN EXTRA 5317 EAST LEAVE GENEVA ABT NOON OR LATER
SALINATURN EXTRA EAST CALEED AT ROPE R 1230 PM
NOTHING ELSE CALEED NOW

ARJ........

People out on line where there was no open office copied their own lineups, as I did at noon or as an updated lineup for my run to Thistle. We used telegraph call letters as shorthand when copying lineups, etc. RA-Helper, KN-Kyune, JF-Soldier Summit, JD-Thistle, NG-Springville, VO-Provo, UN-Roper, etc.

I worked Helper to Thistle one day, returned the next, staying in the RR station/rooming house/beanery at Thistle. Usually, an eight to ten hour day except on Saturday heading back home (Helper) when it was about three hours.

Us peons din't have no radios, and even the ones on engines and cabooses had very limited range. The Complications Dept. was installing repeaters here and there, but it was a long time before radios were considered reliable enough for actual train movements and other vital communications.

View through a motor car windshield with the Book Cliffs receding into the distance, D&RGW, Brendal, Utah, June 18, 1981. *Photograph by R. C. Farewell.*

So "Lineup" was a good time to talk to the gang foremen not at an office. Just before the lineup, get on the DS's wire "Atwood, you there?" "Yeah, Mike." "Talk to me on the message wire after the lineup." "Hokay." You could also ask the DS to give a message to someone, but you never knew when they'd call in, plus we really didn't want to add to the DS's work load.

Section crews ate lunch wherever, and if there wasn't a convenient phone booth, the foreman drove to the closest one for the noon lineup. The reason I tried to be around a gang at noon once or twice a week was that after they got to know me, the guys would occasionally ask "hey, Mike, you wanna try some [great Mexican food]?" Got to the point where maybe every couple'a three weeks a guy would ask "where you gonna be at lunch on Thursday? My wife wants to cook some [whatever] for you." My reply was "I'm gonna be wherever you are on Thursday!" And no, it wasn't kissing ass, several of them could testify that when they did something really stupid, I totally ripped 'em a new one.

The crutch (never heard it called that, but *every* railroad had their own vernacular) is quite commonly used in railroading, and not only by dispatchers. I've got an old Rio Grande timetable showing running times west from Soldier Summit, into TT&TO territory, and down to Thistle for regular freights and "coal" trains that I wrote in on the pages just so I could both accomplish something constructive and to keep from getting run over - worked almost all of the time, too. Section foremen, signal maintainers, etc. all had some similar list to help in planning their work. Watching an old head dispatcher figger running times was awesome: "hmm..., yep..., unh..., they'll meet at Sagers at..." And they did, too. Yes, some guys are just a hell of a lot better engineers/conductors, etc. too. I frequently juggled call times to get the guy I wanted on a snowplow or work train.

Yeah, misread your lineup and you could end up on crutches... The copy of a couple of ETT pages shows a crutch or two. On the bottom of page 4 is a compilation of running times from Soldier Summit to Thistle. A regular "freight train" is one with actual weight per car gross is less than 90 tons per car. A "coal" train is 90 tons or more per car, and is restricted to 50 mph (or lower). A coal train with retainers turned up ("ret") is restricted to 18 mph. Also note on page 5 that I put in times between stations for regular freights.

WESTWARD ▼ ▲ EASTWARD

COND LASS 17 lifornia ephyr eave Daily	Station Number	Mile Post	Subdivision 5 Stations TIME-TABLE No. 8 Oct. 6, 1968	Capacity of Siding	SECOND CLASS 18 California Zephyr Arrive Daily
3 55PM	5000	449.6	2 Ma. Trk. **GRAND JCT**....DNRBKJ	Yard	11 10AM
....	2802	451.7	2.1 DURHAM............	96	....
....	2806	456.9	5.2 RHONE................	103	....
....	2808	460.5	3.6 FRUITA...............W	129	....
....	2812	468.9	8.4 MACK..................	148	....
....	2816	473.1	4.2 RUBY..................	145	....
....	2818	478.0	4.9 SHALE.................	85	....
....	9920	483.3	5.3 UTALINE...............	116	....
....	9922	488.4	5.1 WESTWATER............	98	....
....	9926	498.1	9.7 AGATE.................	150	....
....	9928	504.4	6.3 CISCO...............WY	91	....
....	9930	510.5	CENTRALIZED TRAFFIC CONTROL 6.1 WHITEHOUSE..........	123	....
....	9932	515.6	5.1 ELBA..................	104	....
....	9934	520.7	5.1 SAGERS................	149	....
5 15	9938	528.1	7.4 THOMPSON..........WY	137	s 9 45
....	9940	533.8	5.7 BRENDEL..............J	96	....
....	9942	540.4	6.6 FLOY..................	112	....
....	9944	546.9	6.5 SOLITUDE..............	150	....
5 38	9950	555.2	8.3 GREEN RIVER........WY	133	f 9 18
....	9003	561.5	6.3 SPHINX................	116	....
....	9004	567.6	6.1 DESERT................	115	....
....	9006	574.2	6.6 CLIFF.................	115	....
....	9008	581.4	7.2 WOODSIDE.............	123	....
....	9010	586.6	5.2 GRASSY................	118	....
....	9012	593.1	6.5 CEDAR................W	114	....
....	9014	599.3	6.2 VERDE.................	98	....
....	9016	603.2	3.9 MOUNDS...............J	111	....
....	9021	611.1	7.9 WASH..................	185	....
....	9022	613.0	1.9 WELLINGTON...........	117	....
6 50	9026	619.1	6.1 PRICE...............WY	E120 W 81	s 8 15
....	9028	622.1	3.0 MAXWELL..............	114	....
7 05PM	9032	626.4	4.3 **HELPER**...........DNRBK	Yard	8 03AM
Arrive Daily			(176.8)		Leave Daily

WESTWARD ▼ ▲ EASTWARD 5

SECOND CLASS 17 California Zephyr Leave Daily	Station Number	Mile Post	Subdivision 6 Stations TIME-TABLE No. 8 Oct. 6, 1968	Capacity of Siding	SECOND CLASS 18 California Zephyr Arrive Daily
7 08PM	9032	626.4	CTC 2 MAIN TRACKS **HELPER**.........DNRBK	Yard	8 00AM
....	9038	628.8	2.4 UTAH RY JCT........J	......	....
....	9044	630.4	1.6 CASTLE GATE........	Yard	....
....	9050	638.9	8.5 KYUNE.............W	102	....
....	9054	644.4	5.5 COLTON...........WJ	Yard	....
....	9056	651.4	7.0 SOLDIER SUMMIT.WY	N152 S156	....
8 08	9060	661.0	ABS 2 MAIN TRACKS 9.6 GILLULY..........W	150	....
8 16	9062	665.6	4.6 DETOUR.............	E103	6 48
8 25	9066	672.2	6.6 NARROWS...........	E116	6 39
8 33	9068	676.5	4.3 RIO..................	E108	6 30
8 39	9070	680.9	4.4 THISTLE......DNBJKWY W14.9 E15.9	W145 E123	6 23
8 55	9302	695.8	SPRINGVILLE........J	......	6 06
....	......	698.9	3.1 U.P. CROSSING........	......	....
s 9 05	9310	701.1	2.2 PROVO....RDNBFJKOSWY	Yard	s 6 00
....	......	705.7	CTC 4.6 U.P. CROSSING........	......	....
....	9317	707.2	1.5 GENEVA.............	......	....
....	9319	708.4	1.2 PIPE MILL...........	......	....
....	9321	715.0	6.6 AMERICAN FORK....	175	....
....	9325	720.3	5.3 MESA................	150	....
....	9328	728.6	8.3 RIVERTON...........	130	....
....	9329	733.2	2 MAIN TRACKS 4.6 ENDOT...............	......	....
....	9332	734.9	1.7 MIDVALE.........JWY	Yard E143	....
9 45	......	740.7	5.8 EAST ROPER..........	......	....
....	9350	742.5	ABS 1.8 **ROPER**..........DNRBK	Yard	....
....	......	744.2	1.7 U.P. CROSSING........	......	....
10 00PM	6000	745.1	0.9 **SALT LAKE CITY**...BK	Yard	5 10AM
Arrive Daily			Eastward 119.7 Westward 118.7		Leave Daily

Schedule and train order time for trains at **Provo** apply at passenger station.

Schedule and **train** order time for Westward trains at **East Roper** apply at "End of CTC" sign.

In addition to CTC territory shown in Station column Sub Div 6, trains also operate by CTC, where designated by signs, on Westward Main Track East end **Thistle** and on Eastward Main Track West end **Thistle**.

Two Main Tracks between **Gilluly** and **Springville** and Eastward main **track** between **Springville** and **Provo** signaled for movement with current of traffic only. When operating against the current of traffic within these limits non ABS rules apply.

Two Main Tracks at all other locations are signaled for normal and reverse movements.

Freight trains, yard and other locomotives must make way for passenger trains without unnecessary delay.

Mud Hop

PCDB Form 16 Revised

FOREMAN'S WORK LIST

DELIVER THIS LIST TO YARDMASTER AT END OF EACH TRIP

List all cars switched, including cars moved from one spot to another on same Industry Track, also cars from or to hold or Storage Tracks. When tracks are numbered, use track number instead of name. When car cannot be spotted or picked up, show cause in memo column, using number designated below, and also show in same column on what track cars not spotted were placed.

1. Gate locked
2. Track full.
3. Spot ordered to occupied.
4. Obstruction on track.
5. Oil car connected.
6. No one on hand to direct switching.
7. Ordered placed in preference.
8. Spotted—No more cars wanted.
9. Track in bad order.
10. Switch spiked.
11. Car in bad order.
12. Short of time.
13. Loading not completed.
14. Billing not ready.

SHEET NO.__________ DATE__________, 196__

ENGINE NO.__________ SHIFT COMMENCED__________ A.M. P.M.

NAME OF FOREMAN__________

Initial	Car Number	L Load X Mty.	From Track or Industry	To Track or Industry	Time Set Out or Picked up	Memo.
1						
2						
3						
4						
5						
6						
7						
8						
9						
10						
11						
12						
13						
14						
15						
16						
17						
18						
19						
20						
21						
22						
23						
24						
25						
26						
27						
28						
29						
30						
31						
32						
33						
34						
35						
36						
37						
38						
39						
40						

Yes indeed, in the early 1960s I spent a lot of third-trick hours on the east lead of the GN's Interbay (Seattle) yard and the description of operations is very much the way it was done back then. Especially the rain…

While teletypes were a big step in the right direction, clerical and operator errors still required standing in the rain and recording car numbers as the train pulled in. If a conflict concerning numbers came up during classification, the accepted procedure was to send the long-suffering mud hop sloshing down the tracks in the dark to straighten out the snafu.

At one time I worked for ACI Systems and we won't even think of going there, thank you…

If you're gonna print up switch lists for your model railroad and you're modeling the pre-universal computer days (say 1970s and earlier), print up a whole bunch of 'em. They were the equivalent of today's "post-it" notes and were used by everybody for everything since they were nearly universally available and almost indestructible. Signal maintainers sketching a wiring diagram, a clerk keeping track of the "numbers" he'd bought that day, a water-service foreman drawing new plumbing for a company house, an engineer's note to the track supervisor about a rough spot in the track, groceries to be picked up on the way home, a nearly endless list. Sometimes they were even used to record car numbers on a track out in the yard…

Hardly anybody remembers how labor-intensive everything was back in them days. Hell, the accounting department was several large offices with desks crammed in without hardly enough room to walk between them, and the rattle and crash of a comptometer on each one. Yard offices were a madhouse with clerks trying to decipher train lists and yard checks made in the rain, YM's screaming for the list to make up their switch lists, crew callers, janitors, and a lonely cry from the corner: "Where IS that damn car..."

Form C.S. 803-B

SWITCH LIST-AND-
CONDUCTOR'S REPORT OF CARS DELIVERED

At Station__________ Date__________ 19____ Time__________ M

Train________ Symbol________ Engine No.________ Conductor__________

X Apply Cars	CAR		CLASS	CONTENTS	CONSIGNEE OR DESTINATION	GRO. TONS	TARE	REMARKS (Ice, Bad Order, Etc.)
	INITIAL	NUMBER						
1								
2								
3								
4								
5								
6								
7								
8								
9								
10								
11								
12								
13								
14								
15								
16								
17								
18								
19								
20								
21								
22								
23								
24								
25								
26								
27								
28								
29								
30								
31								
32								
33								
34								
35								
36								
37								
38								
39								
40								

For Binding

Switch lists may have been yesterday's Post-It notes, and universally available, but they were not all the same. Not only did different railroads have different ideas about what they should contain, but the same railroad might have several different formats for different jobs. Here are two that the WP used in the 1960s: one for local and yard work (opposite page) and the other for over-the-road crews to use (right).—Jim Providenza

Scans of WP documents courtesy of Tommy Holt.

Motive Power

First, a disclaimer: I've never ridden any of the newer wide-cab, high-horsepower units, especially the AC's. My cab-riding days were over with the SD40s and T-2 variants. On the other hand, how many guys can say they've hand-fired an NP 0-6-0 working in regular yard service?

Seattle

Equipment in Seattle about 1950 generally operated by the various roads was as follows:

Milwaukee - one 0-6-0 (oil fired), and SW1/NW2 diesel switchers. One wooden cupola caboose, the rest horizontal-ribbed bay window. The local from Tacoma was powered by either a 2-8-0 or a Geep. Electrics were used on passenger trains and mainline freights (which set out/picked up at Van Asselt yard south of Argo).

Great Northern - completely dieselized with a variety of EMD switchers, F-units on passenger and freight trains, plus a handful of Alco FA's. Both wood and steel cupola cabooses, plus some converted cupola-less wood hacks for transfer work.

GN 456 leading a freight west of Spokane on the climb out of the Spokane River Valley to the Central Washington plateau. *Photograph by Philip R. Hastings, Philip Ross Hastings, MD, collection, California State Railroad Museum*

Northern Pacific - mostly steam, 4-6-0's on branch line locals, 2-8-2's on the main line, 4-6-2's and 4-8-4's on local and main line passenger runs, with F-units on the through passengers to the east such as the North Coast Limited and also on through time freights. Geeps were starting to appear in numbers as were various models of EMD/Alco/Baldwin switchers, and 0-6-0's were ubiquitous. Most steam was coal-fired, but some oil. There was a gas-electric for the Grays Harbor local, but when inoperable (frequently), a 4-6-2 substituted. Cabooses were mostly wood cupola type with steel on the mainline. Also a few wood bay window jobs converted from boxcars.

Pacific Coast - 100% steam, one 0-6-0 and several 2-8-0's. Wooden everything: gons, boxes, flats, pulpwood racks, cabooses.

Union Pacific - a couple of 0-6-0's, several diesel switchers, and mostly F-units on freights and passengers. There was one 4-6-6-4 on the night pool train and occasionally a 2-8-0 on a local. A 4-8-2 might show up on a through freight. Both steel and wood cupola cabs.

Five years later the MILW and UP were dieselized, and steam on the NP was fading fast. The PC had been purchased by the GN and dieselized, plus the wood coal cars replaced by steel GS gons and a wooden GN caboose substituted for the ancient wood PC hack.

Rio Grande, 1960s–70s

I do know that the D&RG had a two-point motive power program: maintain the units and put a bunch of 'em on middling-size trains. For the hot trains, enough units to go up the hill at track speed without helpers, which also allowed 70 mph running across the desert and other locations curvature permitting.

Secondary trains got enough power to go up at 20 mph or more to avoid harmonic rocking, and only coal, grain, and trains on Tennessee Pass got helpers. Note that all merchandise trains were generally limited to 4000 tons and we really didn't worry about a unit crapping out. Mostly four-axle power and the biggest question was how much you could shave the minimum running time of 3'10" on the 176 miles from Grand Junction to Helper without the Trainmaster tearing you a new one. Unh huh, we consistently won the Harriman Gold while running a hell of a railroad, a run that came to an end with the SP merger.

"Enough power to go up the hill... which also allowed 70 mph running across the desert..."
D&RGW 5315 at Westwater, Utah, March 21, 1979. *Photograph by Chuck Conway.*

The Rock Island

But where to go to see every size, shape, color, and mechanical condition of locomotives from every damn one of the builders? How 'bout the Rock Island in the '60s, particularly in the Chicago area? You name it, it was out there on the tracks somewhere. Power from EMD, Alco, FM, Baldwin, GE, Davenport, and God knows what else. C415's, BL2's, E's, F's, a couple of Aerotrains, SW's from -1 to ?, seems like they had 'em all.

When I worked in Chicago, our outfit was located between the roundhouse and the suburban line at Blue Island and I watched that wonderful parade of "dummies" from that vantage point and also the Englewood and Polk St. towers.

The units ranged from clean - damn rare - to well camouflaged with native dirt plus spilled liquid highlights. Colors could be any combination and shade of maroon, stainless, yellow, red, and usually with - if any - white striping. But by far my favorite paint scheme was the original red-black-white striped "wings" design.

Anyway, where else could you see BL2's, DL107 and 109's, FM H15-44's, run-of-the-mill E's and F's, and the occasional Aerotrain hauling commuters on two routes to and from all the suburban towns between the LaSalle St Station and Blue Island and Joliet. My, my, my. A rolling museum for sure. Oh, and did I mention that most of the older units were in near-terminal (no, not railroad station) condition? The one oddity I didn't see on the dummies was the pair of AB6 "E-unit-with a cab" that later became frequent power as they were still in use on the Rocky Mountain Rockets I occasionally rode to Denver. Damn right I worked for the Rock Island!

Uhh, what was the question?

On March 14, 1971, Rock Island 421 is pulling a transfer drag of pig flats past 16th Street Tower. It is about to cross the tracks of the Illinois Central and the St. Charles Air Line. The Alco C415 is "well camouflaged with native dirt plus spilled liquid highlights"; its signature "honorary steam engine" black exhaust barely visible against the hazy Chicago skyline. *Photograph by Kevin Idarius, Lloyd Transportation Library.*

Bruce Meyer shot Rock Island's Jet Rocket—now in "dummy" commute service—at Blue Island, Illinois, in 1958. The motive power is one of only three EMD model TLW12 1,200-horsepower passenger engines ever built. The Jet Rocket's articulated Talgo II cars were built by American Car & Foundry. The other two TLW12 locos, and their trainsets built from widened GM bus bodies, were marketed by GM as Aerotrain—an inexpensive modern replacement for existing passenger trains. Shunned by other major railroads due to their rough ride, the two Aerotrains also eventually ended up in Rock Island dummy service. *Bruce Meyer Collection, photo 2018.008.RI.P.047, Lake States Railroad Historical Association at Baraboo, WI.*

The Southern

Several years ago, when I was working for Cyprus we were exporting a lot of raw clay product through the Port of Savannah, Georgia. I went down several times to make sure everything was under control (yeah, right, and the great people and superb food didn't have anything to do with it), and usually stayed in a hotel right downtown above River Street. River Street ran down right on the bank of the river (no kidding), with the "downtown" streets a way above.

View from the side of the road, the River Street Rambler. *Photograph by Steve Smith, NCRails.net.*

The Southern Railway had an industrial lead down the middle of the street that ran to the Port, all in a very touristy setting. To hopefully increase safety, at the same time preserving the ambiance, they painted an SW switcher with a rather colorful scheme proclaiming that it was the "River Street Rambler." To complete the presentation, they mounted loudspeakers on the cab roof and as the engine descended with the street to river level, "Muskrat Ramble" was played for the entertainment of the multitudes.

Rambling down River Street—up close and personal. *Illustration by Kimberly Hoverter Morris.*

Maintenance of Way

Routine

When I was a track supervisor, my work trains frequently picked up/set out cars. A local or drag would set out maybe some cars of OTM (other track material), ballast, rail, ties, or whatever at locations close to where the work was going to be performed. The work train would run to that location, pick up the cars, and then peddle the material as required. The empties might be taken back to the yard or left to be picked up by another train.

Whenever possible, we'd use a local or an industry switcher in this service when the work could be done without seriously impacting revenue traffic. Remember going into the Helper yard office and saying to the conductor of the Scofield, "Hey, Ernie, gotta little bit of work for you today." To which he'd reply, "Oh crap! How many cars of what from where why?" Yep, turned his normal 8-10 hour day into 15:59 just like that. 'Course, later in the week I just might buy a few beers for the crew...

Work train, Soldier Summit, Maintenance of Way section crew sitting on flat car and in the cab of the crane, 1966. *Photograph by Stan Rhine, 2017.055.6933, Colorado Railroad Museum collection.*

We all kinda thought we knew what we were trying to get done, and we'd probably know what (if not exactly how) to do next as soon as the word filtered down from the office. The big problem 50–60 years ago was that everything was made outa cast iron and concrete and there just weren't any gang-sized power tools other than hammers and shovels. Ballast hand tamped, rail moved into position by eight or ten guys equipped with rail tongs, etc. And wheel stops made from scrap, heated and beaten into shape as determined by "I think this's the way we did it last time." Or, as I've said ever since those days, "don't force it, get a bigger hammer."

"No gang-sized power tools..." Denver & Rio Grande section crew at work, September 1963. *Photograph by Philip R. Hastings, Philip Ross Hastings, MD, collection, California State Railroad Museum.*

The signal department was no different. Solid concrete cast-in-place foundations, cast iron relay cases, masts, and signal heads. Track wires and signal cables all buried by hand, and winter work was mostly survival, not improvement. Didn't have no trucks with winches and booms, everybody grab ahold and heave. Know how we moved one'a them cast concrete foundations? Dug all around it, tilted it to one side and threw in dirt, tilted it the other way and threw in more dirt...Then slid it up on the push car on a pair of crossarms.

Yep, hell of a lot easier to open a catalog and buy the assembly needed, but there *was* a certain satisfaction in heating up some metal and whanging the hell out of it—when you're young and foolish.

Switches

When I was a track supervisor, my job was to prevent derailments, not facilitate them. First, the weakest part of the entire track structure is the switch. Don't know the exact figures, but do know I had to budget one hell of a lot of money for switch maintenance. Initial cost and maintenance costs go up geometrically with increases in the frog number and switch-point length. There's a huge increase in switch timber board feet, specialized track material, ballast, and they soak up maintenance man-hours like a sponge.

I've never seen anything larger than a #24 frog in a standard switch, but if anybody did it, it was the PRR. However, the tangential point switch has a #30 or larger. They also have two switch machines to throw the points and one to throw the swing-nose frog. HUGE suckers! Yep, a lot of side-thrust on high-speed switches from passenger trains; think what an 18,000-ton coal train does. Remember watching a BN coal train go through the interlocking at Baird Tower (Lincoln, Nebraska) and afterward there was a nice trail of "filings" ground off the rail on the curved portions.

Anyway, I can't imagine siding after siding with equilateral switches at each end. Why in hell would you set yourself up for all manner of increased costs when the vast majority of movements blow through on the straight side?

Worked in union and management positions for seven different railroads, plus on and near railroads in the supply industry and as a consultant, and the only time I heard "turnout" was when I was in the engineering department at company headquarters, and not very often at that. As track supervisor I even had a small book to record my quarterly switch inspection information, officially issued, titled "Switch Inspection Report." It not only covered points and rods, but closure rails, insulated joints, guard rails, heel blocks, frogs, wing rails, frog heel and toe joints, ties, ballast, surface, and probably other things I've forgotten.

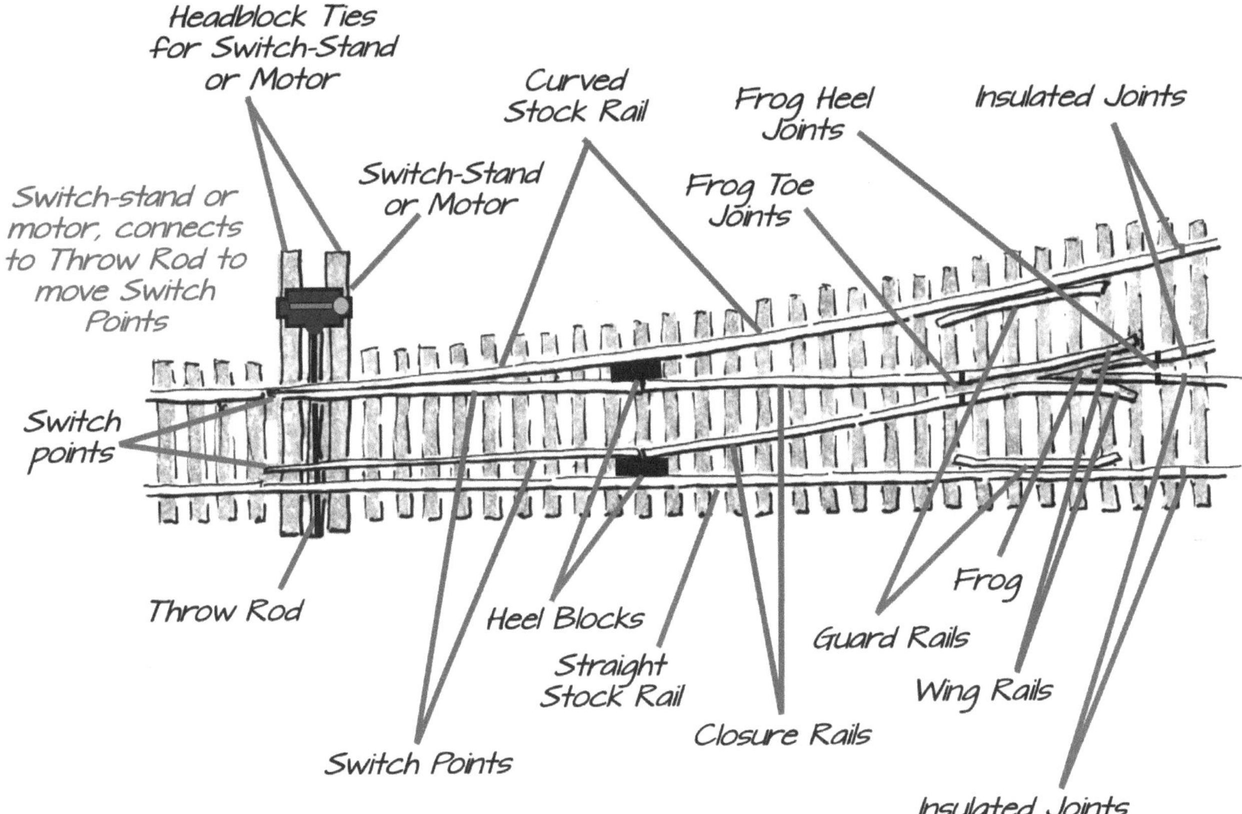

A switch, calling out components to be inspected quarterly. *Drawing by David R. Clemens.*

Defects

First, it was extremely rare to discover a critical flaw. Most defects were slow growing, a soft spot gradually getting worse, etc. On the mainline, broken rails were usually caught by the signal maintainer when he was called out for a red block. Lots'a broken bolts, but again, hardly critical. Did have a chronic problem just west of Gilluly where the tracks were on a sidehill and one curve kept slipping down. If it was questionable when I got there, I'd put a 10 mph slow order on it and get the section gang down to repair it. Finally got fed up with not getting it fixed right, so I had the Foreman check it every night on his way in and if work was required, fix it on overtime. Kept good records of costs and finally proved it was far better to fix it once and for all, rather than shovel all that money over the hill side.

Wide gauge on curves was a gradual development, poor tie condition, etc. The most common problems requiring immediate attention were wash outs/ins, broken angle bars, a piece of the ball of the rail broken out, fires, and so on.

There were always a few hogheads that would report "bad track" or something and we took it seriously before it was serious. Had a reported problem on the eastward track just west of Thistle. I couldn't find it, the foreman couldn't find it, and ol' Jasper Barr an engineer on the Zephyr was getting pissed 'cause we didn't fix it. I rode with him and when he said "right here!" I felt it, but again couldn't find it. Now I was pissed so I put my best section foreman on the engine and he pinpointed it. Hardly critical yet, but if the engineer reported something we had to check it out or they'd kiss it off and never tell us a thing.

Some things I could fix, some things required a section gang, and once in a great while, something serious enough would crop up and a slow order or taking the track out of service was required.

Track Inspection... on a motor car

Track inspection, November 23, 1960, in Ruby Canyon with D&RGW motor car A1296J.
Photograph by Jim Ozment, Western Rail Images.

Usually, an eight to ten hour day except on Saturday heading back home (Helper) when it was about three hours. God said we had to cover our track six days a week, but he didn't say how efficiently. If you're talking about velocity, I think the rules said 20 mph max, and you really couldn't do a good job of inspecting going any faster.

On a motor car your vision is far more concentrated—one track, and basically that's it, but you still can't see the details at speed. That's why the "Saturday AM trip home" was less than efficient. One time did clock my last motor car at 55 mph on the long tangent at Castilla west of Thistle—with a tail wind.

Now I've never been on a trestle as high as the Lawyers Canyon on the Camas Prairie, but been on some damn lofty ones. Yep, it feels just like rolling along on the flat. Hmmm... picture a motor car on the trestle—not much room between it and the end of the ties, right? Now think about doing a tad bit of track inspection and you spot a missing angle bar bolt out there in the middle of the trestle. Stop the motor car, get off on the side on that woefully inadequate bit of bridge timbers, walk back to the joint, install the new bolt/lock washer/nut and really yank on the track wrench to cinch it up tight. Don't think about the wrench slipping and the total lack of railings. Back alongside the motor car and on to the next problem.

Then there's the really fun task of rail renewal out there. Just rolling along...

Reminds me of a situation many years ago up in Soggy Sound country. From Norn Pacific Tacoma Division Special Instructions No. 1, 6/1/67:

NORTHERN PACIFIC RAILWAY COMPANY

TACOMA DIVISION

Special Instructions No. 1

In Effect at 12:01 A. M.
Pacific Standard Time

Thursday, June 1, 1967

These Instructions constitute a part of the Time Table currently in effect.

Employes whose duties are in any way affected by the Time Table must have a copy of The Current Special Instructions and Current Time Table with them on duty.

J. G. DAVIES, Superintendent.

W. E. BUCKLEY, Terminal Superintendent, Seattle.

N. M. LORENTZSEN, General Manager.

E. B. ULYATT, General Superintendent of Transportation.

FOURTH SUBDIVISION

MAIN (PRAIRIE) LINE

1. **Speed Restrictions:**

Zone—Between Double and single tracks:	Maximum Speeds Permitted Freight	 Passenger
15th St. and Tenino Jct.	30 MPH	45 MPH
With helper engines	25 MPH	25 MPH

8. The Army has gun emplacements in the area east of Northern Pacific Prairie Line between Roy and Hillhurst, the firing to be over our main track.

When firing is in progress, army guards will be stationed at the following locations:

950 feet east of MP 15
MP 17
3000 feet east of MP 17
4300 feet east of MP 19

and, on the approach of train or track car, they will immediately arrange for firing to cease and allow train and/or track car to pass through normally.

Guards will not stop trains unless an emergency exists.

Northern Pacific Tacoma Division Special Instructions No. 1, June 1, 1967. *PNRArchives collection at Burien, WA.*

Does this mean motor cars are fair game??? Had a lot of interesting experiences on my motor cars, but never been shot at with 155-mm howitzers.

And off to wreck we go...

When railroads had major wrecks, traffic could be held, detoured, or run back and around, all of which at high cost. If the closure's only gonna be a day up to two days, probably hold everything until the (a) main is back in service or (b) a shoo-fly is built. Detouring is extremely expensive, but depending on the type of traffic involved is sometimes the only alternative, same for circuitous re-routings via home-road trackage. Yep, it's always a lose-lose situation. Remember a derailment on the Grande, we worked 36 hours straight until we got one main open, then "only" 14-18 hour days until the second was serviceable.

Then there was the time we had a huge derailment on Soldier Summit that took over a month to clean up. Had gandies that were *clearing* more per half than I *grossed* for the month, all for the prestige of being a boss... And don't think they didn't let me know it!

For the longest time whenever derailment was mentioned at home, my dad would have to leave the house while uttering a few choice words that got a "Mike!" from my mom. I always thought derailment was the worst swear word anyone could say.

—Christine Trigg

Great Northern Railroad in Washington. *Map by David R. Clemens.*

Way back when before I left Seattle, the GN really got itself caught in the ol' wringer. There were two derailments, somewhere on Stevens Pass and also around Wenatchee, and both the Interbay and Spokane hooks were called out. Then an eastbound freight went into the hole for a meet somewhere, I believe, on the climb up out of the Columbia River valley. Either not enough power or a unit failure and they had to double out of the siding to the top of the grade. There was pretty heavy fog off the river, and when the power returned for the second half of the train, they ran right smack into the cut, spreading it out all to hell over the mainline. Do believe the Division Superintendent was highly pissed as he sent a lot of trains "around the horn" via the SP&S and the joint line up from Portland. Unh hunh, and with the Spokane wrecker west of the mess, couldn't team it up with the Interbay hook to attack the pile-up from both ends.

Sometimes You've Stood There…

Regarding the GN derailments on Stevens Pass. Mike's text doesn't specify where the two wrecks "on the Hill" were located calling out both the Interbay and Spokane Hooks. As I recall the discussion… back when, the two pile-ups which started it all were on opposite sides of Cascade Tunnel. OK, makes sense, Interbay Hook chews into the mess above Skykomish and the Spokane Hook called out to deal with a mess someplace on Nason Creek just east of Cascade Tunnel.

Then Wenatchee yard released an eastbound either with insufficient power (possible) or a unit failure (Mike's speculation) and it tries to climb up to Quincy around Trinidad Loops. She stalls, pulls the front half forward to Quincy at the top of the climb, and as the power rolled back through a tunnel and curves into the fog, it clobbered the back half of the train dumping equipment all over the steep side slopes.

I've stood above the Trinidad Loop watching trains struggle out of the river bottom, up one side of the canyon, through a tight turn back curve, then up the opposite side of the canyon only to disappear into a tunnel as they twist out at the top. I can imagine the crew returning for the back half of the train entering the tunnel in sunshine only to be confronted by fog at the opposite end, and WHAM.

At that point the Interbay Hook is out of the game west of the mess. The Spokane Hook is sandwiched between two wrecks finishing its work up Nason Creek, and the third pile-up has everything west of Spokane clobbered. Thus, management must have "punted" and started sending Seattle traffic via the SP&S around the Columbia River Gorge to Portland.

—Dave Clemens

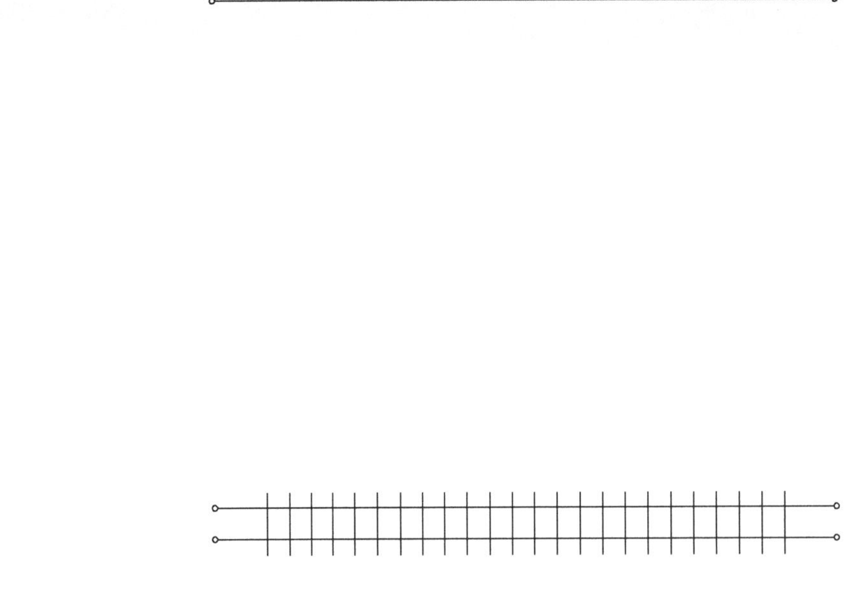

Industrial Traffic Management

PROLOGUE

I think a little "prologue" might be called for before talking about traffic management and traffic managers in the rail environment "back in them days." My experience covered three more-or-less distinct time periods, two of which have a very sharp, well-defined separation. The first two eras are very simply characterized as pre-Staggers and post-Staggers and the transformation from the former to the latter was abrupt, traumatic, and nearly overnight. A large number of traffic managers viewed the pending Staggers legislation with fear and loathing and never adequately made the transition from old to new. They were joined by an equal number of their railroad traffic brethren who also were unable to cope with the new dawn. The third era came about much more slowly and can best be described as the advent of computerized traffic management systems. Indeed, even the term "Traffic Manager" has fallen by the wayside as new terminology and titles have come into common usage: "supply chain management," "third-party services," and "warehouse management systems" became the new rallying cries. I experienced the Staggers upheaval first hand and thoroughly enjoyed the challenges and nearly endless opportunities that arose seemingly daily.

Pre-Staggers can best be characterized as "bureaucracy run amok" as the ICC attempted to protect shippers from their own follies and to shield motor and water carriers from the depredations of a railroad industry that had long since lost any semblance of monopolistic power. Literally thousands of tariff pages of freight rates spewed forth annually as both shippers and carriers sought advantage or protection. Some companies judged their traffic departments by the volume of such production. A little known fact is that tariffs were rarely canceled outright, instead they were merely superseded, and generations of rate clerks spent their working lives searching for the one little misprint that would lower their rates or result in a refund (yep, me too, and I was occasionally successful). Rates were generally "class" rates, and again traffic managers argued interminably before rate committees attempting to gets their shipments a lower classification. The rates themselves applied to all carriers between two rate basis points, penalizing the efficient and protecting the inept. An industry could request a commodity rate based on somewhat unique circumstances, but any other carrier had the option of becoming a party to the rate and any other shipper could demand a similar rate for only slightly similar circumstances. Volume rates were prohibited; in fact, the railroads could only rarely price lower than motor or water carriers as that would be anti-competitive or some such nonsense.

The railroad industry at this time was characterized by a very large number of relatively small carriers by today's standards; routing cars via many junctions was possible with identical rates. Service was just an entry in the dictionary. Thus, railroad traffic salesmen were merely snake-oil hustlers who tried to win carloads by buying shippers dinner, taking them to golf outings, and plying them with liquor in such quantities that cirrhosis was a real occupational hazard. Many industrial traffic managers tended to split their business between multiple carriers as there were no differences in cost and it broadened the base of carriers vying to be allowed to entertain those that controlled the traffic. Of course, this gave the carriers exactly zero incentive to improve service or provide good equipment. When I finally got to the point where I controlled enough traffic to be noticeable, my approach was to give it all to one carrier who was then told "it's yours to lose." And lose it they did if service went to hell. When I worked at Coors I couldn't do much to change the outbound beer routes, but inbound raw materials and supplies were a significant revenue provider for the railroads. One time when the C&S's service really became abysmal, I short-hauled the hell out of 'em until their president went to my boss complaining. My fearless leader thought I was being "a little harsh," but allowed that maybe it might work and so informed the C&S. Service was corrected practically overnight, but they didn't get the traffic back until I was told, for about the third time, "or else!"

And so it went. Mostly everybody was happy because they got to do fun things (except the clerks) and the boat was never rocked too violently. Then on October 14, 1980, the Staggers Rail Act became law. The agonized howls reverberated across the land and forecasts of dire consequences filled the pages of the trade journals. Me? Happiest day of my professional life! After letting my rail carriers get used to the idea, I called them and said "the President signed that sucker yesterday, we need to sit down and start discussing contracts." And discuss it they did, or they lost all that highly-rated refrigerated food and canned goods traffic. A lot of really idiotic (read inefficient!) practices disappeared almost overnight. One such was the "mileage allowance" paid by the railroads to the owners/leasers of private cars. This system encouraged these shippers to route via longer mileage routes to earn more money. These routes were often poor service routes. Railroads had to track private car mileage to calculate the allowance. Shippers had to track mileage to keep the railroads honest, and the railroads had to double check mileage to keep the shippers honest. Probably the dumbest of all, the shippers' rates were set high enough to cover the refunds that were paid back to them months later. Yeah, the bean counters made all sorts of black predictions because there wouldn't be any "payments" to cover the equipment leases. Of course, all this paperwork gave gainful employment to another army of clerks on both sides!

On the other hand, a lot of the old "us genius traffic managers vs. the unwashed management" also disappeared and with it much of the solidarity of the downtrodden in the face of uncaring corporate hierarchy. At the same time a lot of the old guard traffic managers soon retired as clerks and paperwork were turned over to computers. We used to call our counterparts at bitter corporate rivals (e.g., Coors and Budweiser) and ask "how'd you handle..." and receive honest replies of "it may sound silly but we... and it worked!" To round out the scenario, under Staggers railroads were no longer allowed anti-trust exemption and weak railroads were merged, abandoned or sold off to become short lines.

Rates were typically published in "cents per hundred pounds (cwt). There were two generally used forms in the tariff: rates that were based on a carload minimum with further reductions in the rate per cwt. as the minimum weight increased. The second form was a "two part" rate that had a relatively high rate for the carload minimum, with a significantly lower rate for the balance of the shipment over the minimum. The former rates might read "90 cents/cwt, minimum 60000 lbs; 80 cents/cwt, minimum 75000 lbs; and 65 cents/cwt, minimum 95000 lbs." Note that the shipper could ship say 80000 lbs "as" 95000 lbs and the total rate would still be less than if he shipped 80000 lbs at the 80 cents/cwt, 75000 lb rate. The two-part rate clearly lowered costs per 100 lbs significantly as more and more weight was loaded in the car. When I was shipping frozen product from Stockton east, I always moved it Western Pacific as they could provide 140000 lb capacity cars, whereas the ATSF rarely had anything better than 100000 lb capacity. The tariffs also provided for a very wide range of accessorial charges such as diversion, inspection, partial unload, etc.

A very popular group of rates were referred to as "transit" rates. Simplified they allowed product to be milled, processed, fabricated, stored, assembled, etc. "in transit" at intermediate points and then shipped on to the consignee at the through rate rather than as two separate shipments at a higher overall cost.

Rail transportation was made unnecessarily complex for customers and railroads alike, requiring huge staffs. There were long and short-haul routes and rates, government rates, import-export rates, Shippers Order Bills of Lading, and so on ad infinitum. I have a publication that lists 50 "Rules of Railroad Freight Classification" that's guaranteed to perplex the most dedicated transportation professional.

I'm firmly convinced that the railroads would eventually have been nationalized and/or largely abandoned if not given the ability to compete in the market place. We started with the heretofore prohibited contracts, went on to all manner of rates that had service guarantees, car supply guarantees, and the multitude of other items that had been on both the carriers and shippers wish lists. Staggers rail deregulation was followed by motor carrier and steamship deregulation plus liberalization of the regulatory climate. The only regret I have about the passing of the ICC is that they were an incredible treasure trove of historical information on every tiny aspect of rail operation.

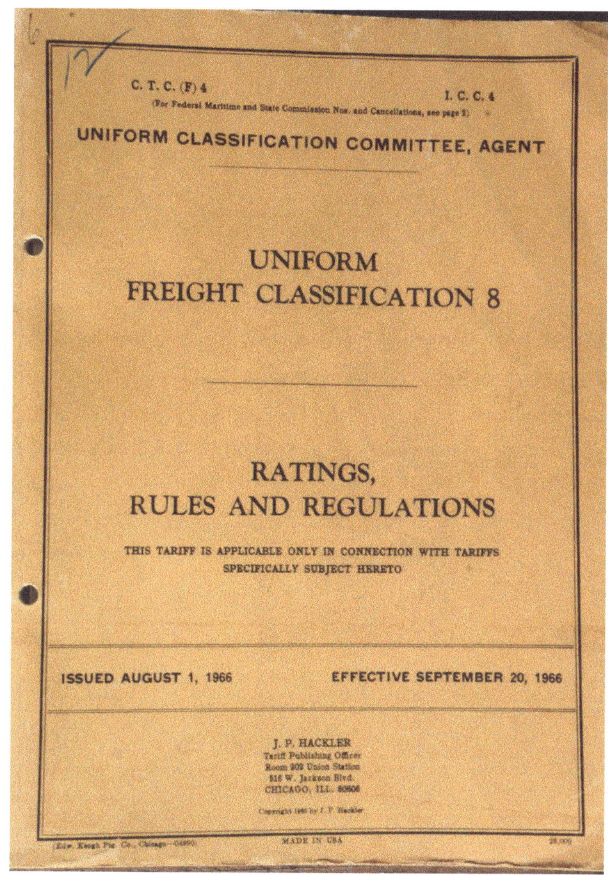
C. T. C. (F) 4 I. C. C. 4

(For Federal Maritime and State Commission Nos. and Cancellations, see page 2)

UNIFORM CLASSIFICATION COMMITTEE, AGENT

UNIFORM
FREIGHT CLASSIFICATION 8

RATINGS,
RULES AND REGULATIONS

THIS TARIFF IS APPLICABLE ONLY IN CONNECTION WITH TARIFFS SPECIFICALLY SUBJECT HERETO

ISSUED AUGUST 1, 1966 EFFECTIVE SEPTEMBER 20, 1966

J. P. HACKLER
Tariff Publishing Officer
Room 202 Union Station
516 W. Jackson Blvd.
CHICAGO, ILL. 60606

Copyright 1966 by J. P. Hackler

MADE IN USA

Uniform Freight Classification 8. *Anthony W. Thompson collection.*

Calculating a freight charge: Even a simple "carload minimum" rate required several steps to figure pre-Staggers. Say a shipper wants to send lampshades from Baltimore, Maryland, to Chicago, Illinois. To compute the freight charge the agent first consults the 900+ page Uniform Freight Classification book. Looking under "lamp shades," he finds the commodity number, 55790. Then in the back of the same book he finds that the carload rating for this cargo is 85. This is one of the essential numbers in the rate.

Next, he turns to another book, the National Rate Basis Tariff. The agent looks under the destination state for this cargo, Illinois, where he finds the "rate base," which in this case is 767. Consulting the appropriate table in the rate book, he finds number 767 in the horizontal column and reads over to number 85 in the vertical column, and this shows, at the intersection of these two, the basic rate, $3.57. This is the rate in cents per hundred pounds (cwt) or "hundredweight."

The cargo of lampshades weighs 10,500 pounds; 105 hundredweights. Multiplying that by $3.57, gives the total shipping cost, $374.85.

—Tony Thompson

Of course, you still have to battle the people that are supposed to be on your side. When I negotiated ocean contracts, I had to pass them to the legal department for review. We had a female attorney who decided that her mission in life was to "improve" such documents with all kinds of format and procedural gobble-de-gook, usually increasing the paperwork from three pages to 30 in the process. The standard contract form was handed down by the Federal Maritime Commission and no damn changes allowed. About the third time I had one of them returned to me, I went to the VP-Legal and recited my tale of woe, which caused him no end of merriment. His solution? "Give 'em to my secretary and she'll sign my name and whatever you do don't tell Felicia (or whatever her name was)."

I left transportation as all the acronyms came into being: 3PL (third-party logistics), WMS (warehouse management systems), ERP (enterprise resource planning [???]), etc., and the titles changed from Traffic to Transportation Manager to Director of Logistics, Supply Chain Manager and so on, each more grandiose than the last. I've sort of kept up with the morphology through continued reading of various trade magazines and web sites, but dialing someone in India (who *speaks* English, but doesn't *understand* English) to solve a problem just isn't the same as calling "uncle" Walt down at the Rio Grande and hashing out the various intricacies that produce a win-win solution, naturally over a cold one or three.

So, there you have it: my brief overview of "that's the way we always used to do it"; industrial traffic management as practiced long ago and far away…

Traffic Manager Responsibilities

So, you are a traffic manager at a large rail served industry. What is your day like?

Yard check. Yeah, that's where you start… you actually have to SEE what is where if you want it to be right. Back to your desk, match waybills to the spots you wrote down on a switch list; identify off-spot cars.

Determine cars to be pulled, spotted, respotted.

Obtain advance train list from railroad showing inbound traffic for today. Work up switch list for the RR crew showing all pulls, spots, respots, and any other special handling. A knowledgeable manager will work the list as far as possible to minimize excessive switching by the train crew (generic empties, sequential cuts, etc.).

Meet conductor, compare lists, finalize any last-minute changes.

Make up outbound train list as train departs and transmit to the railroad's freight agent (unofficial, but prepares everybody for the inevitable screw-up).

If time permits (you gotta whole hell of a lot of other stuff to do), start the yard check for tomorrow's activity.

"Working the switch list" is something I did at Coors to get extra work out of the C&S train crew while simultaneously reducing their work load, all within both the union and tariff rules. Not to mention occasionally buying a beer or two after work at the Goose Town Tavern.

Traffic Management–Coors

Coors employee Ronald Peck caught one of the plant's SW8's shoving empty RBL's across Clear Creek and down to the transfer tables in the packaging building. Inbound barley and rice were stored in the elevator building on the left. *Photograph by Ronald Peck, 2017.039.35661, Colorado Railroad Museum collection.*

First, remember that Coors was NOT a typical industry alongside a typical stretch of track. We had (if I remember right) at that time approximately 800+ RBL cars assigned to us for outbound loading, plus inbound there was a whole hell of a bunch of cars of barley, rice, new bottles, cars of aluminum for the can plant (the largest in the US at that time), coal for the power plant, not to mention cars of minerals for the porcelain division, LPG tank cars as standby gas supply in the winter when we were subject to natural gas shut-off when the temperature dropped below X degrees, and miscellaneous car loads of all kinds of crap that went to central receiving. All in all, close to a couple of hundred cars per day.

How many industries other than steel mills, auto plants, etc., ran two to five switchers around the clock?

May 29, 1982: With polished brass bells, four of the cleanest units in railroading rest between shifts at Coors massive brewery in Golden, Colorado. All are SW8s.—Mike Chandler.
Photograph by Mike Chandler.

Coors had a constant inbound stream of empties arriving every day. Some of these had a load of pallets (before we went to slip sheets). Should explain here that each car had 60 pallets as assigned equipment, but the tariffs allowed consolidating 300 pallets in one car for return. There were also cars of returning bottles and/or kegs. We had a 7-track yard where the C&S spotted inbound traffic and pulled outbound loads. As all cars were assigned, there was absolutely no requirement for cars to be assigned to particular traffic routes. We just loaded 'em out as they came in. In those days, (don't know what they do today), when things slowed down in the winter, we allowed the RR's to load reasonably controlled back hauls of "clean" products (such as wine from Modesto), to improve car utilization. But we were never short of empties, and it was the railroad's responsibility to shovel in empties in order of arrival (i.e., our demurrage started when they delivered).

Outbound routes were by delivering carrier, primarily, with the Rio Grande participating in northern California traffic to the WP and SP, plus local to Grand Jct. and Helper. Once in a while I'd have to short-haul a railroad to get their attention on service matters, mostly on inbound stuff, but usually outbound was on auto pilot.

When I started, empties came in on specified tracks, cars with returns (kegs, bottles) on another track, grain and so on, inbound materials, and on and on. The C&S delivered twice a day, and you couldn't specify "this car, then these three cars, then these two cars" to track two. Sure, you could ask for several cars to be delivered to ONE track, but that's it. What I did get - along with my copy of the inbound "Beer Train" list - was the morning C&S yard check. My, my, frequently cars were kind'a grouped by my internal destinations. "Hey, Tony, if you guys pull your tracks as follows (one pull per track), and then when the first beer run arrives and you group these cars and those cars, you can go home, as far as I'm concerned."

The guys I worked with at Coors just couldn't figger out how I got it done. Then I started blocking outbound traffic, and then arranged setouts at the Rio Grande's North Yard. Oh my, a humongous amount of wailing, but in the end, it worked for everybody. Also, because of my background, I knew who to call - when it was really important. "Supt. KC Division, I goddam well NEED this car, it's 16th ahead of the cab on train XXX, due in at XXX and I don't see why you can't get it onto train XXX." Typical response: "If that's the way it's blocked, it's done," because I spoke the language.

If you don't have assigned cars, you have to ask for the type of car and then specify the routing so that car service rules can be followed. You just have to know what's shipping and when so the cars can be ordered for timely shipping. It's also important to trace your traffic every day - even with a big fleet like Coors, you got so that you could spot something going astray.

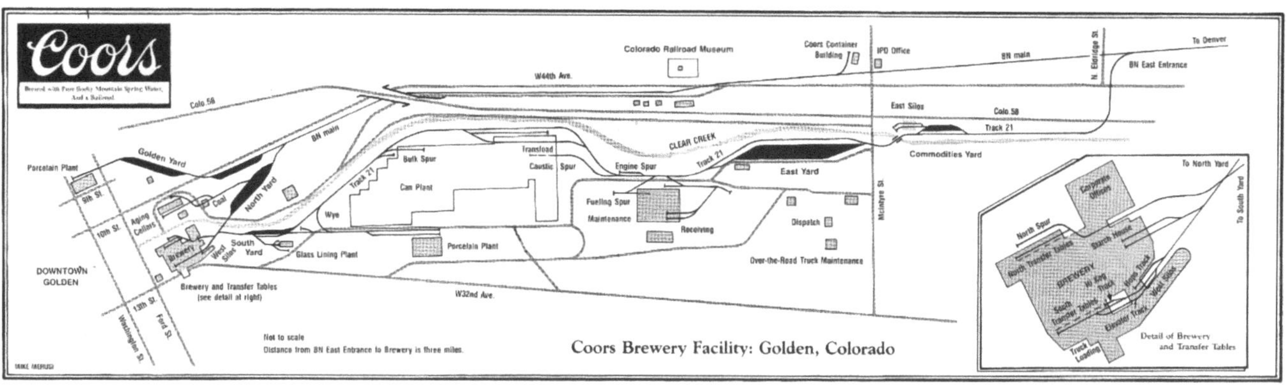

The layout of the Coors warehouse facility, Golden, Colorado, in 1985. *Mike Merusi, ©2020 Railfan & Railroad Magazine/White River Productions, used with permission.*

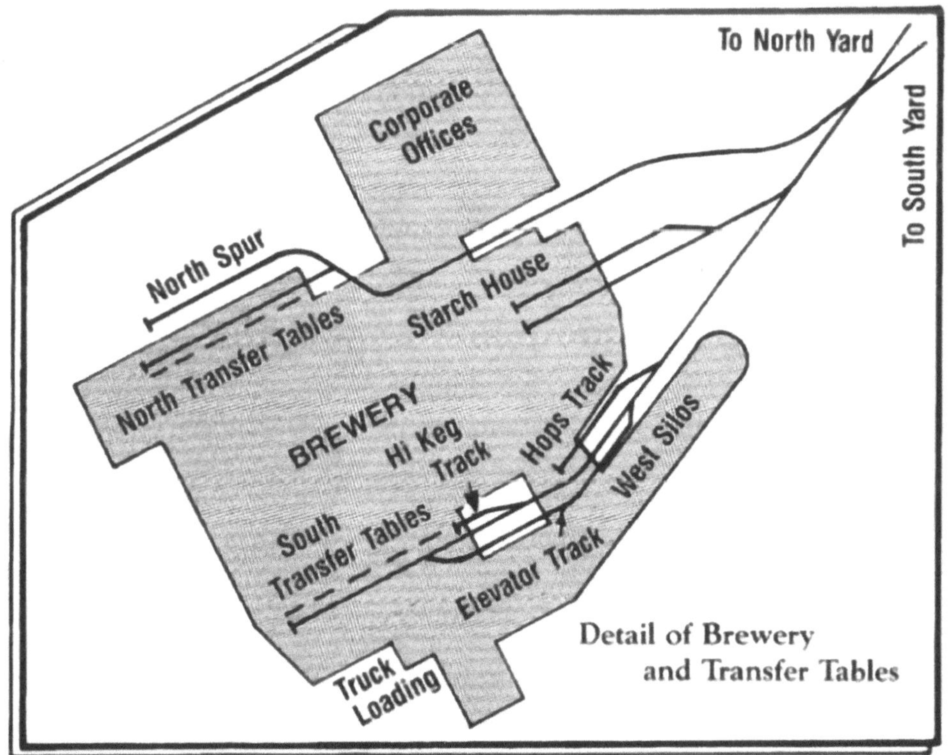

Coors Brewing Co. in the early 70s had (still has) a unique system for loading box cars with beer. A railroad track served 7 loading doors on one side of the warehouse and 6 doors on the other. A set of two transfer tables served each door so that individual cars could be spotted and pulled as required.

The "inside" table would hold a 60-foot RBL car next to the loading door, and upon completion of loading, the table would be run out from the door to push out the "outside" table that was aligned with the switching lead and align itself with the lead, allowing the load to be pulled by a switch crew. An empty was then spotted on the "inside" table, which was returned to the door, pulling the "outside" table back into alignment with the lead.

The catch is that not all cars were loaded at the same rate. Most product was loaded directly off the production lines, but some product was only run say one or two shifts per day (quarts, 8 oz, etc.) while kegs came from a different part of the brewery. A "mixed" car might be loaded in 3 hours, while a "straight" car of 12 oz cans would take less than an hour (7200 cases per car— at a six-pack per day, it'd take you almost 79 years to drink it all!) Thus, the crews had to very carefully plan their spotting sequence so that they didn't have to run to the yard to get rid of their loads before all their empties had been spotted.

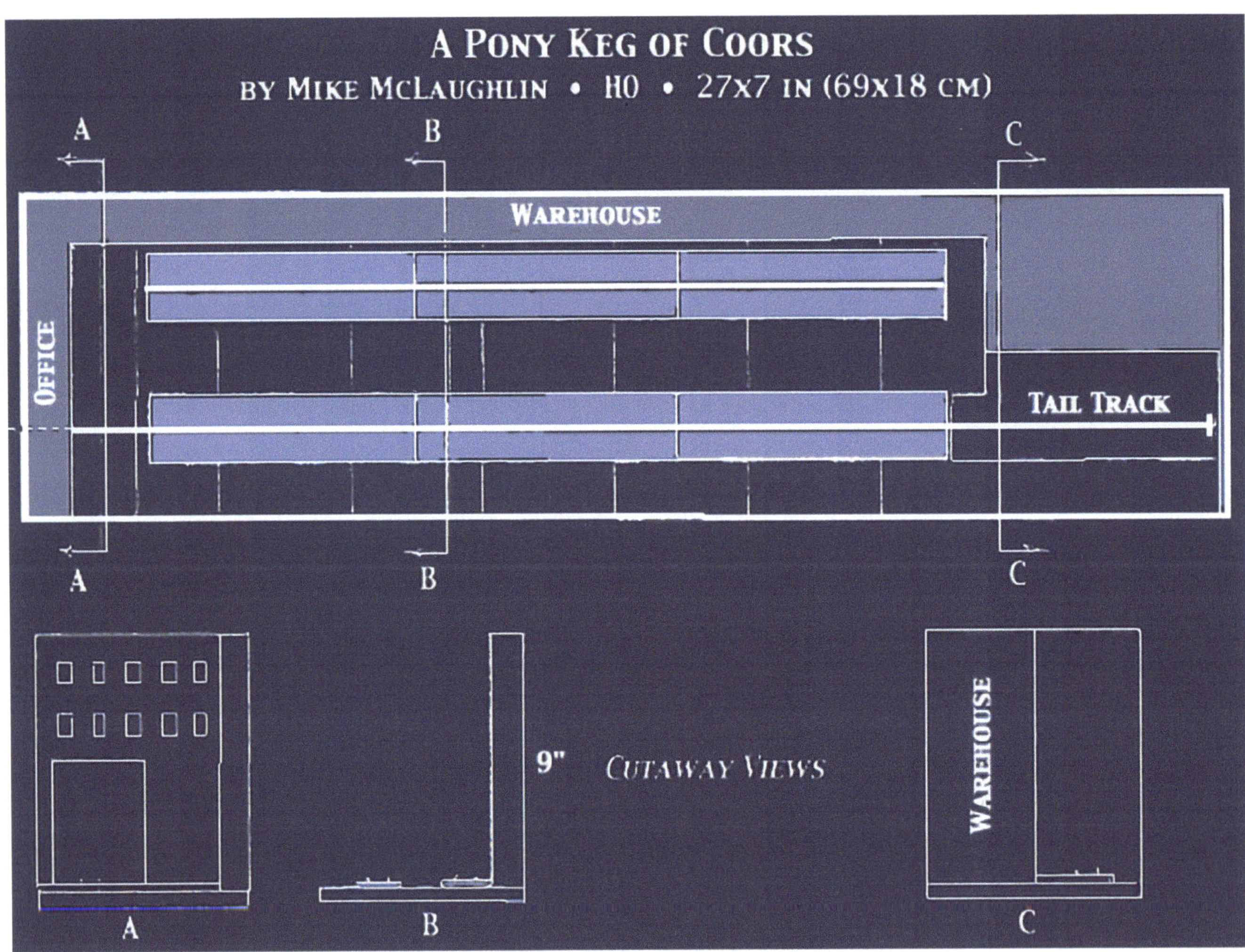

Describing how the Coors transfer tables worked, Mike drew up a condensed plan, showing how the system might look if reduced to ¼ of its size and modeled in HO Scale (1/87th actual size). Mike pointed out that "It just so happened" that the cubic dimensions of such a model would equal that of a pony keg of beer!

In 1971 Coors tested the Evans Air-Pak system and calculated potential savings…

DISTRIBUTION LIST:

*308-A. Babb	200-E. Edlund
319-E. Barnhardt	*301-W. Hays
*103-C. Buck	*405-H. Martin
*308-J. Coors	308-M. Nelson
322-Joe Coors	200-D. Parker
326-P. Coors	*308-G. Veber
321-Bill Coors	*308-S. Zorichak
*307-E. Werth	308- Q.C. File

* Denotes Members Present

*100-N. Kuhl ✓*304-M. McLaughlin

RESEARCH AND DEVELOPMENT COMMITTEE

Meeting No. 36
November 18, 1971

2. <u>Project No. 60 - Air-Pak Equipment</u>

A report was presented by Norm Kuhl and Mike McLaughlin stating the success of Evan's Air-Pak System placed in the ends of one car. Distributors were exceptionally enthusiastic with the system since the loads arrived with much less damage and were faster to unload. Savings of over $90,000,000 could be realized over the next 10 years by switching the present and future cars to air-pak. This included loading savings of $428,000, glued six-pack savings of $86,749, damaged claim reduction of $813,000, side panel repairs of $1,104,000 and reduction in car fleet of $1,466,000. Even without the glued six-pack savings considered it was felt that air-pak would save money over the $1,950,000 needed to convert the present 965 car fleet.

The following decisions were made:

(A) All new cars to be built by the railroad in 1972 for our use were to be equipped with air-pak, not side panels, with no additional cost to us.

(B) Sufficient cars of the present fleet were to be equipped with air-pak to accommodate the market test of the glued six-pack in February or March of this year.

(C) Implementation of the program was to be turned over to the Pul-pak Sub-Committee of the the Packaging Committee since they were geared to coordination with distributors.

Meeting adjourned.

Jeff Coors, Chairman

11/19/71
jb

Coors R&D Committee monthly meeting notes, November 19, 1971, condensed to show relevant material. *Michael J. McLaughlin collection.*

Beer Train headin' home from Coors, passing the Colorado Railroad Museum in Golden, Colorado. *Photograph by Philip R. Hastings, Philip Ross Hastings, MD, collection, California State Railroad Museum.*

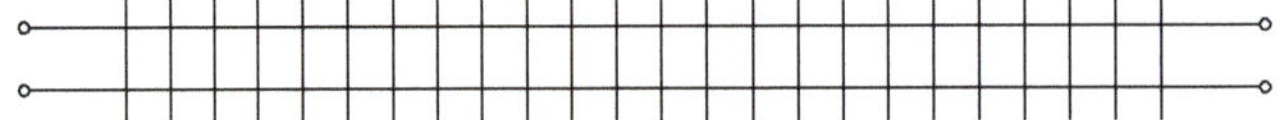

Traffic Management–Leprino Foods

I *think* the Western Pacific was supplying Fruit Growers Express reefers when I was working for Leprino Foods and Western Grocer. Now Leprino Foods is not a household name like Coors, but maybe it oughta be. Headquarters in Denver, largest producer of mozzarella cheese in the county, and makes a bunch of cheese byproducts too.*

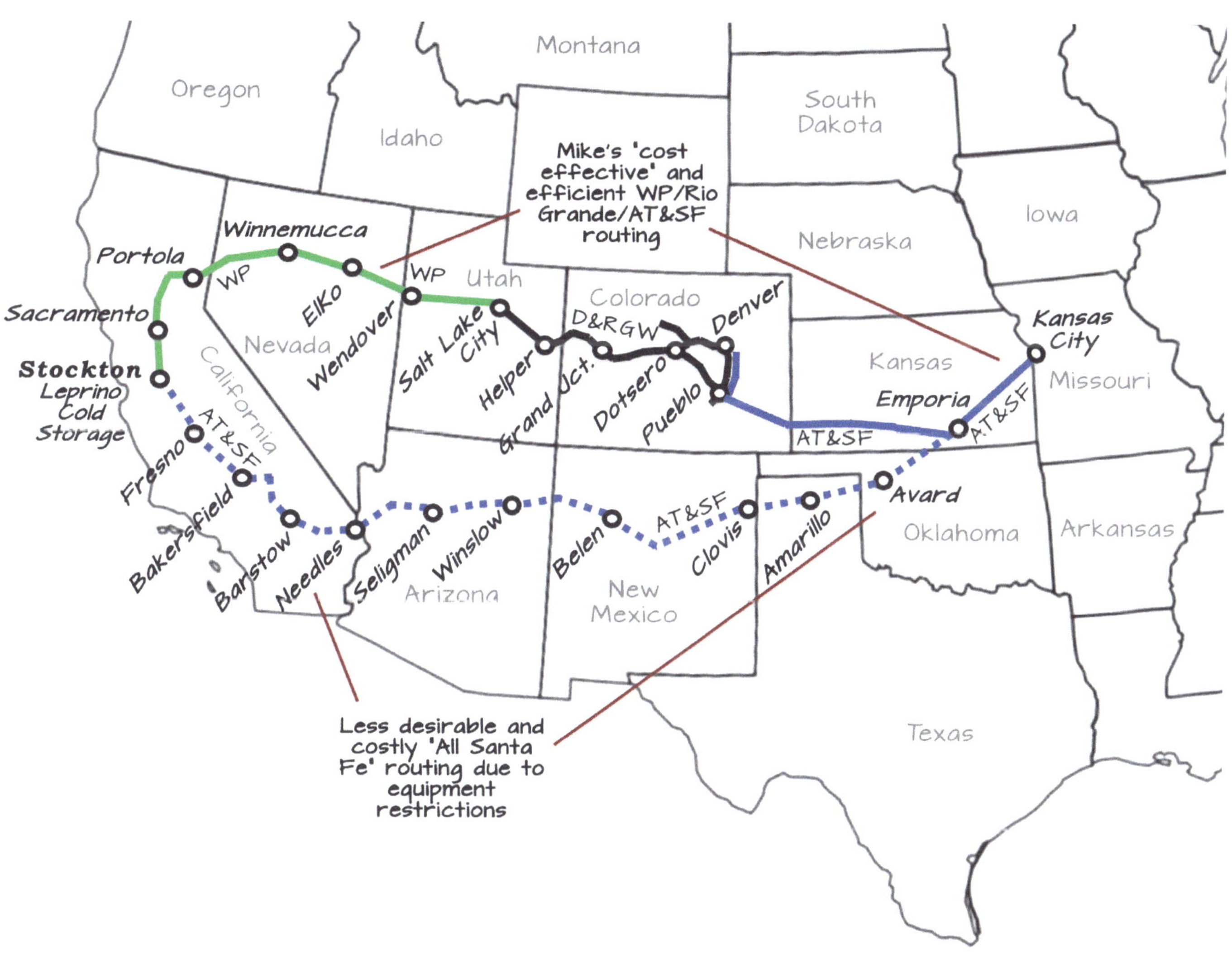

How the Santa Fe managed to short-haul itself by not listening to the customer...
Map by David R. Clemens.

I believe the FGE cars carried special reporting marks to keep 'em separate from other cars. The WP cars were much larger than the typical mechanical reefer of the era. Say, maybe 80-85 tons vs. 55-60 tons as furnished by the ATSF. Note, John Santa Fe did have some larger reefers but I couldn't talk 'em outa any. I got absolutely great service from the WP, due in no small part to a guy named Larry Gomez who worked in their SF sales office. He was a Portagee from the Napa Valley, and on his way home he used to check my reefers at the cold storage to make sure they were running and had the proper temp dialed in. Unh hunh, and the occasional quart of booze to the night yardmaster at Stockton made sure that they went out on the first hot train...

The only opportunity to [load Santa Fe MTC refrigerator cars] was when I was shipping cheese from Stockton to the caves at Kansas City on the ATSF. Unfortunately, the Santa Fe cars were of restricted weight capacity, whereas the cars the WP furnished had a substantially higher load limit. The rate was a two-part affair wherein the base rate was 90,000 lbs at $X per cwt and the balance moved at about 0.60X, a significant savings at max gross weight. Since cheese always weighs out instead of cubing out, I shipped WP-DRG-ATSF, keeping my buddies at the Grande and WP happy, and the Santa Fe guys less so. Oh yeah, and screw the Yoon Pacific.

After the UP-WP merger in 1982 I continued to ship the same route. When the Yellow Peril started running the WP trains directly into UP's North Yard, the WP guys used to put a Rio Grande block on the back of the trains and drop the block at Salt Lake City's Grant Tower where it was picked up by a DRG switcher. Took quite a while before Uncle Pete's geniuses figgered that one out...

When Leprino Foods started shipping cheese out of Horseheads, NY, I went back and met all the local people in the Horseheads-Elmira area, rode with the switch crew, and listened to the trainmaster bitch (he had SEVEN seniority boards to deal with when calling crews: Erie, Lackawanna, Erie-Lackawanna, Lehigh Valley, Pennsylvania, Penn Central, and Conrail). But when I needed a reefer and the car distributor in Buffalo ignored me, that same trainmaster would "steal" a prepped reefer out of a through train for my product ("gotta protect MY shippers").

The primary requirement was to think and talk like a railroader, and never, ever, claim something's hot when it isn't. Plan ahead, try to do things the railroad's way, and when a true emergency arises, tell it the way it is and if you've been up front all along, they'll usually work with you. I remember spending a three-day weekend on the phone with the BN trying to get 16,000 tons of talc ore to Portland to meet a ship after a horrendous freeze-up in Montana, and my trains got power while two intermodals sat in sidings—the BN man said "hey, us guys what work nights and weekends gotta stick together!"

And again, having the WP sales rep deliver a bottle of good scotch to the night yardmaster in Stockton certainly didn't hurt productivity...

*Note: Leprino Foods is still the biggest cheese maker you've never heard of. To give just one example, the company currently supplies the mozzarella cheese for the four largest pizza restaurant chains in the United States.

Interchange—1950s/60s Style

SEATTLE

Freight interchange in Seattle itself was "really quite simple." Within the Seattle terminal, major interchanges occurred in the waterfront area south of the central business district in Seattle's Tide Flats area. All railroads interchanged directly with one another behind Sears, Roebuck. Stacy Street was the location of Milwaukee, Pacific Coast, and NP primary freight yards, and a small Union Pacific "downtown" yard serving local industries and their freight house a block away just north of Atlantic Street. The Great Norn had their transfer tracks alongside the NP yard. All roads crossed each other on the northern end at Atlantic Street. Had a great ol' wooden pedestrian bridge over all the trackage from Sears, Roebuck to Alaskan Way on the waterfront.

The Great Northern classification yard was several miles north, so transfers were run along the water's edge south from Interbay Yard to the downtown pier area, along tracks immediately adjacent to Alaskan Way across from the piers, and into the central yards. The UP reached its downtown yard by running transfers north from Argo on a track sandwiched between the "GN track" and the Milwaukee's two waterfront tracks adjacent to Alaskan Way.

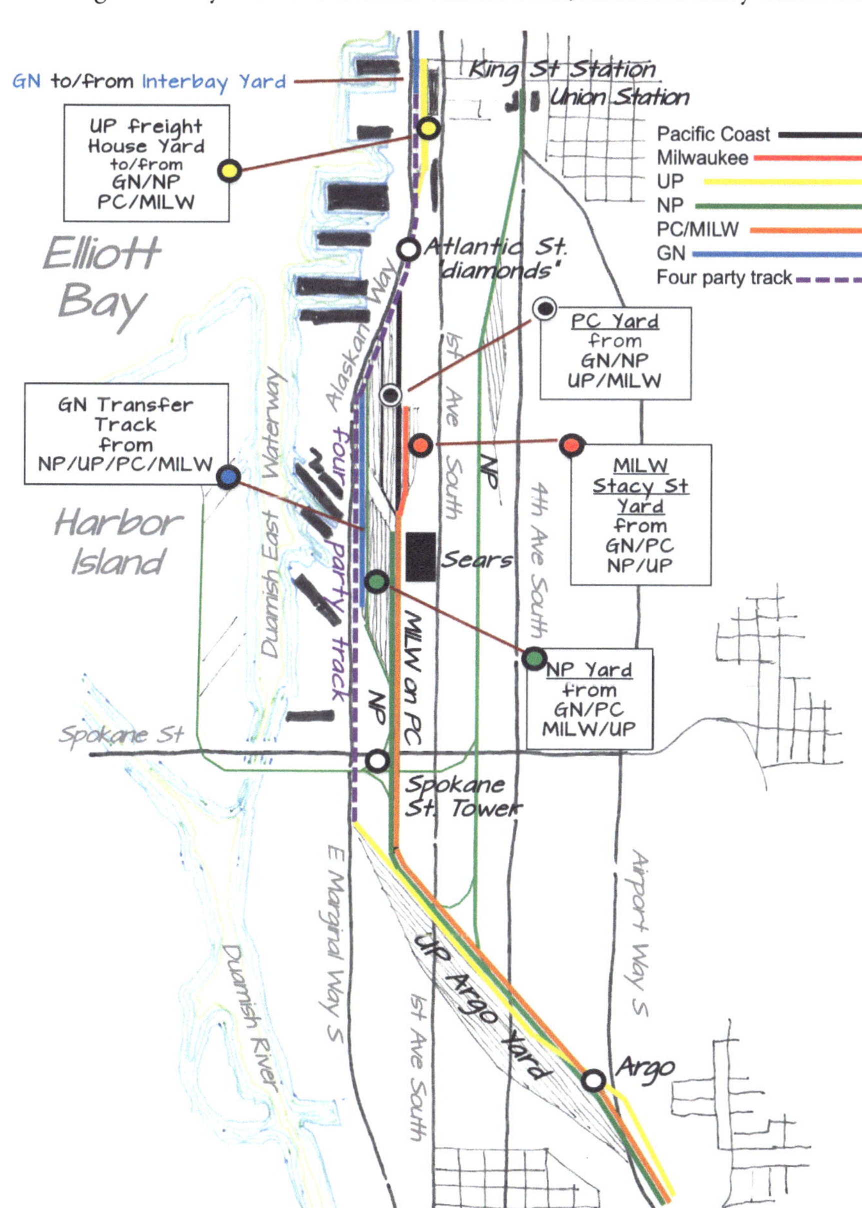

South Seattle Interchanges. *Map by David R. Clemens.*

All railroads delivered directly to each other's freight yards and the GN transfer. The Yoon Pacific transfer jobs worked both ways between their main yard at Argo and the freight house yard, while the GN transfers delivered to everybody and returned to Interbay with the traffic delivered to their transfer tracks by the other roads.

Yep, rode on switch engines of all but the Big G. I remember riding a Milwaukee switcher handling interchange in Seattle one afternoon. Push a few cars into the UP yard, back to their own yard, pull a cut for the PC and push it through the crossover into the interchange track, back again to the MILW yard and pull a cut for the NP/GN/waterfront across the diamonds at Atlantic Street. Shove the NP's into their yard, back again across Atlantic Street (with the flagman's blessing—CMStP&P: two motions with green flag/lantern) onto the "four-party" waterfront tracks, shove down into the "GN track," pull back and then push on down the waterfront with cars for the barge yard serving Bellingham and Port Townsend lines plus the MILW switched piers in the area. Pull a cut back from the waterfront and push it across the Atlantic Street crossings and into the CMStP&P Stacy Street yard. This activity was accompanied by switching movements on the NP north end leads (an 0-6-0 and a VO 660), the PC 0-6-0, a UP EMD switcher, all briefly blocked by a GN transfer.

MILW SW1200 #618 at Stacy Street Yard; the Sears, Roebuck warehouse is to the right. *Photograph by Dan Perkins, DRP009-045, PNRArchive collection at Burien WA.*

Great Northern operated an interchange job all three shifts between Interbay and the NP, MILW, PC, and UP. This job handled traffic in both directions. The crew went on duty at Interbay, where cars for the NP were in track 4, the MILW in track 3, and UP and PC in track 2. The caboose was on the north end of track 4. The crew doubled the train together with the PC cars on the head end. Most trips were about 60 cars. The carmen connected all the air hoses and confirmed that the brakes on the cars applied and released during the air test.

The PC cars, if any, were set out to the Bemis Pocket, next to the MILW just south of Atlantic Street. At Whatcom Avenue Yard the job pulled through track 5. MILW cars went to track 4, UP to track 7, and NP to track 8. The crew set the caboose at the south end of track 6, coupled up the track, and went to beans. The carmen hooked up the air hoses and made an air test. When the crew got back, the drag left for Interbay. At Interbay the crew pulled into track 6, cut off, and took the engine to the roundhouse. The job often worked less than eight hours, which was why it was a high seniority job.

—Mac McCulloch

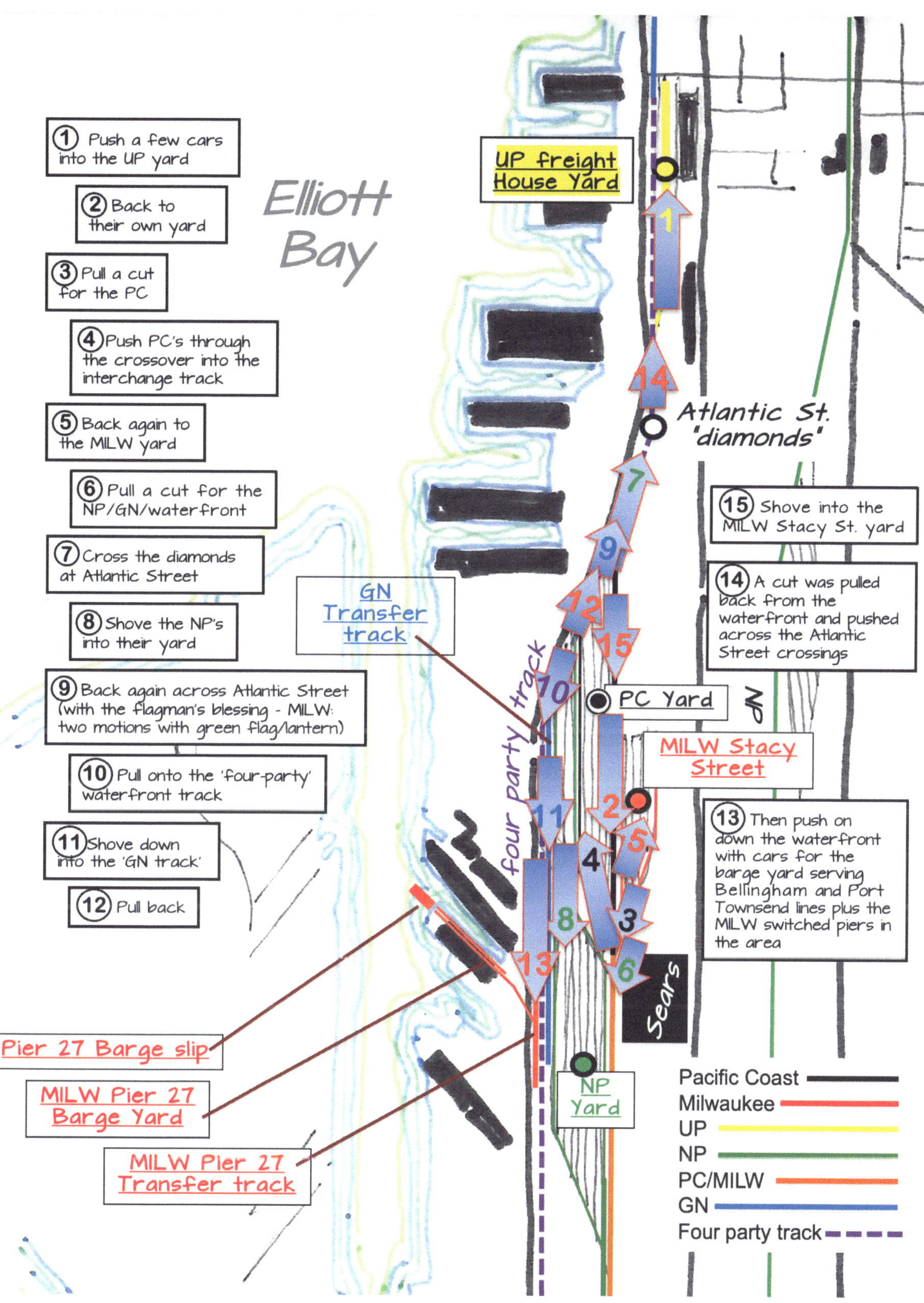

Mike's Afternoon Ride: MILW South Seattle transfer runs, a choreograph of seeming chaos orchestrated with the similar moves by the other four railroads' switch crews.
Map by David R. Clemens.

Most interchange movements were one-way and to specific tracks. Deliveries were made to the other road and the crew returned light. The exceptions were the GN which delivered to the various yards and then pulled the transfer track on the waterfront, and the UP which ran transfers both ways between Argo and the central area. Although in both cases, the transfer/downtown switcher still delivered to the other yards, while they in turn delivered to the GN and UP. In this era, all per diem accounting was based on cars on-line as of 12:01 AM. Thus, most railroads participated in the "midnight shove". Interchange traffic was collected up to the last minute, and then delivered to the connecting roads just prior to the witching hour. Obviously, high volume/priority interchange required multiple deliveries throughout the day, but the "shove" was a fixture in countless terminals.

What's in a [railroad] name?

History!

Whatcom Avenue does not appear on any Seattle street maps of any recent vintage. Only through a deep dive into the Internet did I discover that East Marginal Way South, running along the west side of the tracks Mac McCulloch calls Whatcom Avenue Yard and Mike McLaughlin described as the Four Party Tracks, was once named Whatcom Avenue. The street was renamed sometime after 1941—the Great Northern's name for the yard tracks remained unchanged, regardless.

—Linton von Beroldingen

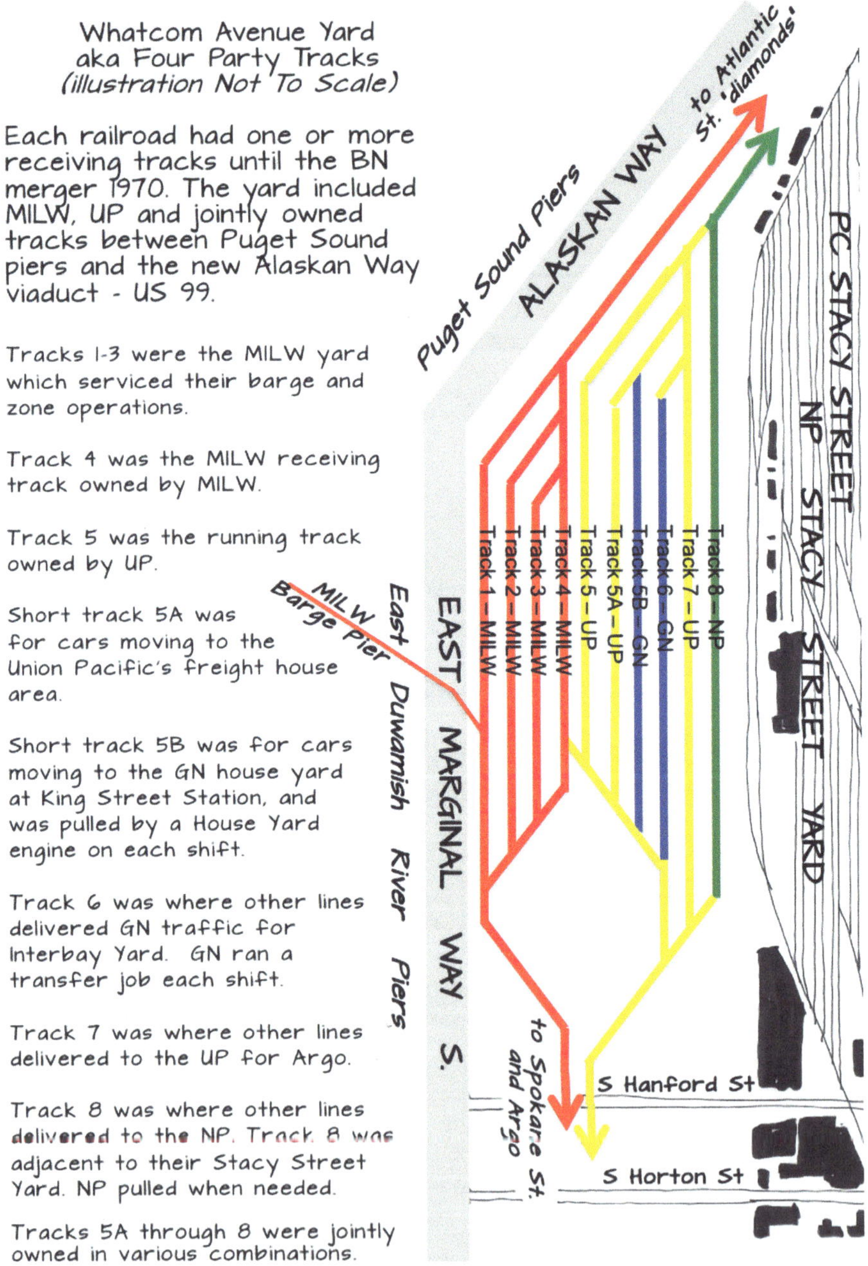

Whatcom Avenue Yard
aka Four Party Tracks
(illustration Not To Scale)

Each railroad had one or more receiving tracks until the BN merger 1970. The yard included MILW, UP and jointly owned tracks between Puget Sound piers and the new Alaskan Way viaduct - US 99.

Tracks 1-3 were the MILW yard which serviced their barge and zone operations.

Track 4 was the MILW receiving track owned by MILW.

Track 5 was the running track owned by UP.

Short track 5A was for cars moving to the Union Pacific's freight house area.

Short track 5B was for cars moving to the GN house yard at King Street Station, and was pulled by a House Yard engine on each shift.

Track 6 was where other lines delivered GN traffic for Interbay Yard. GN ran a transfer job each shift.

Track 7 was where other lines delivered to the UP for Argo.

Track 8 was where other lines delivered to the NP. Track 8 was adjacent to their Stacy Street Yard. NP pulled when needed.

Tracks 5A through 8 were jointly owned in various combinations.

Puget Sound Piers
ALASKAN WAY
to Atlantic St. 'diamonds'
PC STACY STREET
NP STACY STREET YARD
Track 8 – NP
Track 7 – UP
Track 6 – GN
Track 5B – GN
Track 5A – UP
Track 5 – UP
Track 4 – MILW
Track 3 – MILW
Track 2 – MILW
Track 1 – MILW
MILW Barge Pier
East Duwamish River Piers
EAST MARGINAL WAY S.
to Spokane St. and Argo
S Hanford St
S Horton St

Whatcom Avenue Yard/Four Party Tracks. *Text by Mac McCulloch, map by David R. Clemens.*

But away from Stacy Street...

Through the 1950s and into the late 1960s, railroad to railroad interchange of carload traffic followed a definite choreograph. A multitude of interchange points were established, in part a result of ICC regulations which enforced nearly open routing at common rates between most points. In addition, most terminal areas had "reciprocal switching" wherein cars arriving on one line-haul road were spotted at an industry on another line at no additional cost to the shipper/consignee. As an example, eight interchanges existed in the Seattle area amongst the four trunk lines and the shortline Pacific Coast Railroad:

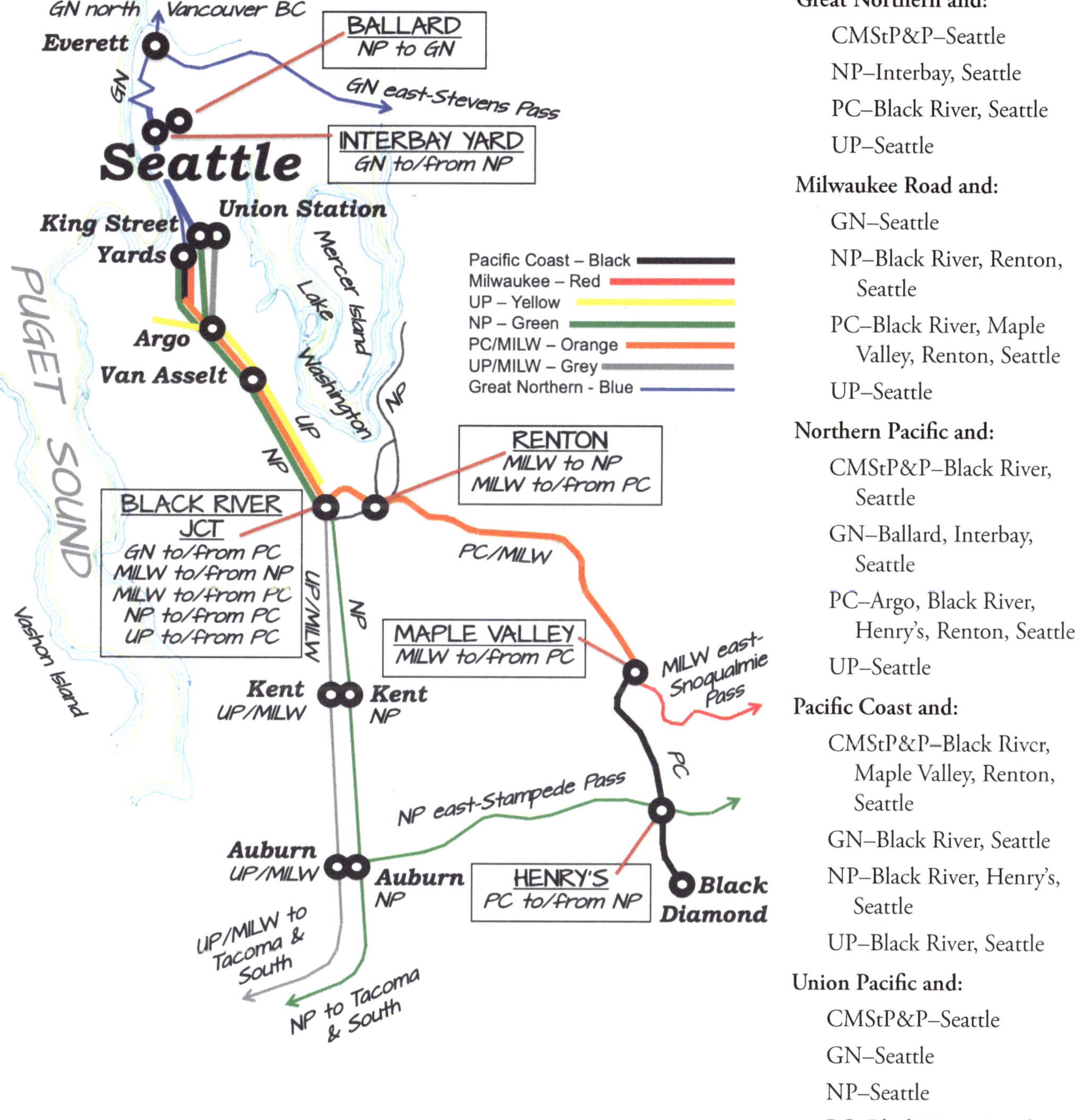

Great Northern and:
- CMStP&P–Seattle
- NP–Interbay, Seattle
- PC–Black River, Seattle
- UP–Seattle

Milwaukee Road and:
- GN–Seattle
- NP–Black River, Renton, Seattle
- PC–Black River, Maple Valley, Renton, Seattle
- UP–Seattle

Northern Pacific and:
- CMStP&P–Black River, Seattle
- GN–Ballard, Interbay, Seattle
- PC–Argo, Black River, Henry's, Renton, Seattle
- UP–Seattle

Pacific Coast and:
- CMStP&P–Black River, Maple Valley, Renton, Seattle
- GN–Black River, Seattle
- NP–Black River, Henry's, Seattle
- UP–Black River, Seattle

Union Pacific and:
- CMStP&P–Seattle
- GN–Seattle
- NP–Seattle
- PC–Black River, Seattle

Seattle's Outlying Interchanges. *Map by David R. Clemens.*

The physical location of these interchanges (other than Seattle itself) was:

Argo—in Seattle adjacent to the UP yard, about three miles south of the central yards.
Ballard–northwest Seattle, just north of the ship canal.
Black River–about ten miles south of Seattle close to Renton.
Henry's–twenty-eight miles southeast of Seattle where the PC crossed over the NP main line east to Stampede Pass.
Interbay–site of the GN yard in northwest Seattle, just south of the ship canal.
Maple Valley–twenty-two miles southeast of Seattle where the CMStP&P and PC separated.
Renton–twelve miles southeast of Seattle at the south end of Lake Washington.

Note that in some instances, a railroad listed a point as an interchange, while the correspondent line didn't:

MILW–Renton–NP: NP didn't;
NP–Ballard–GN: GN didn't;
NP–Argo/Renton–PC: PC didn't.

These exceptions were usually for specific, directional traffic that might require expedited handling.

Generally, the "outlying" interchanges were also essentially directional. For example, at Henry's, eastbound coal traffic was given to the NP by the PC; south industrial traffic from/to Renton was interchanged at Black River; and GN cars for their freight house on Terry Avenue (switched by the NP) interchanged with the NP at Interbay.

ADDENDUM

Switching Zones: Interchange Before the BN merger

Zone Defense!

By mutual agreement Seattle was divided into switching zones and most zones were switched by one road in the interest of all to minimize the number of switch jobs operating over congested trackage and to reduce operating costs.

A couple of additional notes to further explain the map:

Zone 3, switched by MILW, included their barge slip at Pier 27

Zone 4 is the west side of Harbor Island, 407 acres of artificial land

Zone 9 is the east side of Harbor Island; after 1963 it included the Alaska Hydro Train barge slip.

—Mac McCulloch

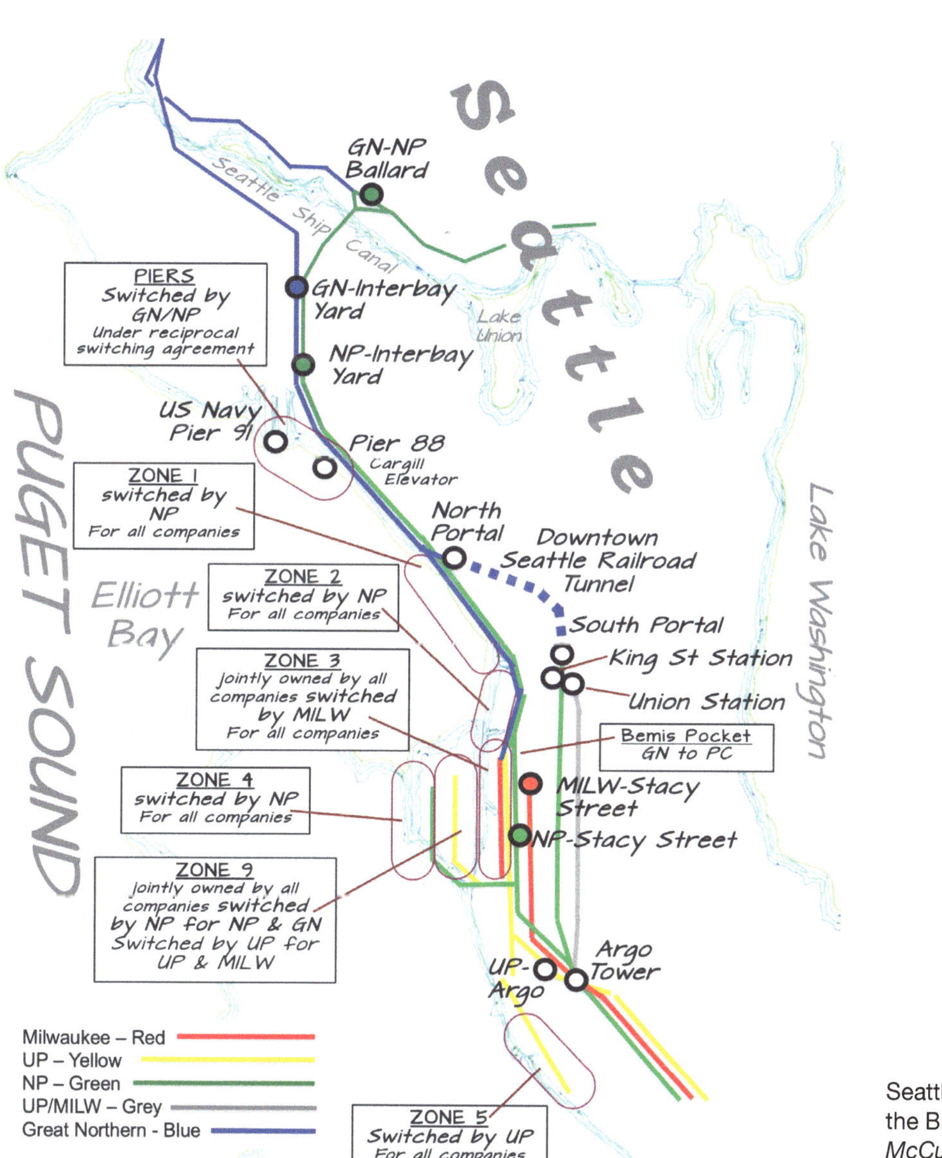

Seattle Switching Zones before the BN merger. *Text by Mac McCulloch, map by David R. Clemens.*

Seattle Interchange Locations and the 1970 BN Merger

Whatcom Avenue Yard: *Established in 1918 and expanded in 1941 for joint operation, was the principal interchange until sometime after the BN merger in 1970.*

Pacific Coast Railroad until 1970: *Interchange with GN made to the Bemis Pocket near Atlantic Street. Interchange between NP and PC was in the PC yard which lay adjacent to Stacy Street.*

Argo: *When Whatcom Avenue interchange was closed after the merger, BN delivered to the MILW and UP at Argo Yard. The BN interchange job handled cars in both directions.*

King Street Station: *King Street Station was a separate company, owned 50-50 by GN and NP. Freight traffic to and from KSS was interchanged with each parent. GN delivered an occasional car of company material to King Street Station on track 11 of the house yard. King Street Station delivered to track 21 of the house yard. NP had a similar arrangement.*

By post-merger agreement, the UP was granted trackage rights to the Cargill grain terminal south of Pier 88, enabling them to deliver directly to the grain terminal tracks. The UP now also operates trains directly to and from Terminal 5, which was formerly an exclusive NP area, eliminating the interchange formerly required.

—Mac McCulloch

And change continues... In 2022, when this photo was taken, the Lander Street pedestrian overpass is long gone. The Sears warehouse, that landmark of South Seattle railroading, is now the "mother church"—the headquarters of Starbucks Coffee. Tourists flock to the plaza in front of the building to take selfies. The derelict spur that served the warehouse, buried in brick paving where it crossed Lander Street at the back or "railroad side" of the building, is about all that remains to say that this was once part of another, different nationwide enterprise that helped define an era. *Photograph by Jim Providenza.*

Interchange—1950s/60s Style

D&RGW

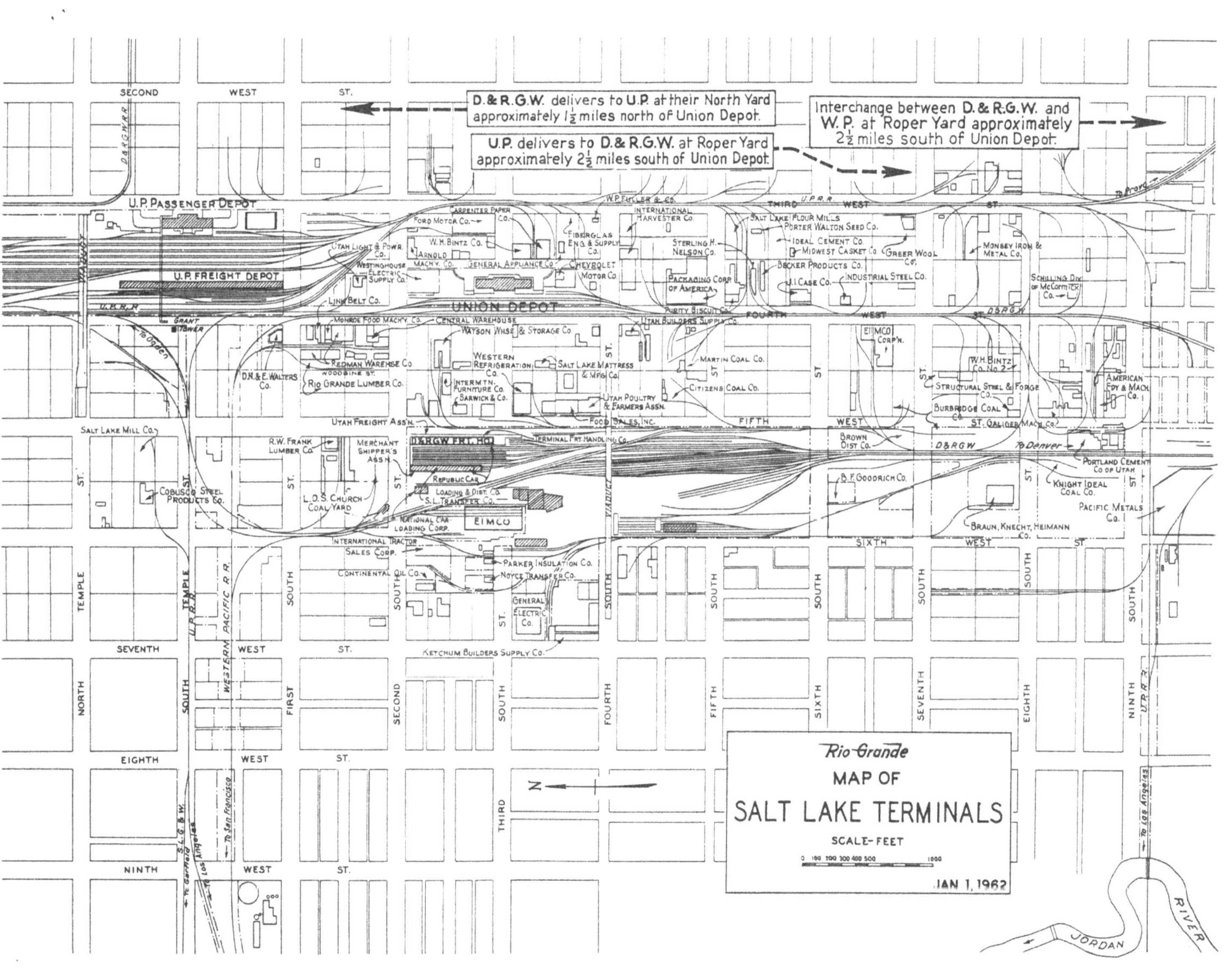

Denver & Rio Grande Western 1962 “Map of Salt Lake Terminals” provides a broad overview of railroading in Salt Lake City. *Michael J. McLaughlin collection.*

Salt Lake City:

Other railroads had their interchange "dances."

The WP began and ended its 900 mile plus run from Oakland directly into D&RGW's Roper Yard, having no yard of its own in Salt Lake City. On the other hand, the UP and the D&RGW had a pair of runs between North Yard (UP) and Roper at Salt Lake. Each delivered to the other road and returned light. The UP transfer was called the "creeper" as their top speed was approximately 5 mph—that crew made a day's work out of a 15-mile round trip. When the union rules were modified to allow bi-directional loaded movements, it was implemented immediately.

The Rio Grande Salt Lake Superintendent called his counterpart at the UP and asked, "How'll we do this?" The answer was, "How about we run in the morning and you take the evening?" "Okay, let's start tomorrow." Service was doubled and concomitantly reductions in expenses were achieved. Meanwhile, in Denver similar arrangements would take several months, due to the headquarters-to-headquarters animosity between the D&RGW and the UP in Omaha.

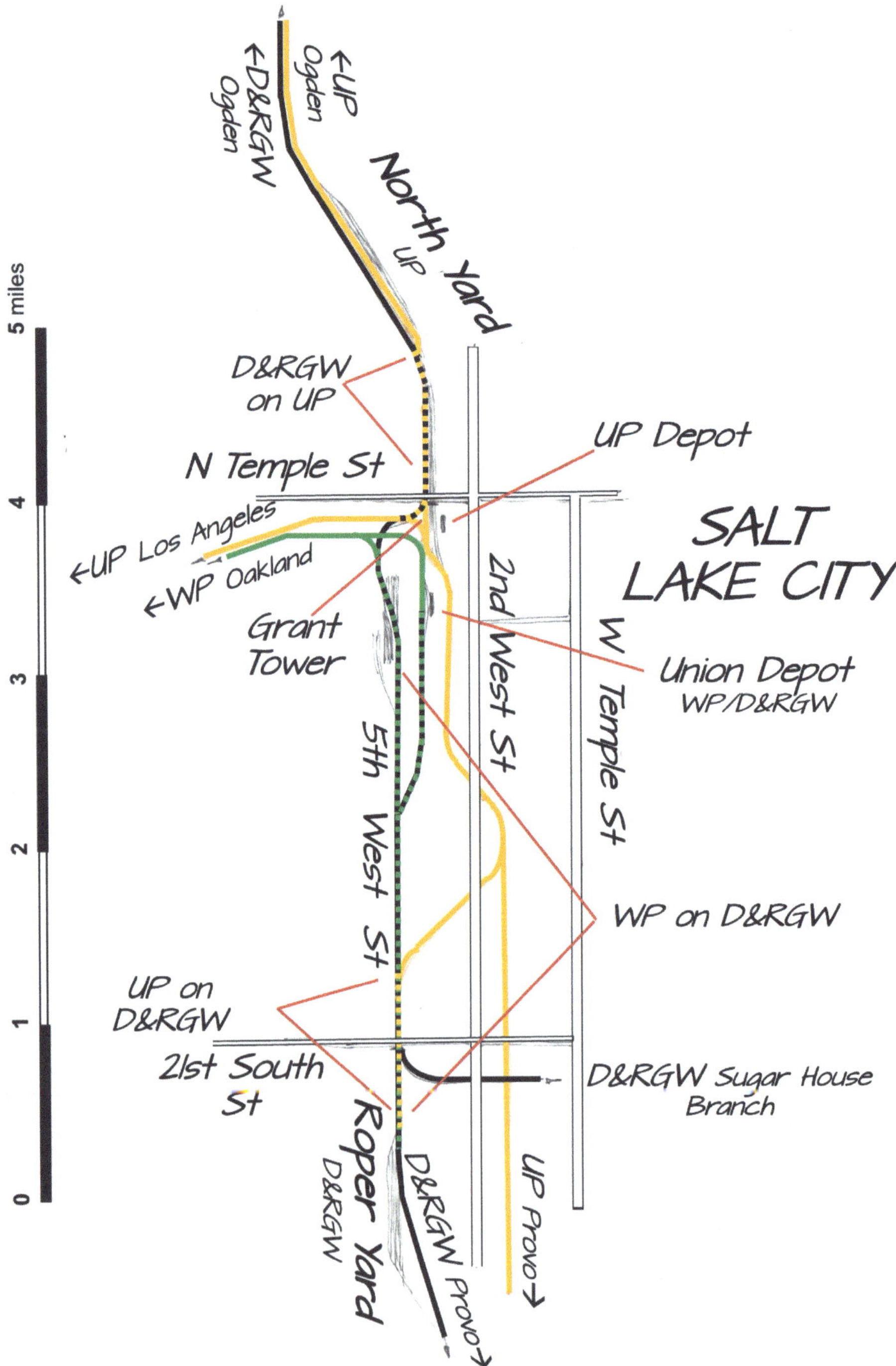

D&RGW, UP, and WP in Salt Lake City. *Map by David R. Clemens.*

Denver:

D&RGW 3123 and 3096 lead the "South Local" at 7th Street Yard on July 9, 1985. *Photograph by Chuck Conway.*

The Rio Grande in Denver in the 1950s had some 11 different interchange points with four other railroads and there were two joint yards, each hosting a pair of lines! Traffic was routed as follows:

1. CB&Q to D&RGW, westbound (Moffat Tunnel) only, 38th Street Yard to North Yard via Prospect.
2. D&RGW to CB&Q from the Moffat line, at 38th Street via the Belt Line/stockyards.
3. D&RGW to/from CRI&P within North Yard (joint yard with the Rock Island).
4. D&RGW to UP at the Rio Grande yard at 11th Street, except Moffat Tunnel traffic.

4A D&RGW to UP at 47th & York (east of the UP yard) via the Belt Line, Moffat Tunnel traffic only.

5. UP to the D&RGW at 38th Street via the Belt Line/stockyards, except Moffat traffic.

5A. UP to D&RGW at 48th & York via the Belt Line, Moffat Tunnel traffic only.

6. CB&Q/D&RGW both ways (except Moffat traffic) at 11th Street.
7. C&S/ATSF to D&RGW at 7th Street.
8. D&RGW to C&S/ATSF at 11th Street.
9. D&RGW to/from C&S/ATSF at Fox Junction.

Whew!

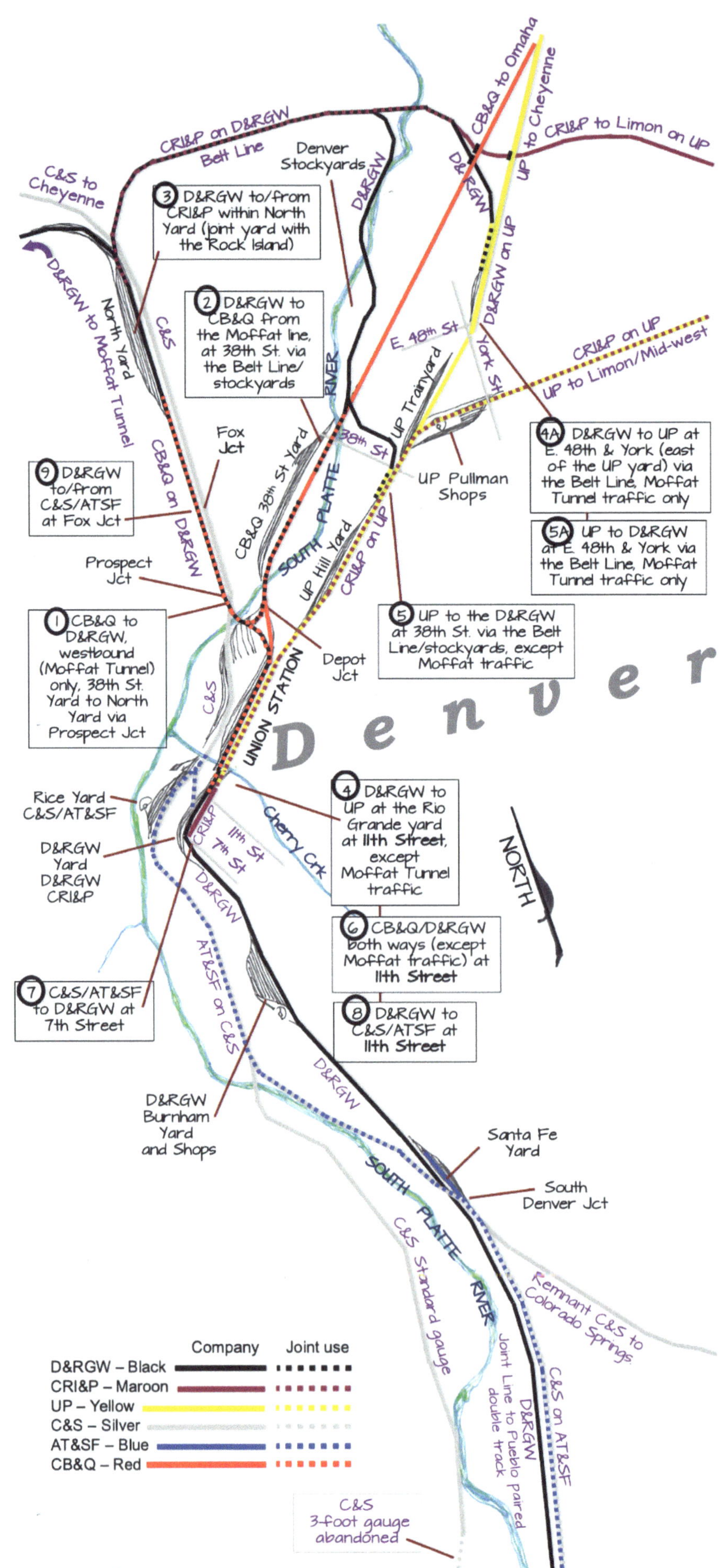

Denver interchanges and yards 1950s–1960s; track ownership and joint use as indicated. *Map by David R. Clemens.*

Perhaps a bit of history about D&RGW interchanges might clarify things (I hope!). There are two main dates to remember: 1934 and 1951. Prior to 1934, ALL D&RGW traffic to and from the south went out of Burnham. That's why most of the interchange was done at 7th/11th Streets, which are just a few blocks north of Burnham. Before 1934, a lot of the RI business would have gone through Colorado Springs. Why take it to Denver only to drag it over the Palmer Divide? After the completion of the Dotsero Cutoff in 1934, more RI business came to Denver, but still had to go through 11th Street and Burnham before going west. Likewise, Q and C&S/ATSF business utilizing 7th /11th Streets and Burnham. The UP was never a huge factor in D&RGW interchange business, since the two companies loathed each other.

With the completion of the Dotsero Cutoff, the number of scheduled freights west jumped from 2 to 6. Much of the increase came from the Q and RI, both of which took advantage of this shortcut (compared to the Royal Gorge route) for transcontinental shipments. And with these increases, something besides the 7th/11th Streets/Burnham operations was definitely in order. The war years only exacerbated the problems and after the D&SL was merged into the D&RGW in 1947, plans were made for a new yard (North Yard) just north of 48th Avenue and south of Utah Junction. Concurrent with the construction of North Yard was the building of the Rock Island cutoff, which allowed RI trains to be directly interchanged with the Grande and North Yard became a joint D&RGW/RI agency in 1951. The Q also ramped up its transcontinental business through North Yard and both cuts and entire trains were interchanged as noted in 1 and 2 of Mike's list. As noted earlier, the C&S/ATSF continued to interchange at 7th St until the '70's when most interchange was between 31st St and North Yard. And eventually, all UP interchange occurred via York St.

—Chuck Conway.

On June 3, 1982, Chuck Conway shot D&RGW 130 as it passed through Fox Junction. The EMD built the SW1200 for the Rio Grande in 1964. It would serve the railroad for 31 years. *Photograph by Chuck Conway.*

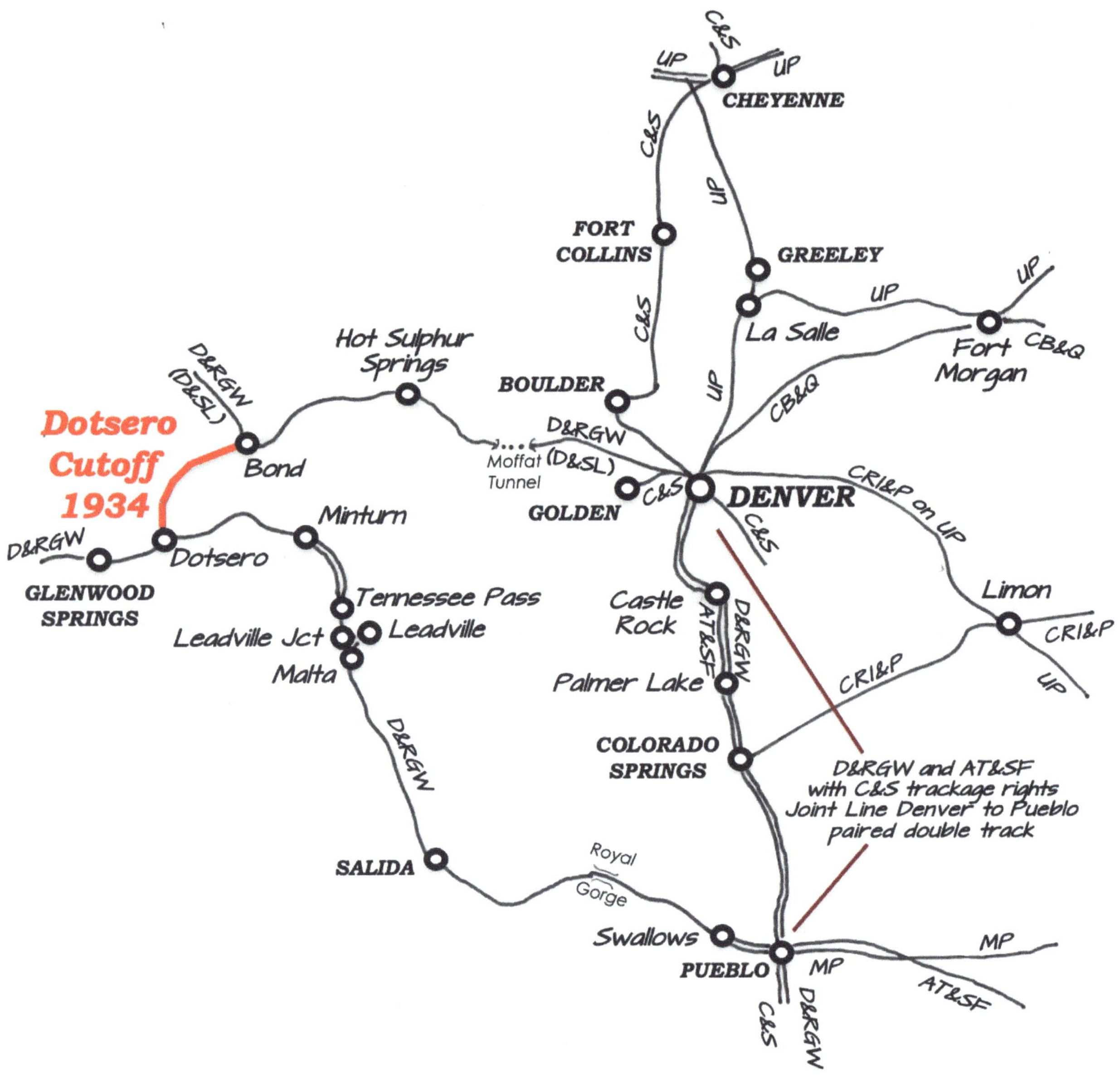

Denver Area railroads, highlighting the Dotsero Cutoff. *Map by David R. Clemens.*

All interchange movements to foreign yards/interchange tracks were uni-directional, returning light. Long-distance transfers had cabeese, the others were engine only. Note that some interchanges were restricted to specific traffic—via Moffat Tunnel only, everything except Moffat Tunnel, etc.

Frequently, traffic to be interchanged bypassed its ultimate destination, moved through the "official" transfer, and backtracked to the terminal passed earlier. An example was the Coors traffic movements between the C&S and the D&RGW. Outbound cars from the Golden brewery pulled into Denver on the C&S "beer train" on trackage rights on the Rio Grande main line, past North Yard, returned to C&S tracks at Prospect Jct. and terminated at Rice Yard. The D&RGW cars were switched to the 7th Street interchange, placed on a transfer, and run back to North Yard. Only then could the traffic be dispatched west as required. Following elimination of union rules prohibiting road trains from making set-outs and pick-ups within terminals, North Yard was made an interchange point. Thus, the beer run would stop on the main in front of the yard tower, back through the crossovers, and set out the D&RGW's (as previously blocked by the Coors switchers) on whatever track the Rio Grande YM directed. Frequently, the cars were set directly to the outbound train, and in any case were out of town in hours rather than days.

Friendly and Unfriendly Connections

The term interchange refers to the act of physically passing cars from one railroad to another. Assume a carload of candy that originated at a factory served by the Chicago Burlington & Quincy (CB&Q) at Chicago moving to a distributor in Salt Lake City served by the Denver & Rio Grande Western (DRGW) interchanged at Denver Colorado. On the waybill this car would show the route CB&Q – DEN – DRGW and would be physically interchanged at Denver at a location mutually agreed as between the carriers.

This example illustrates "friendly connections." The CB&Q and the DRGW were friendly connections to each other at Denver. They were non-competitive and each was an extension of the other. By contrast, the Union Pacific was not a friendly connection to either the Q or the Rio Grande at Denver. The Q was a direct competitor for traffic to and from Chicago, and the Rio Grande was a direct competitor for traffic to and from Salt Lake and points west. For the UP to deliver traffic to and from competitive points east of Denver to the CB&Q meant that the UP would be short-hauling itself, a situation to be avoided at almost all costs since short hauling meant loss of revenue to the carrier being short hauled. Of course, if a customer was located at a station on the DRGW or the Burlington but not on the UP, the traffic had to be handled on a joint UP-CB&Q or UP-DRGW route.

—Mac McCulloch

The above examples of long-distance interchange traffic can be extrapolated upward to terminal areas such as Chicago where transfer runs sometimes died on the 16-hour law before returning to their home yards. In some terminals, interchange had to carried out through an intermediate carrier: via Alton & Southern, via Canadian National, etc. Conversely, the outlying point of Henry's, Washington provided a "low key" interchange between the Pacific Coast and the Milwaukee for a couple of cars of coal now and then.

Regardless of location or volume, structured interchange of carload traffic was an integral and complicated part of railroading.

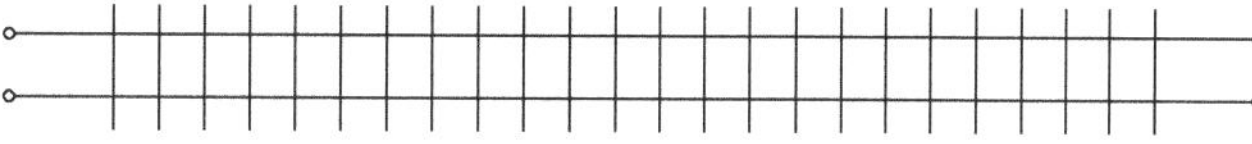

Grant Tower—North Platte Hump

Towers… One note: "Electro mechanical" is just that—a combination of mechanical interlocking with electric (or pneumatic) switch and signal execution. Pistol grip handles and mechanical bed below. NX is completely electric with relay logic (interlocking) rather than mechanical, and it has a totally different type of panel. And this in turn is different from the "standard" electric interlocking, where each switch and signal are controlled by a separate lever.

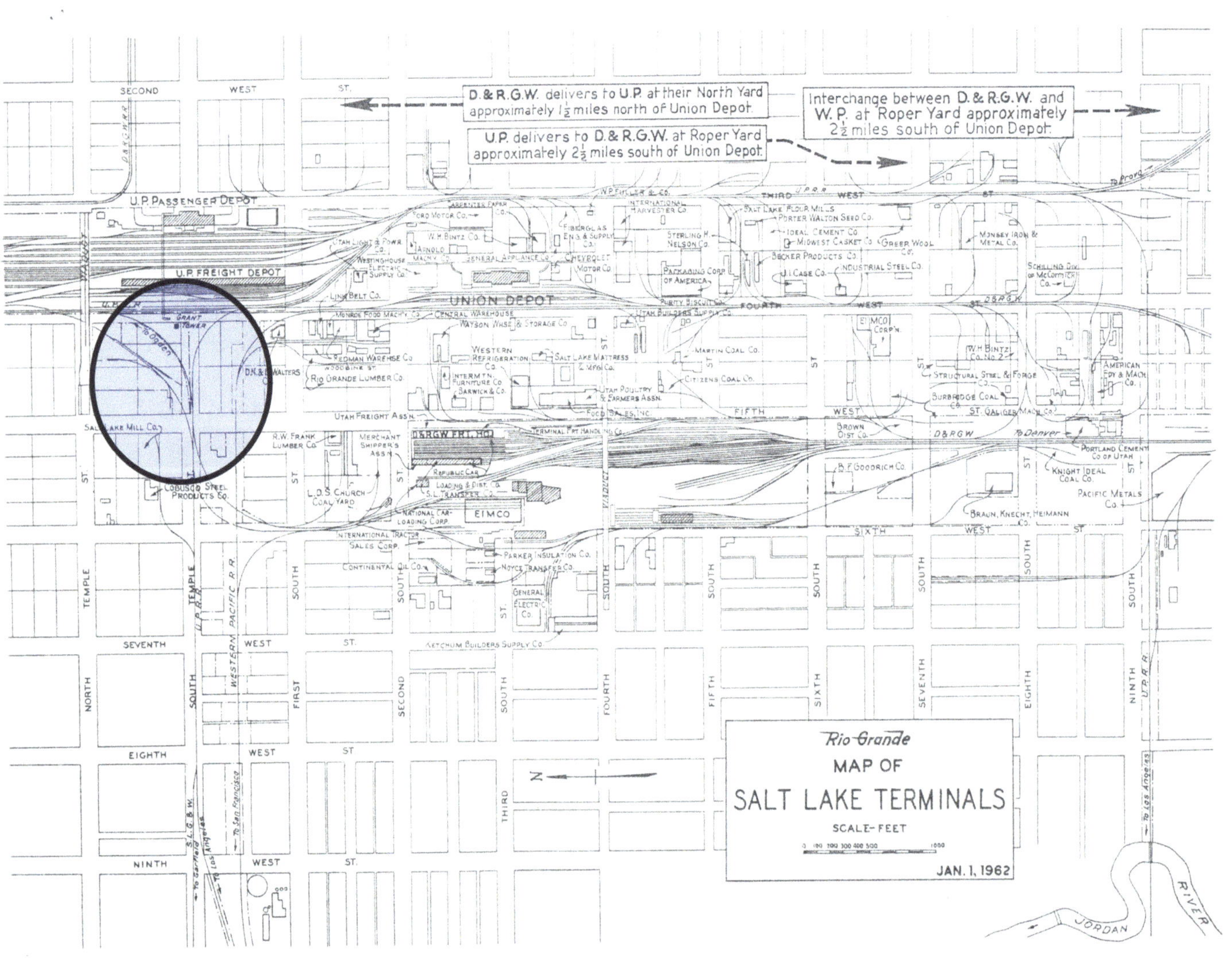

Denver & Rio Grande Western 1962 "Map of the Salt Lake Terminals" with the location of Grant Tower highlighted in the upper left. *Michael J. McLaughlin collection.*

Grant Tower

Grant Tower in Salt Lake (D&RGW) was an NX machine, although now is CTC operated from Omaha. It controlled the RG-WP-UP trackage next to both depots, plus the freight main junction/crossings with the passenger line of the UP/WP. I spent a lot of time there in both union and management. A fascinating place; one morning the operator held a UP Provo Sub empty ore drag for a mainline UP freight which died in the plant. The Provo train extended back down 3rd West (now 4th West), blocking *all* the major street crossings, and rush hour yet. The cops, UP Trainmaster, and Superintendent were all screaming their heads off while the operator and I shrugged and made comments about UP locomotive maintenance.

The tower was just north of Salt Lake's notorious 2nd South hooker strip. (Remember the congressman who got caught in a sting by a policewoman disguised as a hooker?) After work, the maintainer and I would stop for a beer in a bar on 2nd South right at the Rio Grande depot trackage crossing. Met a different group of women, to be sure—"Okay, traffic's picking up, let's get out and wiggle it." One absolutely miserable rainy day, they decided to party rather than "work"; and that was one of the more interesting afternoons I ever spent—the railroad paid me for this?

While Mike might disparage UP's locomotive maintenance practices, it was hard to beat the UP when it came to fielding one-of-a-kind locomotives. Heading this freight is a GE U30C; while not unique, it and its sisters are almost lost among UP's fleet of around 800 variants of EMD's model SD40. Trailing the 2914 is low-nosed GP20 485, followed by a DD35A and two GP9B's—both rostered only by the UP. *Photograph by Blair Kooistra.*

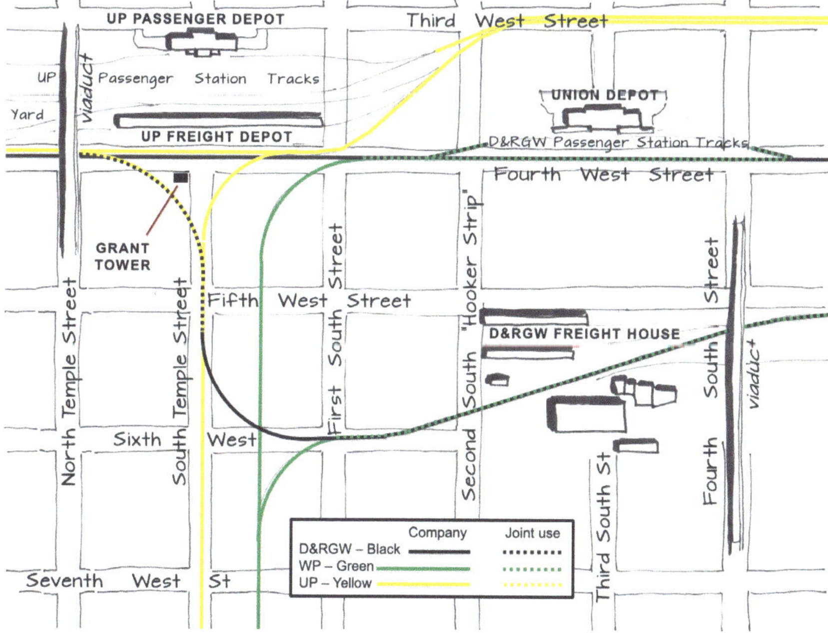

Grant Tower and the tracks it controlled in Salt Lake City. *Map by David R. Clemens.*

At 8:30 one night, the operator is lining a WP movement through the plant at Grant Tower.
Illustration by Kimberly Hoverter Morris from a Jaime Schmidt photograph.

North Platte Hump

The original westbound hump yard was typical of the era: manually controlled retarders and switch machines. Two signal maintainers built an "automatic switching" system that lined turnouts for each car from hump crest to bowl track. It was absolutely the goddamnedest thing I ever saw. It was a literal representation of the hump trackage made from tubing. At each "switch" there was a solenoid that opened one "route" (tube) or the other. As each car was programmed into the system, a series of steel or brass balls was selected. They were loaded, all automatically, into the top of the model and cascaded down through the tubes as the car moved off the hump. Magnetic sensors (steel or brass balls) threw the turnouts on the hump tracks and also the corresponding solenoids on the model. The balls then dropped to the next switch where they were held, the sensor determined switch position, and they crashed down again. At the bottom, the balls were pumped back up to the appropriate hopper at the top of the "machine." When in full operation, the noise was deafening.

It was about 12–15 feet high, and GRS actually took out a patent (joint with the maintainers) on the thing. I saw it when I took some engineers from Coors to look at Bailey Yard (the eastbound hump). Much to the disgust of the UP tour guide, we were more impressed with the "mechanical monstrosity" than with the most sophisticated hump yard in the world. I wonder what happened to it?

TEST MODEL BALL MACHINE at North Platte

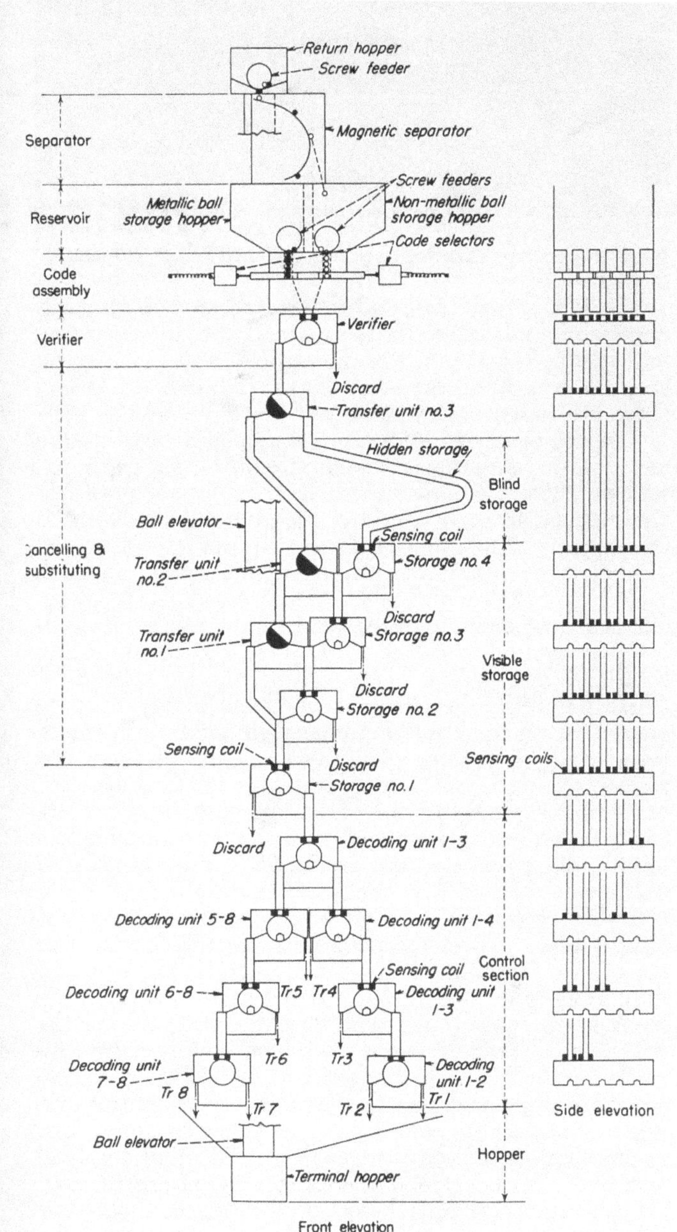

Courtesy of Control Engineering

Fig. 2—Plan of the ball machine

In its April 1955 issue, *Railway Signal & Communications* magazine ran a 5-page article on the pilot installation of the UP's automatic switching system at North Platte. The machine was controlling movement onto 8 of the 42 westbound hump yard tracks. UP expected the complete installation for all tracks to be in service by the end of 1955. The article goes on to describe the use of an analog computer and radar to control the hump yard retarders in the same pilot program—in 1955! *Photograph and plan from the* Railway Signal and Communications *article, from the Jim Atkins collection.*

Hiking Sticks

No, not the sticks or poles you might want to use while taking a hike on one of the mountain trails in the Rockies around Victor, Colorado; rather the poles supporting signal and communications lines!

Inasmuch as communications pole lines usually carried signal wires in signaled territory, I'd like to provide some additional information concerning this aspect. First, some background: I began climbing on the Great Northern in western Washington, hiked sticks all over the Rio Grande, was one-half of a "line gang" on the Rock Island in Iowa plus working Chicago and other locations, wore hooks and belt on the Boston & Albany around Boston, and even as a management employee back on the D&RGW found myself on top to a pole more than once. —Letter to the Editor, *Railroad Model Craftsman*, August 19, 1992.

Memories… A wasp nest the size of a basketball on a pole at the west portal of the Cascade Tunnel, hiking 80's in the Wasatch mountains, bugs—especially chiggers—in Iowa, climbing a 60 in the median of Route 128 [Boston, MA], which was already terminal from errant automobiles, building a new pole line at 30 degrees below in the Rockies, and the near disaster of having a newly-strung wire sag and get snagged by a truck on a city street crossing. If I'd been between it and the pole I'd have been cut in half.

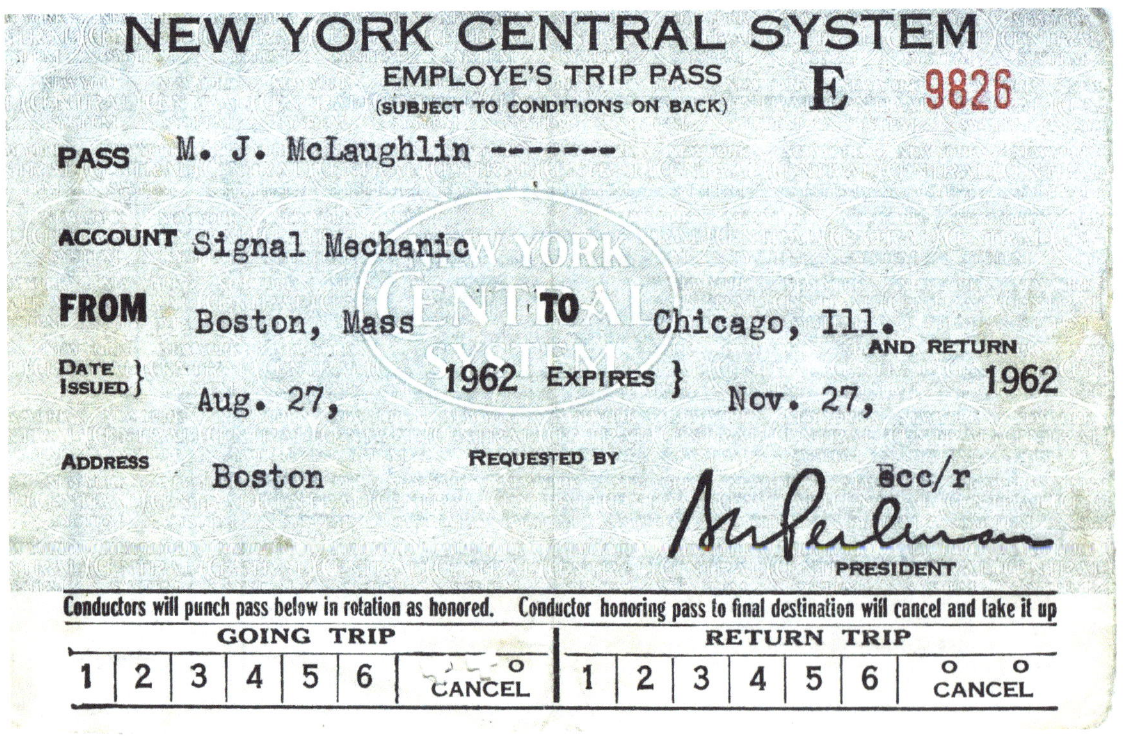
NEW YORK CENTRAL SYSTEM

EMPLOYE'S TRIP PASS

(SUBJECT TO CONDITIONS ON BACK)

E 9826

PASS M. J. McLaughlin -------

ACCOUNT Signal Mechanic

FROM Boston, Mass TO Chicago, Ill. AND RETURN

DATE ISSUED Aug. 27, 1962 EXPIRES Nov. 27, 1962

ADDRESS Boston REQUESTED BY Scc/r

PRESIDENT

Conductors will punch pass below in rotation as honored. Conductor honoring pass to final destination will cancel and take it up

GOING TRIP							RETURN TRIP						
1	2	3	4	5	6	CANCEL	1	2	3	4	5	6	CANCEL

The reverse of this employee pass notes that it was "Not good on the Twentieth Century Limited"; the fine print begins "[The user of] this free pass ASSUMES all risk of injury or death…" *Michael J. McLaughlin collection.*

Railroads, ballparks, and pole lines… In Boston, Fenway Park backs up to the B&A right-of-way. When there was a game and we were working in the area, we could climb a convenient pole on Lansdowne Street and swing over into the stands. The primary purpose wasn't to watch the game (we could only do this for a couple of minutes) but to get a cold Knickerbocker beer before the foreman caught us.

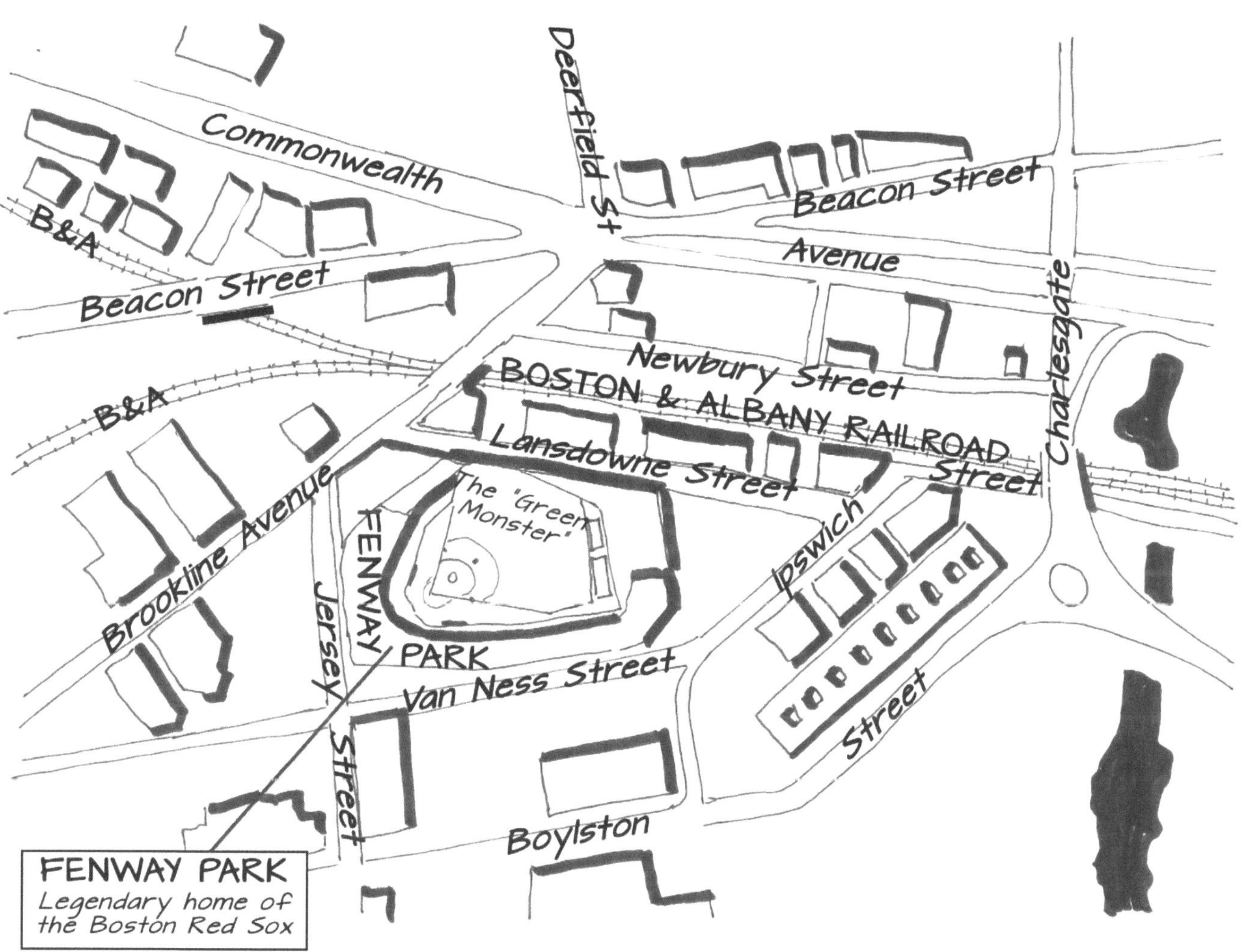

Fenway Park and The Boston & Albany. *Map by David R. Clemens*

Forty Years Ago, Today

Before the specifics, a little background: I've worked all over the country in railroad and supplier/consultant jobs on everything from the shortest short lines to mega-systems; from below sea level to 10,000 feet; from the land of the eternal drizzle (Seattle) to desert summers (120° F) to mountain winters (-50° F); on ratty branches, single track mainlines, multiple-track properties with incredible traffic. On section gangs, in towers, on trains and in headquarters. Mostly signal, but also operating, maintenance-of-way, and once qualified as a rules examiner. Which is not to say I'm any more infallible than the next person stepping up to the lectern. The one thing I've learned is that every railroad does things their way, and there are always exceptions.

From*:* "Is CTC the Only Way to Run a [Model] Railroad? Hell No!"

Hey, amigos,

Forty years ago today, Carol, Christine, and I arrived in Denver and forty years ago tomorrow, I started my first management-position railroad job, on my 29th birthday. Oh, my...

May 1987, a BN track inspector "sets on" his speeder at Washtucna, Washington, on the former SP&S. *Illustration by Kimberly Hoverter Morris based on a Blair Kooistra photograph.*

Sure, not always working in Denver, but it's always been home base, well, also lived in Utah, which was an equally great place to be, but the Rocky Mountains have been home for four decades. Buffalo in the winter, Houston in the summer, but when the project was done, I got to go home to Colorado.

Can't imagine a better place, where we got our daughter through a super university including an incredible year in Europe at the University of Madrid, saw her be involved in international affairs in both the western hemisphere and Europe.

Been involved in a lot of "stuff," guess I din't always make what others might have considered the "correct" decision, but it was MY decision, and there were a couple of "wrong" decisions that I'd probably make again.

Well, hell, forty years is forty years, done it my way, guys...

Mike

May 16, 2006, email to Dave Clemens and Jim Providenza

Mike McLaughlin, Glenwood Springs, Colorado, 2007. *Photograph by Mike's daughter Christine Trigg.*

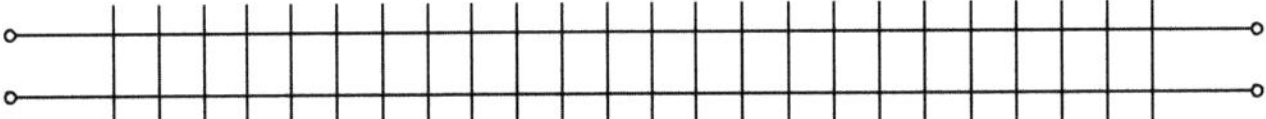

7

ADDENDUM

EXTRA GN 83 EAST

Jim Providenza

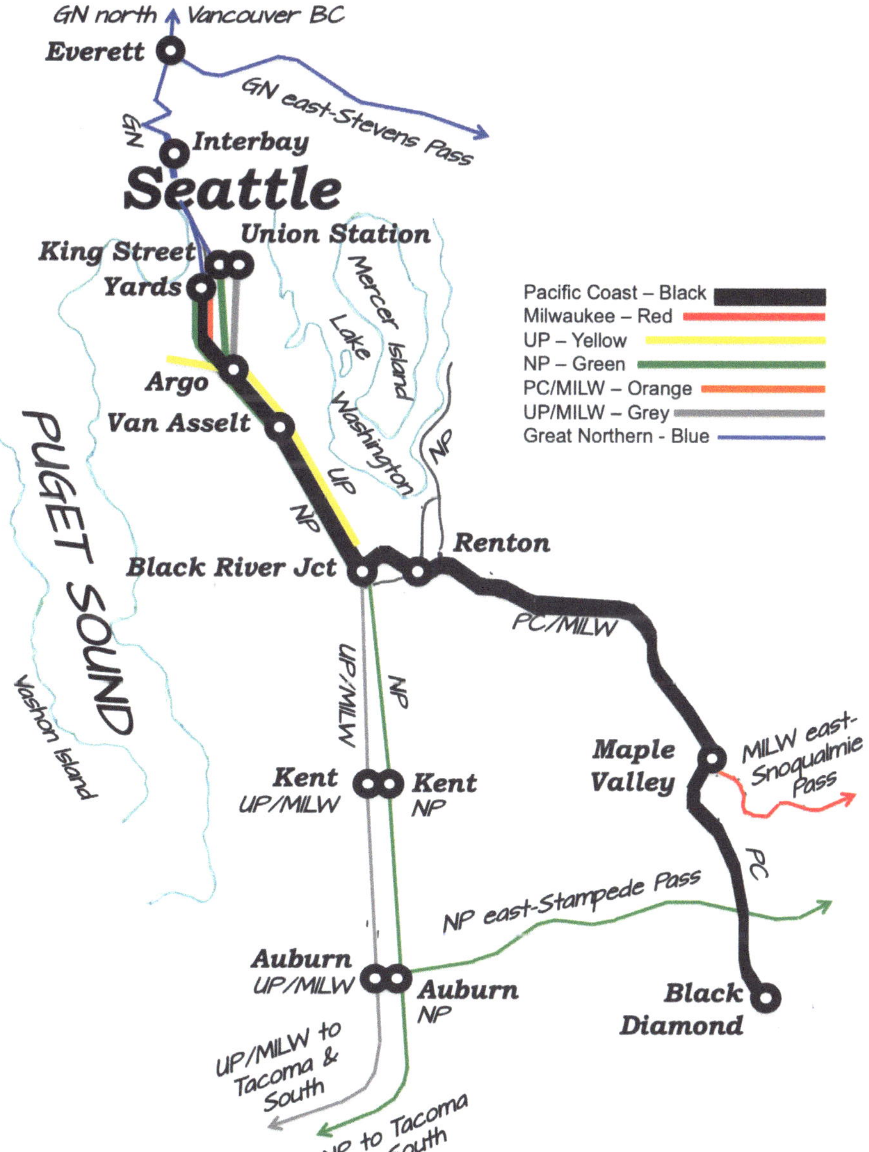

The route of Extra GN 83 East. *Map by David R. Clemens.*

The Pacific Coast Railroad, long a creature of a steamship line, and with a narrow gauge cousin of some repute in Central California, was in essence a coal hauling short line between a large coal wharf on the Seattle waterfront and coal mines some 35 miles inland. But in the way of such things, it hosted the CMStP&P for 23 miles between Maple Valley, WA, and Seattle on electrified track with automatic block signals, which was even double tracked west of Renton, WA. It was bought in 1951 by the Great Northern, which rapidly replaced steam locomotives and composite wood drop bottom gondolas with diesel switchers and steel rolling stock. Other "betterments"—to use a railroad term—followed a bit more slowly…

As he did on any number of occasions on the Seattle area trunk lines, Mike sometimes ended up in a Pacific Coast cab or caboose, befriended by railroaders who recognized another willing victim, smitten with the love of railroading. On at least two occasions he seems to have spent time with Pacific Coast crews as they went about their daily chores.

October 21, 1955, was apparently one such day, and Mike had saved a big chunk of the paper that the Pacific Coast train crew was given as they made their way along the line. Buried deep in a storage box, overlooked by some well-meaning souls helping to "get rid of all this junk" after Mike's death, the handwritten train order forms created with a steel stylus and double-sided carbon paper, and the other railroad paper typed with all-caps billing typewriters, were never intended to last any longer than the day they were issued. That this record survived over 60 years seems on reflection no less than a minor miracle. It allows us to recreate some small bit of "what it was like back in the day," as Mike used to say.

As we dig into the documentation, looking to flesh out what the day was like, we find that back in the day was actually a time of transition for the railroads around Seattle. The "Great Norn," having just purchased the Pacific Coast, was making significant changes in motive power, rolling stock, and facilities. The trunk lines themselves were replacing steam locomotives with new diesels.

The 21st of October was a Friday. The morning was cool, and in fact daytime temps would get no higher than the mid-50s. But contrary to accepted wisdom (and Mike's oft repeated sobriquet of "soggy Sound"), it was not raining. Fog was reported in the morning, but eventually the sun broke through and there was good visibility during the day (*Farmer's Almanac*, Historical Weather Data).

At 7:10 am Train Order Operator Bisiack, who was working at Renton, repeated back the morning Foreman's Train Location, a list of trains expected to run between Van Asselt and Maple Valley before 4:01 pm. This "lineup" was put out by the dispatcher over the authority of the Superintendent, William Coliton, whose initials were "W P C." Our first unanswered question is why Mike included this with the other paper he saved from the day. A lineup was a document issued for section crews, signal maintainers, and other employees who worked along the tracks. It was not issued to or normally used by train crews. Regardless, the lineup gives us a framework to consider the extra's movements.

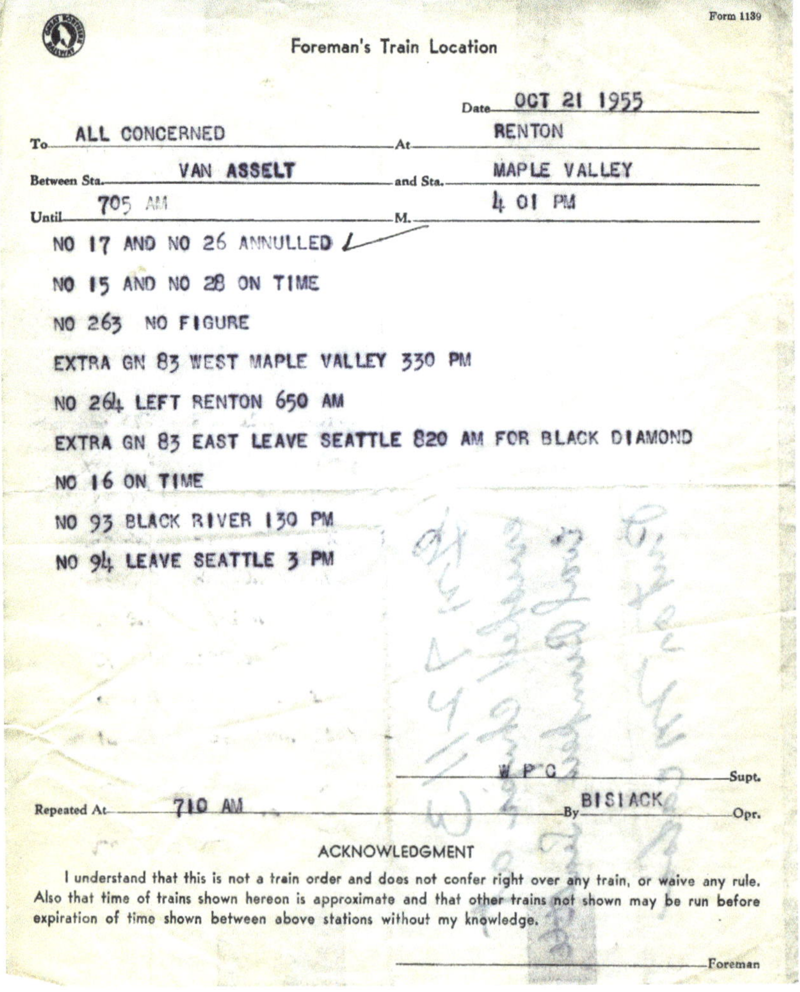
Form 1139

Foreman's Train Location

Date OCT 21 1955

To ALL CONCERNED At RENTON

Between Sta. VAN ASSELT and Sta. MAPLE VALLEY

Until 705 AM M. 4 01 PM

NO 17 AND NO 26 ANNULLED

NO 15 AND NO 28 ON TIME

NO 263 NO FIGURE

EXTRA GN 83 WEST MAPLE VALLEY 330 PM

NO 264 LEFT RENTON 650 AM

EXTRA GN 83 EAST LEAVE SEATTLE 820 AM FOR BLACK DIAMOND

NO 16 ON TIME

NO 93 BLACK RIVER 130 PM

NO 94 LEAVE SEATTLE 3 PM

W P C Supt.

Repeated At 710 AM By BISIACK Opr.

ACKNOWLEDGMENT

I understand that this is not a train order and does not confer right over any train, or waive any rule. Also that time of trains shown hereon is approximate and that other trains not shown may be run before expiration of time shown between above stations without my knowledge.

Foreman

Some scheduled trains are annulled, some trains are on time; at least one—No. 263—the DS has no information ("no figure") on. With the exception of the last two lines, trains are listed by direction with westbound trains listed first. Thus, we find EXTRA GN 83 WEST MAPLE VALLEY 330 PM listed several lines above EXTRA GN 83 EAST LEAVE SEATTLE 820 AM FOR BLACK DIAMOND, even though GN 83 will run as an extra east before it will run as an extra west. We will come back to the lineup shortly.

GN 83 was the last of nine EMD SW1 switchers the GN purchased. Built in 1950, it served the GN and successor BN until it was retired in 1983. In 1955 it would still have been painted in its as-delivered "Simplified Empire Builder" paint scheme of olive green and Omaha orange.

GN 83 at the Pacific Coast Stacy Street Yard in March 1970. *Photograph by Dan Perkins, DRP005-075, PNRArchives collection at Burien, WA.*

The extant paperwork from the crew for Extra GN 83 for October 21st does not include clearances/orders for the run from Seattle to Maple Valley. We have a very good idea of what they would have looked like based on a clearance and orders from 3 days earlier, which were also found in the storage box. That clearance, to C&E Ex GN 83 East at Spokane Street, listed 3 orders for the train: number 3, number 6, and number 430, and was okayed at 8:20 am on October 18th.

Order number 3 annulled two scheduled trains, No. 17 Maple Valley to Argo and No. 26 (its reverse movement to continue to Tacoma) Argo to Black River.

Order number 6 authorized C&E Engine GN 83 to "run extra Argo to Renton" and stated that "all first class trains due Argo at or before 820 am have arrived or left."

Order number 430 was a slow order originally issued on October 12th addressed to C&E Eastward Trains at Spokane Street: "Do not exceed 15 MPH through Argo Interlocking Plant."

Considering the information on the Foreman's Train Location form, we can be sure the crew of the 21st received an order very much like number 3 and they needed a running order similar to number 6. Whether they would have received order 430 depends on the nature of the problem requiring the slow order and whether it would have been corrected in the intervening 3 days. They would also receive another order giving them authority to run from Renton to Maple Valley.

The first clearance and order we do have was issued at 11:30am on October 21, 1955, addressed to Extra GN 83 East at Maple Valley, with one order, number 10.

A PACIFIC COAST R. R. CO. A
CLEARANCE FORM A

1130a M., Oct 21 1955

To CE Exa Gn 83 East at Maple Valley

I have 1 orders for your train.

No. 10 No. No. No. No. No.

No. No. No. No. No. No.

There are no further orders for your train.

Block

OK 1130 am WPC — O'Neil

SUPERINTENDENT — OPERATOR OR SIGNALMAN

FORM PC A1

Order number 10, a particular type of Form G "running order," gave Extra GN 83 East authority to run from Maple Valley to Black Diamond and return to Maple Valley. The order was copied, and the clearance issued, by H. V. O'Neil. Based on the fact he also typed up and gave the crew the following agent's message, it is a reasonable guess that his position at Maple Valley was that of Agent-Operator. In fact, this is not quite correct, as we shall see.

Form PC249½

FORM 19 PACIFIC COAST R. R. CO. FORM 19

TRAIN ORDER No. 10 Oct 21 1955

To CE Eng Gn 83

To

To

To

AT Maple Valley

X OPR.: M.

Eng Gn 83 run Extra Maple Valley to Black Diamond and return to Maple Valley

WPC Supt.

Made Complete Time 1130a M. O'Neil Opr.

CONDUCTOR AND ENGINEMAN MUST EACH HAVE A COPY OF THIS ORDER.

MVALLEY OCT 21 1955

BOW

AT BLACK DIAMOND SPOT 1 GN GOND AT RAMP AND THEY WILL LOAD SOME NUT IN IT AND FINISH LOADING AT BUNKERS. CAR TO COME OUT TODAY FOR SEATTLE.

FROM B DIAMOND UCR 20431-PC 9073-9036-9059-9028-9012-9042-9026-
9064-9017-9033-9043-9016-9025-9056-9071-9001-9055
9069-9047-9040-9002-9066 SEATTLE

CALL YOURSELF AND STEGER FOR MAPLEVALLEY EXA 6.45 AM MONDAY AT LANDER ST.

H V O

Conductor Joe Bow. Seattle Times *photograph, 1947, photo MVHS_PC0080, PNRArchive collection at Burien, WA.*

The agent's message is chock-full of information. The fact that it is given to the crew at Maple Valley tells us the agent there handles freight agent duties for the coal mine at Black Diamond. It is addressed to BOW, and a first guess is that these are the initials of the conductor on Extra GN 83 East. But further digging turns up a contemporary photograph of Pacific Coast Conductor Joe F. Bow sitting at his desk inside a Pacific Coast caboose.

The message is signed HVO, from which we glean the first and middle initials of "Operator" O'Neil. The last line in the message, "Call yourself and Steger for Maple Valley EXA (extra) 6:45 am Monday at Lander St." gives us the last name of the engineer, lets us know they are the regular crew on this job, and that they are next called for duty after the weekend at Lander Street in Seattle. So, is Mr. O'Neil a crew caller as well? In fact, he is much more: Hugh V. O'Neil is the Chief Dispatcher for the Pacific Coast, as testified to by Pacific Coast Dispatcher Train Sheets of the time period. He is working out of his office at the new Pacific Coast depot at Maple Valley. This third Pacific Coast depot at Maple Valley is only two years old in 1955.

Chief Dispatcher Hugh O'Neil on the platform of the second Maple Valley depot in 1944.
Photographer unknown, photo MVHS_PC0057, PNRArchive collection at Burien, WA.

The body of the message also has a lot to tell us about "how it was back in the day." The first line starts out, "At Black Diamond spot 1 GN gond…" Ah, what GN gondola? If you look back at the lineup, you will note there is some handwriting showing through from the back of the page. When you turn it over, it looks like this:

GN 72113
crushed chips at
coal Bunkers Seattle

Put on Meadow

Since the lineup was issued at Renton, Conductor Bow must have picked it up at that station. Did he receive a verbal instruction from Operator Bisiack and write it down on a handy piece of paper—the back of the lineup in Renton? Did he use the form he already had to make a note later in the day?

The 1953 Official Railway Equipment Register (ORER) identifies GN 72113 as one of a series of 400 hoppers, AAR classification HK, "equipped with doors lengthwise to rail." This sounds like a ballast hopper, as opposed to a GS (general service) gondola and so might or might not be the car listed by Agent O'Neil in the message to the Extra GN 83's crew. This leaves us with a second question destined to remain unresolved at this distance: what is the crew supposed to do with GN 72113 at the coal bunkers in Seattle?

Pacific Coast 9065. *Location, date, and photographer unknown, photo WWAPC0567, PNRArchive collection at Burien, WA.*

The rest of the main body of O'Neil's message tells the crew what cars to pull from Diamond Mine to be taken to Seattle. First out is a UCR 20431, a Utah Coal Route gondola. UCR was a jointly-owned subsidiary of the Utah Railway and the Union Pacific Railroad. The car is a 40-foot GS gondola, "coal dump, steel." The 20431 is followed by 22 Pacific Coast cars in the 9000 series. These cars are not listed in the 1953 ORER, but are in a copy from 1961. They are described as "GS, gondola, steel, drop bottom, 40' Capacity 100,000 lb." In 1955 they are almost brand new and had 25 percent more capacity than the old Pacific Coast composite wood/steel cars they replaced.

O'Neil's message says nothing about spotting new cars for loading. Trying to answer several questions that came up, I reached out to Dave Sprau, train dispatcher on the BN and predecessor lines who worked at Maple Valley intermittently from 1970–1980. Dave commented about spotting empties at Black Diamond, "the reason there is nothing in writing about them at Black Diamond is, the crew routinely spotted empty coal gons at the bunkers and at other places there, without being told to do so. It was a part of their job that was completely understood without anything having to be said; empties can be jostled around, just about any place, relying on general knowledge about the correct thing to do and this is one of those cases.

PC steel gondola and GN caboose X1 (the former PC 53) at Pacific Coast Coal Company Black Diamond tipple in 1955. *Photographer unknown, photo WWAPC0463, PNRArchive collection at Burien, WA.*

"Loads are a different matter; they come under all sorts of demurrage and freight rate rules, and really are not supposed to be moved without some kind of authority, even if it is only a message pending being furnished waybills and a list."

Finished with their work at Black Diamond and having returned to Maple Valley on order number 10, the crew received a fistful of new train orders for their return to Seattle with the loaded coal gons:

A PACIFIC COAST R. R. CO. A

CLEARANCE FORM A

430 P M., Oct 21 1955

To C&E Exa Ym 83 West at Maple Valley

I have 4 orders for your train.

No. 12 No. 14 No. 16 No. 18 No. No.

No. No. No. No. No. No.

There are no further orders for your train.

Block

OK 430pm WPC — SUPERINTENDENT

Loveless — OPERATOR OR SIGNALMAN

FORM PC A1

Form PC249½

FORM 19 PACIFIC COAST R. R. CO. FORM 19

TRAIN ORDER No. 12 Oct 21 1955

To C&E Eng Ym 83

To

To

To

AT Maple Valley

X OPR.: M.

Eng Ym 83 run Extra Maple Valley to Argo. All regular trains due at Maple Valley Renton and Black River at or before 245 pm have arrived or left except No 94

WPC Supt.

Made Complete Time 245 pM. O'Neil Opr.

CONDUCTOR AND ENGINEMAN MUST EACH HAVE A COPY OF THIS ORDER.

Form PC249½
FORM 19 PACIFIC COAST R. R. CO. FORM 19

TRAIN ORDER No. 14 Oct 21 1955

To C&E Extra GN 83 West

To

To

To

AT Maple Valley

X ... OPR.: ... M.

All first class trains due at Maple Valley at or before 355 pm have arrived or left

Made Complete Time 355 p M.

CONDUCTOR AND ENGINEMAN MUST EACH HAVE A CO

Form PC249½
FORM 19 PACIFIC COAST R. R. CO. FORM 19

TRAIN ORDER No. 16 Oct 21 1955

To

To C&E Westward trains

To

To

AT Maple Valley

X ... OPR.: ... M.

No 25 due to leave Black River Oct 21st is annulled Black River to Argo

No 18 due to leave Argo Oct 21st is annulled Argo to Maple Valley

WPC Supt.

Made Com Time 425 p M. Loveless Opr.

CONDUCTOR AND ENGINEMAN MUST EACH HAVE A COPY OF THIS OR

Having received the clearance and these 4 orders at 4:30 pm, the crew will recheck the schedule shown in the current time table, Pacific Coast Time Table No. 16 of 1954, to determine if the DS has given them sufficient authority to complete the run to Seattle. We will also look at a copy of the Milwaukee Road Coast Division Time Table No. 28 of 1953, which will help us to better understand some of the Milwaukee train movements. Keep in mind that the Milwaukee time table gave no authority for movement of trains over the Pacific Coast; it is just for information.

Form PC249½

FORM 19 PACIFIC COAST R. R. CO. FORM 19

TRAIN ORDER No. 18 Oct 21 1955

To C&E Extra GN 83 West

To

To

To

AT Maple Valley

X OPR.: M.

Extra GN 83 West has right over Extra CMStP&P 2440 East Maple Valley to Renton

WPC Supt.

Made Com Time 4 20 p M. Loveless Opr.

CONDUCTOR AND ENGINEMAN MUST EACH HAVE A COPY OF THIS ORDER.

THIRD SUBDIVISION EASTWARD 5

Time Table No. 28 JAN. 15, 1953 STATIONS	Distance from Tacoma	See Rule 6-A	Office Hours Also see page 15	FIRST CLASS			SECOND CLASS			
				52	16	18	84	264	94	82
				U. P. R. R. Passenger 457	Passenger	Passenger	U. P. R. R. Time Freight 691	Time Freight	Way Freight	U. P. R. R. Time Freight 681
				Daily	Daily	Daily	Daily	Daily	Daily Except Sunday	Daily
SEATTLE	37.6	P	Via U. P. R. R.		2.30PM	10.00PM				
STACY ST. YARD -0.7-	36.6	BKORTV WXZP							12.50PM	
SPOKANE ST. TOWER -1.7-	35.9		Via P. C. R. R.						12.45	
ARGO (U. P. CROSSING) (N. P. CROSSING) -1.7-	34.2	IP	Via P. C. R. R.		2.18	9.39			12.35	
VAN ASSELT -4.3-	32.5	P				9.36			12.30	
BLACK RIVER (N. P. CROSSING) -6.9-	28.2	IJPRVXY	Continuous	A 11.42AM	A 2.10PM	A 9.29PM	A 4.10AM	A 4.55AM	A 12.20PM	A 7.30PM
KENT -5.0-	21.3	PX	7.45 AM to 4.45 PM Except Sat. & Sun.	11.34	2.01	f 9.20	3.56	4.42	12.05PM	7.10
AUBURN -4.6-	16.3	PX	7.00 AM to 11:00 PM Except Sat. & Sun.	94 **11.28**	1.54	f 9.12	3.45	4.32	15-52 **11.30** **11.15**	83 **6.50**
BENROY -2.5-	11.7	P	No Office	15 **11.23**		9.06	3.35	4.22	11.05	6.35
SUMNER -1.7-	9.2	PWX	7.00 AM to 9.15 PM Except Sat., Sun. and Mondays	11.20	1.45	s 9.02	3.28	4.16	11.00 10.00	6.25
NORTH PUYALLUP -5.5-	7.5	P	No Office	11.17	1.42	f 8.58	3.23	4.12	9.55	263 **6.15**
TACOMA JCT. -2.0-	2.0	JKPRVX	Continuous	L 11.11AM	1.36	8.51	L 3.10AM	L 4.00AM	L 9.40AM	L 6.05PM
TACOMA	0.0	BKPRVX	6.00 AM to 10.00 PM Except Sat. & Sun.		L 1.30PM	L 8.45PM				

Passenger trains must not exceed a maximum speed of 70 MPH. Other trains 50 MPH.

Third Subdivision schedule, Chicago Milwaukee St. Paul & Pacific Railroad Coast Division Time Table No. 28

Order number 12, made complete at 2:45 pm, gives Extra GN 83 West the authority to run from Maple Valley to Argo. It is also a register check, telling the crew that all regular trains (trains listed on the timetable schedule) due at the junctions at Maple Valley (Milwaukee Road), Renton (NP) and Black River (UP), have arrived or left except second class eastward train No. 94. Even though it is a completed order, it has no effect until delivered to the crew via a clearance.

Order No. 14, completed at 3:55 pm, is a further register check, and lets the crew know that all first class trains (presumably including CMStP&P train 16) due at Maple Valley at 3:55 pm have arrived or left.

Dave Sprau explained the dispatcher's reason for issuing these two orders when he did: "The register check in order 12 informs of the passing of superior trains at the time the order was issued. No radios or other communication in those days, so O'Neil probably did not know for sure when X 83 west would come down the hill into MV (Maple Valley), and so he had order number 12 ready at 2:45 pm. No. 16 is due at Renton 3:38 pm, Indian 3:46 pm, Maple Valley at 3:53 pm, and the possibility existed that X83, if it arrived MV at say 2:50 or 3:00 pm, could have gone to Renton or Indian for No. 16, or at least would have seen them pass MV. But that didn't happen, so O'Neil issued order No. 14 after No. 16 passed, to take care of that situation."

2

EASTWARD

CAR CAPACITY			SECOND CLASS			FIRST CLASS					FIRST SUBDIVISION TIME TABLE No. 16 Effective November 14, 1954	
			86 C.M.St.P. &P Daily	94 C.M.St.P. &P Daily Except Sunday	264 C.M.St.P. &P Daily	18 C.M.St.P. &P Daily	16 C.M.St.P. &P Daily	28 C.M.St.P. &P Daily	26 C.M.St.P. &P Daily			
Siding	Other Tracks									Distance from Seattle	STATIONS	Telegraph Calls
Yard	500	....	....	....	....	....	....	....	....	0.0	SEATTLE Main Street 2.0	....
Yard	0	....	....	L 2:05 PM	....	....	....	....	....	2.0	SPOKANE STREET TOWER N. P. Crossing 1.4	....
0	0	....	....	2:10	....	L 9:25 PM	L 3:23 PM	L 9:53 AM	L 8:29 AM	3.4	ARGO TOWER N. P. and U. P. Crossings 2.0	G
CMSt P&P YARD		....	L 4:30 PM	2:15	L 4:45 AM	9:28	3:26	9:56	8:32	5.4	VAN ASSELT 4.3	....
0	13	....	A 4:40 PM	A 2:45 PM	5:15	9:34	3:31	A 10:01 AM	A 8:40 AM	9.7	BLACK RIVER U. P. Crossing 2.4	BI
70	200	....	....	....	5:25	s 9:41	263 s 3:38	....	....	12.1	RENTON N. P. Crossing 3.4	RN
0	0	....	....	....	5:38	....	....	....	....	15.5	ELLIOTT 1.7	....
95	0	....	....	....	5:45	9:50	3:46	....	....	17.2	INDIAN 1.3	....
0	5	....	....	....	5:49	....	....	....	....	18.5	CEDAR MOUNTAIN 3.8	....
79	17	....	....	....	A 6:00 AM	A 9:59 PM	A 3:53 PM	....	....	22.3	MAPLE VALLEY	DS
			.10 25.8	.40 11.5	1.15 12.8	.34 33.4	.30 37.8	.08 47.4	.11 34.4		Time Over Subdivision Average Speed per Hour	

DOUBLE TRACK (Spokane Street Tower to Renton)

AUTOMATIC BLOCK SIGNALS (Argo Tower to Maple Valley)

EASTWARD TRAINS ARE SUPERIOR TO WESTWARD TRAINS OF THE SAME CLASS.

EASTWARD

CAR CAPACITY		SECOND CLASS									SECOND SUBDIVISION TIME TABLE No. 16 Effective November 14, 1954	
Siding	Other Tracks									Distance from Maple Valley	STATIONS	Telegraph Calls
79	17	....	....	....	....	....	....	....	....	0.0	MAPLE VALLEY 4.6	DS
	7	....	....	....	....	....	....	....	....	4.6	DANVILLE 1.0	....
	10	....	....	....	....	....	....	....	....	5.6	HENRYS 2.0	....
Yard	Yard	....	....	....	....	....	....	....	....	7.6	BLACK DIAMOND	....
			....	....	....	....	....	....	....		Time Over Subdivision Average Speed per Hour	

EASTWARD TRAINS ARE SUPERIOR TO WESTWARD TRAINS OF THE SAME CLASS.

Pacific Coast Railroad Employee Time Table No. 16 schedule.

WESTWARD

3

FIRST SUBDIVISION TIME TABLE No. 16 Effective November 14, 1954 STATIONS		Distance from Maple Valley	FIRST CLASS 17 C.M.St.P. &P Daily	15 C.M.St.P. &P Daily	27 C.M.St.P. &P Daily	25 C.M.St.P. &P Daily	SECOND CLASS 85 C.M.St.P. &P Daily	93 C.M.St.P. &P Daily Except Sunday	263 C.M.St.P. &P Daily		Signs
SEATTLE Main Street 2.0		22.3	....	....	....	....	....	....	....	....	PBRVZXJ
SPOKANE STREET TOWER N. P. Crossing 1.4	DOUBLE TRACK	20.3	....	....	....	....	....	A 12:45 PM	....	....	DNPIJV
ARGO TOWER N. P. and U. P. Crossings 2.0	DOUBLE TRACK; AUTOMATIC BLOCK SIGNALS	18.9	A 7:35 AM	A 9:13 AM	A 2:48 PM	A 8:24 PM	....	12:35	....	....	DNPIJV
VAN ASSELT 4.3	DOUBLE TRACK; AUTOMATIC BLOCK SIGNALS	16.9	7:30	9:08	2:45	8:21	A 4:40 AM	12:30	A 4:10 PM	....	PX
BLACK RIVER U. P. Crossing 2.4	DOUBLE TRACK; AUTOMATIC BLOCK SIGNALS	12.6	7:20	8:58	L 2:40 PM	L 8:14 PM	L 4:30 AM	L 12:20 PM	4:01	....	DNPBIJRVX
RENTON N. P. Crossing 3.4	DOUBLE TRACK; AUTOMATIC BLOCK SIGNALS	10.2	s 7:15	s 8:53	....	....	....	....	16 **3:38**	....	DPBRXZYI
ELLIOTT 1.7	AUTOMATIC BLOCK SIGNALS	6.8	....	....	....	....	....	....	3:20	....	P
INDIAN 1.3	AUTOMATIC BLOCK SIGNALS	5.1	7:07	8:43	....	....	....	....	3:16	....	P
CEDAR MOUNTAIN 3.8	AUTOMATIC BLOCK SIGNALS	3.8	....	....	....	....	....	....	2:58	....	P
MAPLE VALLEY	AUTOMATIC BLOCK SIGNALS	0.0	L 7:00 AM	L 8:35 AM	....	....	....	....	L 2:50 PM	....	DNPBJ KRVX
Time Over Subdivision Average Speed per Hour			.35 32.4	.38 29.8	.08 47.4	.10 37.8	.10 25.8	.25 18.5	1.20 12.6		

EASTWARD TRAINS ARE SUPERIOR TO WESTWARD TRAINS OF THE SAME CLASS.

WESTWARD

Distance from Maple Valley	SECOND SUBDIVISION TIME TABLE No. 16 Effective November 14, 1954 STATIONS					SECOND CLASS				Signs
0.0	MAPLE VALLEY 4.6	....	....	....	....	....	....	....	....	DNPBJKRVX
4.6	DANVILLE 1.0	....	....	....	....	....	....	....	....	P
5.6	HENRYS 2.0				....	....	....	....	....	V
7.6	BLACK DIAMOND	....	....	....	....	....	....	....	....	XP
	Time Over Subdivision Average Speed per Hour	....	....	....	....	....	....	....		

EASTWARD TRAINS ARE SUPERIOR TO WESTWARD TRAINS OF THE SAME CLASS.

Order No. 16 informs the crew, and any other westward trains at Maple Valley, that train No. 25 is annulled Black River to Argo, and its opposite movement, No. 18 is annulled Argo to Maple Valley. No waiting around at Maple Valley for trains that will not run! The Columbian, trains No. 17 and No. 18, has been discontinued on this part of the Milwaukee Road—between Avery, Idaho and Tacoma, Washington—since January of this year. Train No. 25 was No. 18's train from Tacoma where it runs "westward" over the PC from Black River to Argo. Leaving the PC at Argo, it went into Seattle Union Station over the UP. Departing from Seattle on the UP, it runs as No. 18 on the PC from Argo to the connection with the Milwaukee main at Maple Valley to head east—before it was discontinued. Annulling orders for the schedules listed in the current timetable is a daily occurrence until a new timetable with a revised schedule takes effect. Retired dispatcher Sprau offered a further insight: "O'Neil apparently thought X83 West would be into Seattle and tied up long before No. 25 was due at Black River, and he probably was correct, but obviously Dispatcher Loveless erred on the side of caution and wisely issued order No. 16 as a precaution. Better that X83W have it and not need it, than need it and not have it."

Train order 18 was issued 10 minutes before the Clearance Form A was okayed by the dispatcher and gives Extra GN 83 West "right over" Extra CMStP&P 2440 East between Maple Valley and the beginning of double track at Renton. CMStP&P 2440 is a nearly new EMD GP9, built in June 1954.

Sprau again: "Extra CMStP&P 2440 East is destined east of Maple Valley; and per standard procedure for eastward Milwaukee freight trains, Dispatcher Loveless needs to issue a running order via the Milwaukee's operator at Tacoma Junction for this train to run extra from Black River to Maple Valley. In order to do this without improper conflict between the two opposing extras, order No. 18 was issued giving X GN 83 West, which undoubtedly would arrive Renton far ahead of X 2440 E, right of track to that point - where double track rules take over, and since each train will then be on a separate track, no conflict exists between there and Black River."

With these orders in hand the crew has to confirm the status of No. 94. A caveat is in order at this point. The schedules of the two different railroads are oriented differently, if one may use the term in such a fashion. On the Pacific Coast, "railroad east" is away from Seattle; west is toward the city. CMStP&P Time Table No. 28 for the Milwaukee Third Subdivision defines east as toward Seattle from Tacoma; the move from Seattle to Tacoma is considered a westbound movement.

From CMStP&P Time Table No. 28 we learn that No. 93/94 is a daily except Sunday Tacoma (Tide Flats Yard) to Stacy Street Yard (Seattle) and return Second Class Way Freight. It is scheduled to depart Tacoma at 9:41 am, join the PC at Black River at 11:42 and arrive at the Milwaukee's Stacy Street Yard at 12:50 pm. It departs Stacy Street for Tacoma at 2:00 pm, Black River Jct. at 2:45 pm and arrives at Tacoma at 5:00 pm… if it is on time. The times, train numbers and direction of trains 93/94 shown in the CMStP&P time table are "for information only"—it is the Pacific Coast time table that is in effect between Maple Valley and Stacy Street as is confirmed on copies of Pacific Coast Dispatcher's Record of Train Movements (Train Sheet) from the time period.

So, the crew of Extra GN 83 West is potentially concerned with the movement of No. 94 only from Spokane Street Tower (where CMStP&P freights to/from Stacy Street Yard join the PC) to Black River Jct., as No. 94 is on the schedule only between those two stations. Since Black River Jct. is on the double track portion of the Pacific Coast and the crew of Extra GN 83 West presumably would not have to worry about eastbound movements, they should be free to depart. At Renton they will get on the double track for the rest of the way to Seattle, assuming they have no further work along the way. But as Dave Sprau points out: "Of course at Renton in the single track zone, or at Black River on a switch move if X 83 W has to cross over or otherwise occupy the 'other main track,' then they DO have to be concerned about OPPOSING superior trains on that track."

Since Extra GN 83 West got no helping orders against No. 94, there apparently was no conflict anticipated between the two trains. Extra GN 83 West can head to Renton, ducking under the classic wooden covered bridge at Allentown and then ride the double track to the PC yard at Seattle.

But what if… Extra GN 83 West does have work at Renton? This was quite common, and this PC local was often referred to as "The Renton Rocket" for just that reason. Refer back to the Dispatcher's Record of Train Movements shown in Chapter 13, A Day on the Pacific Coast. On that day in 1952, the crew spent over four hours switching the industries at Renton and another 45 minutes at the interchange at Black River. They finally got back to Stacy Street at 10:40 pm after being on duty for almost 14 hours.

Would the fistful of orders "our" crew now has have covered such an eventuality on this particular Friday? Most likely. Arriving at Renton with work to do, they will immediately get off the main track—they "had right over" and thus were superior to the opposing Extra CMStP&P 2440 East up to Renton, but not at Renton. If they have several hours of work at Renton, and then have to work any of the interchanges with the four trunk lines at Black River Jct. (if that requires they cross over to the eastward main track), they need to determine if No. 94 has gone by Black River Jct. How will they know this? Black River Jct. is a register station (note the letter R among the other letters in the far right column of the schedule page of PC Time Table No. 16, which signifies trains will sign a register book as they pass this location.) They will physically check the register book to make sure No. 94 has passed by before doing any work at Renton or Black River Jct.

The crew's next concern would have been No. 25 and No. 18. This is where Order 16 may come into play. Since these trains have been annulled, Conductor Bow knows that he does not have to take them into his planning for his eventual return to Stacy Street Yard, regardless of whether or not the crew has work to do in Renton and Black River Jct.

Eventually the crew will tie their train down in the yard in Seattle and park GN 83 by the yard office. The Pacific Coast switch job will take care of spotting the inbound cars. The coal in the gondola cars will make its way to the PC coal wharf for transloading into a ship or perhaps to the University of Washington, another Black Diamond coal customer.

A coal collier, Pacific Coast coal wharf and loading tower, and a composite steel and wood coal gondola pose for Tom Krontz at Pier 43 on a typical "soggy Sound" March 31, 1951. Almost everything in the photo will be gone within the next two years. *Photograph by Tom Krontz, P11.14.77, Maple Valley Historical Society collection, Burien WA.*

On July 30, 1973, Dave Stanley photographed Operator Ted Pope at work at Tacoma Junction. While the motive power and the typewriter have changed from those used in 1955, the method of authorizing train movements on this portion of the Milwaukee Road and Pacific Coast RR has not.

We can follow the procedures that had been ongoing here since the 1920s—the operator copying a train order for an eastbound freight as it was dictated by the Pacific Coast Dispatcher at Maple Valley and then hanging the train order delivery forks—and we can stand with Dave "as the head end crew and then the rear man pick up their orders on the fly at sunset before hitting Snoqualmie Pass for a night run east."

3032
3032

Salt Lake City, Utah
September 14, 1968

Mr. O.B. Thornton,
Train Dispatcher,
Roper, Utah

Formal investigation will be held in the Conference Room, Utah Division Office Building, Roper, Utah, at 3.00PM, Monday, September 16, 1968, to develop facts and place responsibility, if any, in connection with Motor Car SL A-221 being struck in the vicinity of the West Switch at Kyune by Extra East 3051 at about 3.00PM, September 13, 1968.

Your presence as a principal is required at this investigation, together with representative of your choice if desired.

Richard E. Davis
Superintendent

Receipt acknowledged:

____

CC:-Mr. M.J. McLaughlin
Track Supervisor - Helper

Please arrange to attend as a witness.

RED

8

ADDENDUM

THE LOST MOTOR CAR STORY

Jim Providenza and Dave Clemens

We were each of us certain we had a copy of the story Mike wrote to us about his wrecked motor car. Positive, in fact. Unh huh... But in truth we never could find it, either on paper or in an email. We believed this story was about the second motor car that Mike "lost" on the Rio Grande. Struck by a train, someone screwed up... but we don't really know—assuming Mike did write it—which accident it was about. Because, you see, it happened to Mike twice.

At one point in some correspondence, Dave Clemens asked Mike, "You don't happen to recall what you were doing that particular day, do you?"

Mike replied in a May 6, 2010, email, "Hell no, but most likely horsing that goddam motorcar over Soldier Summit; since it was May, wondering if it's ever gonna warm up; checking the track for broken bolts and other problems; wondering if I could just happen to be where a section gang was working at lunch time; examining switches... and waiting interminably for trains.

"Got blocks in CTC territory (but remember I got my first motor car hit while having a valid CTC block), figgered running times based on lineup information in ABS (but remember I got my second motor car hit when a student dispatcher made an error on the lineup), and waited a hell of a lot. Also helped to know the foibles of the various dispatchers. The worst DS on the road never got anyone into a jackpot because everybody knew he was a flake and triple checked *everything* he did."

Based on Mike's comment that he had lost his first motor car while running in CTC territory, this is the accident referenced in the September 1968 letter on page 224. Kyune was smack in the middle of the CTC territory between Helper and Soldier Summit. From his reply to Dave, Mike's second motor car got hit on a May morning and was in ABS signaled territory. So, this second collision occurred somewhere between Gilluly and Thistle, west of Soldier Summit—the line was automatic block signal territory between those two points at the time.

In a postscript to a 1992 letter to Jim Providenza, Mike added, "Found a couple of extra prints of my *last* motor car after a right-of-track dispute with the Helper local just west of Thistle. The local won. A long story, not to mention the one hit at Kyune, and the one almost hit at Castle Gate." And another time, "And how come good ol' rules-examiner-qualified me had *two* punted into left field, to mix a metaphor?"

The accident we do have at least some second-hand knowledge of is through Mike's daughter, Christine Trigg, as well as from a few comments he made at various times.

Mike bailed out in time to avoid being hit himself, and felt lucky that all he ended up with was a hole in his leg from a rough landing along the right of way. The motor car itself wasn't so lucky, of course. Christine vividly remembers his injury, and told us there were a number of pictures of the wrecked motor car. Where are they now? We don't know.

Christine told us: "What you have written down is about what I remember as well. I remember him saying that he looked around [a curve] and saw the light from the engine and knew the only thing he could do was leap from the motor car. He said the train was not where it was supposed to be. I remember asking him if there had also been a derailment.

"I can picture the mangled, yellow car from visiting the train yard. I also recall that my dad actually found his lunch box/dinner pail wedged inside the wreckage. I wish I was a talented artist and could draw it for you!"

With a comment like that, we asked Kim Morris for help…

Having been sent a scan of Kim's sketch, Christine replied, "The motor car is perfect because it wasn't wrecked beyond recognition…just crumpled. And thank you for including the lunch pail. I am certain my dad would be quite pleased with this depiction!"

As Mike concluded in 2009 about a motor car "stuffed and mounted" at the depot museum at Ritzville, Washington: "Better parked by the depot than out on line being punted down the track by a predatory freight!"

The artist's depiction of the wrecked motor car. *Illustration by Kimberly Hoverter Morris.*

9

CABOOSE

Rock Island Train 162, Calmar, Iowa, 1964. *Photograph by Philip R. Hastings, Philip Ross Hastings, MD, collection, California State Railroad Museum.*

Glossary and Abbreviations

Many of the terms and abbreviations listed here are still in general use in the railroad industry. It is indicated where terms are specific to the 1950-1980s timeframe that this book centers on.

16 Hour Law: *see* Hours of Service

AAR/Association of American Railroads: a trade organization formed in 1932.

ABS/Automatic Block System: A system using signals along the right-of-way to keep distance between trains and to prevent a following train from running into the train ahead of it.

ACI System: A colored bar code system for tracking railcars across the North America. Developed by General Telephone & Electronics, it was required for use on railcars starting in 1967. The initials stood for **A**utomatic **C**ar **I**dentification and, while its marketing name was "KarTrak," the system was most often called by the initials ACI. It was not successful and its use was discontinued by 1977.

Air Test: Train brakes are controlled by the engineer, using compressed air. An air test is made by the engineer "applying the brakes" from his air brake control stand in the locomotive while employees physically walk the train to check that the brake shoes on each car have made contact with the wheels.

ammeter: An instrument for measuring electric current. Diesel-electric locomotives are equipped with ammeters to determine the current draw of the traction motors. To be "in the red" is to have traction motors drawing an excessive amount of current which, if continued for a specific amount of time, will cause damage to the motors. Similar to red-lining on a car's tachometer.

ATSF/AT&SF/Atchison, Topeka and Santa Fe Railroad: Often called "the Santa Fe," the ATSF was formed in 1859 and merged into the Burlington Northern Santa Fe (BNSF) railroad in 1996. One of the largest railroads of its time, it ran from Chicago to Los Angeles and San Francisco through the Southwest.

B&B Gang: Group of railroad employees responsible for maintenance of bridges and buildings.

BCE/British Columbia Electric Railway: Operated in the southern portion of the Canadian province of British Columbia between 1897 and 1958.

beanery: A restaurant, sometimes financially supported by a railroad, usually open 24 hours, where railroaders can get a meal at any time.

beans: Slang for food or to eat, as in "going to beans."

Big G: Nickname for the Great Northern Railroad.

blue flag: A blue flag placed on a piece of rolling stock warning employees that other employees were working on the equipment. The car was not to be moved or coupled to until the blue flag had been removed by the employee (or a member of his/her craft) who had placed it on the rolling stock.

bootleg: A bootleg ground connects the neutral side of the electrical receptacle to the conductive metallic casing of an appliance or lamp. This can be a hazard because the neutral wire is a current-carrying conductor, which means the exposed casing can become energized.

Boston & Albany Railroad: Running from 1867–1968, a New York Central subsidiary which allowed the New York Central to access New England via Boston, Massachusetts.

brace and bit: In the days before power drills were suitable for use in the field, linemen had to use a "brace and bit": a combination of a crank turned by hand with a chuck on one end and a round base on the other to drill holes.

brass: Slang for management.

BRT/Brotherhood of Railroad Trainmen: A union formed in 1883; it became part of the United Transportation Union in 1969.

brush hook: A tool resembling an axe with a 12- to 16-inch curved blade and a 3- to 4-foot-long handle, used to clear heavy brush and undergrowth from along the railroad right-of-way.

build: To create the physical plant of the railroad from one place to another. This includes grading the right-of-way, laying track, and building all supporting structures, such as bridges, depots, and roundhouses.

C&S/Colorado & Southern Railroad: A subsidiary of the Chicago, Burlington & Quincy Railroad, which operated in Colorado, Oklahoma, and—through its own subsidiary the Fort Worth & Denver—Texas from 1898–1970, when it was absorbed into the new Burlington Northern Railroad.

CB&Q/Chicago, Burlington & Quincy Railroad/"the Q": Founded in 1848, for the majority of the 20th century the CB&Q was jointly owned by the Great Northern and Northern Pacific railroads. Serving the Midwest, it became part of the Burlington Northern Railroad in 1970.

cabeese, crummy: Slang for caboose.

call board: A large board, using either chalk or moveable blocks, that maintains a roster of active employees in a particular occupation and the jobs available for that position. As employees at the top of the list complete a job to which they have been assigned, their names are rotated to the bottom of the board to eventually work their way back to the top and a new job assignment.

car knocker: A railroad employee who inspects or repairs rolling stock, so-called because he uses a hammer to tap or knock on truck assemblies and other metal parts to check their soundness.

cat head: Slang used by Mike McLaughlin, meaning fused cut-out. This is not a common slang term used by linemen to describe a fused cut-out and may have been a local or D&RGW-specific slang term.

chat ballast: Chat is a gravel-like waste product created by crushing ore or other rock. Chat ballast is ballast using chat.

class rate: A shipping rate where a single price applies to any of a number of similar commodities.

classification tracks: A railroad yard has specific tracks designed and used for specific purposes such as arrival/departure tracks, repair-in-place tracks, and classification tracks. Classification tracks are the tracks on which cars arriving in one train are sorted into other departing trains based on their next/final destination.

clearance: A document issued by the train dispatcher authorizing a train to leave its initial or an intermediate station and which may officially deliver one or more train orders to the train crew.

CMStP&P/Chicago, Milwaukee, St. Paul & Pacific Railroad: also known as MILW or Milwaukee Road, operated in the Midwest and Northwest from 1847 to 1986.

CN/Canadian National Railway: Formed as a Crown Corporation by the Canadian Government in 1919 to take over several bankrupt Canadian railroads. Like its major competitor the Canadian Pacific, CN serves all of Canada and parts of the United States. It was privatized in 1995.

comptometer: The first commercially successful key-driven mechanical calculator. Patented in 1887, comptometers were produced until the mid-1970s.

cow and calf: A pair of switch engines, semi-permanently paired together; the "cow" has a cab with controls while the "calf" is cab-less.

CP/Canadian Pacific Railway: 1875 to present. Like its major competitor, the Canadian National, it serves all of Canada and parts of the United States.

CRI&P/Chicago, Rock Island & Pacific Railroad: Also known as Rock Island, served the Midwest from 1847–1980.

critter: Slang for a small internal combustion locomotive used for industrial switching. Often of indeterminate origin.

crutch: On some railroads, the name for handwritten personal notes on a timetable to aid an employee in estimating the time that various types of trains will take to travel from one location to another.

CTC/Centralized Traffic Control: A system of authorizing the movement of trains using signals spaced along a main line which are controlled remotely from a central location.

cut in the air: The act of connecting the air brake hose of a locomotive to that of a car or cars and opening hose valves to allow compressed air from the locomotive to charge the air brake system in the cars.

cut lever: A rod connected to a coupler which, when operated, opens the coupler to disconnect coupled cars.

demurrage: A fee payable by a customer to a railroad for failure to load or unload a freight car in the allotted free time after the car was spotted at the customer's industry.

direction: *see* railroad direction

Dispatcher's Record of Train Movements: Also known as the "train sheet," the dispatcher's official record of all train and equipment moves over a division.

doodlebug: Slang for a gas-mechanical or gas-electric powered passenger car designed to replace steam-powered local passenger trains.

double the hill: The act of splitting a train into two parts and moving it up a grade one part at a time when the locomotive pulling the train does not have enough power to make it up the grade in one trip.

drag/drag freight: A low-priority train which will take longer to travel over the main line and may have switching work to do.

D&RGW/Denver & Rio Grande Western Railroad, aka the Rio Grande: Originally started as a 3-foot narrow gauge railroad in 1870 and converted to standard gauge about 10 years later, it ran between Denver, Colorado, and Salt Lake City, Utah. It merged with the Southern Pacific Railroad in 1988.

D&SL/Denver & Salt Lake Railroad: Formed in 1902 to build directly west from Denver through the Rocky Mountains. Acquired by the Rio Grande in 1934, the D&SL via Dotsero Cutoff significantly reduced route miles for transcontinental traffic from Denver to the west coast.

DS: The train dispatcher who is responsible for and controls the safe movement of trains over a section of the railroad.

dwarf signal: A signal mounted low to the ground used in yards or sidings to indicate the direction of a turnout or to give authority to proceed.

dynamic braking: Using the momentum of the train and the kinetic energy of the turning wheels of a diesel-electric locomotive to drive its traction motors as generators to create electrical energy that is dissipated through a resistance grid, creating heat; this activity, in turn, slows the train.

Employee Time Table/ETT: A document containing the schedule and additional operational information. The schedule lists all trains operated regularly (i.e., "daily" "daily except Sunday") and the list of stations and their locations (mile posts). The schedule grants authority for the movement of the trains so listed.

flag protection: When a train is stopped on the mainline and needs to be protected from possible following and/or approaching trains, a crew member acting as the "flagman" will take flagging equipment (red flag/lantern, fusees, and track torpedoes) and walk from his train a specified distance in the direction needed. He places the torpedoes on the track and stands with a red flag and/or a lighted red fusee to stop any approaching train.

flanger/flanging: Plow or element of a plow used for removing snow and ice from between rails; the act of doing so.

flat wheel: A wheel that has a flat spot worn in the tread due to excessive braking in which the wheel slid along the rail.

FM/Fairbanks, Morse Co.: A minority builder of diesel locomotives. From 1945 to 1963, it built railroad locomotives with its proprietary opposed piston two-cycle diesel engine, which had been used extensively in US submarines during World War II.

fused cutout: A combination of fuse and switch used in an electrical distribution network to protect transformers or other devices from power surges and overloads.

fusee: A flare with a spike in one end to allow it to stand upright. It is used by a flagman as a warning or "stop" signal to an approaching train. The spike allows the fusee to be dropped from a slow-moving caboose and land upright between the rails so it can be clearly seen.

gandy/gandy dancer: Nickname for a member of a maintenance-of-way section gang. The name supposedly came from the Gandy Tool Company, which made a range of maintenance-of-way tools used by section gang members, and the coordinated movements the gang members needed to use to manually maintain track. Interestingly, there is no hard evidence of the existence of the Gandy Tool Co.

geep (pronounced "jeep"): A four-axle locomotive manufactured by the Electromotive Division (EMD) of General Motors, having a model number starting with the initials GP for General Purpose (GP7, GP9, GP40, et al.).

GN/Great Northern Railroad: The northernmost of the US transcontinental railroads, the GN ran from St. Paul, Minnesota, to Seattle, Washington. Incorporated in 1878, it merged with the other "Hill Roads" in 1970 to form the Burlington Northern.

gondola/gondola freight car: a freight car with a floor, sides, and ends, but no roof.

GS gondola: a type of gondola freight car with fixed sides and ends and a series of trap doors in the floor that allow the car to carry such things as coal or gravel, which can be dumped, as well as more common items such as wood or steel beams. The initials "GS" was one of a series of initials used to define specific types of railroad cars. All of these definitions were spelled out in an appendix to the Official Railroad Equipment Register (*see* ORER).

Harry Bedwell stories: Harry Bedwell (1888–1955) was a railroader and railroad fiction author. His popular "Eddie Sand" stories, featuring a railroad telegrapher, often appeared in *Railroad Magazine*. His novel, *The Boomer*, published in 1942, is considered by many to be the best railroad novel ever published.

head end traffic: Express, mail, LCL packages and baggage that move in specialized cars at the head end of a passenger train.

head room: The length of track past the points of a switch needed for a locomotive with or without cars, to clear the switch so that it can be lined from one track to the other.

high ball: A signal to proceed, named after the earliest signals in which balls were raised on masts to indicate authority to proceed.

Hill Roads: Railroads in the Pacific Northwest, Intermountain West, and Midwest under the control of or associated with James J. Hill: Great Northern RR; Northern Pacific RR; Spokane, Portland & Seattle RR; Chicago, Burlington & Quincy RR; Colorado & Southern RR; and Fort Worth & Denver RR. These railroads were merged together to form the Burlington Northern Railroad in 1970.

hoghead: Slang term for a locomotive engineer, regardless of the equipment being driven (steam, diesel, or electric locomotive).

hotshot: A train with the highest priority to get over the road.

hours of service: Federal law regulating the maximum hours railroad employees are allowed to work continuously without rest. The number of hours vary depending on the employee's job and have changed over the years. Until the 1970s, train and engine crews were allowed to work up to 16 hours without a break, thus the "16 hour law."

house car: A railroad freight car with a floor, four sides, and a roof, and with side or end doors, for lading requiring protection from the weather. House cars include boxcars and refrigerator cars.

hump: A portion of a freight yard which has a grade to permit cars to roll into classifications tracks without being shoved by a locomotive.

ICC/Interstate Commerce Commission: Established in 1887 by the Interstate Commerce Act, replaced by the Surface Transportation Board in 1996. The ICC was established to insure fair and non-discriminatory railroad rates and came to have broad powers that had adverse effects on railroads' ability to generate a reasonable return on equity.

Interlocking/Interlocking Plant: A location where two tracks cross each other, equipped with an interlocking machine. The interlocking machine is built with an internal logic (mechanical, electrical, or later digital) which allows the tower operator to only select one route crossing of the tracks at a time, to prevent collisions between trains on opposing tracks.

LCL/Less than Car Load: Up until trucking took over package delivery from railroads in the 1960s, the term LCL meant Less than Car Load, where the car in question was a boxcar. With the advent of firms such as UPS and FedEx, the similar term is Less than Truck Load or LTL. The boxcar or truck carries shipments from many different customers going to a specific city where they would be dispersed to individual recipients.

line a switch: to move the point rails of the switch from one side to the other (e.g., from left to right), changing the route from the track straight ahead to the track diverging to one side.

lineup: The list of trains the dispatcher expects will run over a given portion of the railroad during part of a day.

lining bar: A steel pry bar, ranging in length from 5 to 6 feet, used by members of a section gang to shift track alignment or raise ties and rail.

loads-empties-tons: A numerical expression of the consist of cars in a train; for example, a train with 35 loaded cars and 14 empties with a gross weight of 3,500 tons would be described at 35-14-3,500.

logging show: The location where a logging company is conducting large-scale timber harvesting.

mud hop: One of several types of clerks at a yard office, tasked with recording cars out in the yard for the yardmaster to make sure all cars are properly accounted for. Yard tracks are notoriously undermaintained, frequently with little ballast, hence the nickname.

New York Central: formed in 1853, it served New England, the East Coast, and the Midwest to Chicago. It merged with its arch-rival, the Pennsylvania Railroad, in 1968 to form Penn Central, which went bankrupt in 1970.

NP/Northern Pacific Railroad: Ran 1864 to 1970 from St. Paul, Minnesota, to the Pacific Northwest. With the Great Northern and their jointly-owned subsidiaries, including the Spokane, Portland and Seattle and Chicago, Burlington and Quincy, the NP merged to create the Burlington Northern Railroad.

NX machine: an interlocking machine designed so that the tower operator selects the eNtrance and eXit points of the interlocking plant and the internal logic of the machine automatically lines all signals and switches for the route through the interlocking plant.

Opr: The abbreviation authorized by the Book of Rules for a Train Order Operator.

ORC/Order of Railway Conductors: A union formed in 1868, which became part of the United Transportation Union in 1969.

ORER/Official Railroad Equipment Register: Published quarterly, a listing of all railroads in the United States, Canada, and Mexico; their connections to each other for car interchange; and the dimensions and capacities of all active freight cars. Used to determine which car to supply to a customer for a shipment and how to route the car to its destination.

"OS" or "On Sheet": Train order operators report the passing of a train by their station to the dispatcher. The operator would fill out his station record and tell the dispatcher the train was "on sheet." Using telegraph, an operator would key the letters O and S followed by the station name, the train, and the time. The same abbreviations and sequence continued to be used when telephone supplanted telegraph.

outfit: a railroad maintenance-of-way car that employees who work out on the railroad line live in; a group of such cars that include bunk, dining, machine shop and storage cars.

over the road: To travel from one station to another.

pin lifter: *see* cut lever

pole road: An early logging railroad where the rails of the track were made from peeled logs.

PRR/Pennsylvania Railroad/"Pennsy": Formed in 1848, it grew to be the largest single railroad in the Unted States, accounting for over 10% of the freight car fleet in the post-WWII era. In 1968 it merged with arch-rival New York Central to form the Penn Central, which went bankrupt 2 years later.

puzzle switch(es): Any of several specialized switches allowing transit to and from multiple possible routes using very complex trackage. It could take a person some time to "puzzle out" the route through such trackage, hence the term.

Q or "the Q": *see* Chicago, Burlington & Quincy Railroad.

railroad direction: Railroads established nominal directions of travel for their main lines, either East/West or North/South. Trains were listed in the timetable schedule by direction. These railroad directions did not change regardless of the actual compass direction at any specific location of the tracks involved.

RBL: An insulated house car. Like the initials GS for a type of gondola freight car, the initials RBL specified a specific type of refrigerated house car. The AAR Classification of Cars appendix in the ORER lists 9 different types of refrigerator cars, each with an initial letter code of R, followed by additional letters such as RA, RB, etc. An RBL is described as a refrigerator car with a minimum of 3" of insulation and without ice or mechanical refrigeration.

retainers (in the 20 pound position): A pressure retaining valve which is manually operated to limit the release of air pressure from a car's brake cylinder after the engineer puts the automatic train brake in the release position. Setting the retainer to "the 20 pound position" keeps 20 pounds of air pressure in the car's brake cylinder.

reverse lever: The removeable handle of a diesel locomotive control stand that determines the direction that the locomotive moves. It has three positions: forward, reverse, and neutral. When it is removed from the control stand, the locomotive cannot be moved.

roadmaster or track supervisor: Supervisor of maintenance-of-way employees.

salt chuck: A Pacific Northwest/Canadian term, possibly from Chinook jargon, for a body of salt water.

SD (as in SD40): A six-axle locomotive manufactured by the Electromotive Division (EMD) of General Motors, having a model number starting with the initials SD for Special Duty (SD7, SD9, SD40, et al.).

shoofly: A temporary track built around a section of damaged track.

short haul: To route a freight car by a shorter route on one railroad when a longer route would be possible, giving another railroad a larger percentage of the total "haul" and the fee. The expression "to short haul oneself" is similar to "shooting oneself in the foot."

slack: The amount of built-in free movement in a railcar's draft gear and couplers. Thus, when a freight train starts, movement proceeds from one car to the next as the slack is "pulled out," until the entire train is moving.

Sperry Rail Services: Formed in 1928, the Sperry company was the first to develop induction and ultrasonic methods of non-destructive rail testing to find flaws that were not visible to the eye. The testing equipment is housed in self-powered railcars that travel over a railroad's lines under contract. Rail found to have a defect was marked for immediate replacement. Thus, "Sperry rail" refers to a piece of rail that is defective.

spotting a car: the act of physically placing a freight car at the loading or unloading location at an industry.

Staggers: The Staggers Rail Act of 1980 is a federal law deregulating the American railroad industry, largely replacing the regulatory rate structure developed by the Interstate Commerce Commission.

string chart: A graphic representation of train movements comparing time on one axis vs. distance on the second axis. String charts are used to develop and analyze train schedules.

time table or timetable: Two types of time tables are used on a railroad. A **public time table** is for use by the public and lists passenger trains and their arrival and departure times at passenger stations. The public time table does **not** grant authority for the actual movement of these trains. An **Employee Time Table** is for the information and governance of employees of the railroad issuing it. Under certain rules and methods of train dispatching, an Employee Time Table **does** grant authority for those trains listed in the schedule portion of the time table to run across the railroad.

Time Table and Train Order operations: from the 1850s until the 1980s, a method of authorizing the movement of trains. The time table authorized the movement of "regular" trains listed in its schedule pages. The train dispatcher authorized the movement of "extra" trains, not listed in the schedule, using train orders which were dictated first by telegraph and then by telephone to operators at stations who in turn gave the written orders to the train crews.

torpedo: a small package of black powder which is clipped to a rail and causes an audible explosive signal when run over by a locomotive. This signal alerted the engineer of possible danger ahead.

tow path: A path next to the tracks for employees to walk on; the term originates from a path along a canal used by horses towing canal barges.

track chart: a profile of a portion of a railroad, in either vertical or horizontal format.

train order: A document issued by a train dispatcher, in a specified format, authorizing the movement of trains. The authority granted by a train order supersedes that conferred by the time table schedule.

train register: Under rules for Time Table and Train Order dispatching, a book maintained at stations or junctions in which train crews completed entries to indicate that their train had arrived or departed; the information is used by other train crews to determine whether they can safely move on the main line.

train sheet: *see* Dispatcher's Record of Train Movements.

trainmaster: Supervisor responsible for operation of trains in a designated territory.

transition era: Generally the period after World War II and before 1960 when the diesel-electric locomotive replaced the steam engine.

TTX/Trailer Train Corporation: A corporation formed and jointly owned by a majority of trunk line railroads in the 1950s to purchase and manage a fleet of flat cars for intermodal service. Thus a "TTX flat" is a flatcar designed and used for intermodal service.

turn: A local train that starts at one station, goes to another, and returns to the first, usually in one work day.

unit train: A freight train in which all the cars carry the same commodity and travel together from the origin to the destination.

UP/Union Pacific Railroad: Operating from 1862–present, a Class 1 railroad and the eastern half of the original transcontinental railroad. The Central Pacific Railroad built the western portion. During most of the period covered by this book the Union Pacific operated between the Midwest, Los Angeles and the Pacific Northwest. In 1982 the UP bought the Western Pacific and gained entry to central California and the San Francisco Bay Area.

USRA: (1) **United States Railroad Administration**, the name of the nationalized railway system in the United States during and just after World War I; (2) **United States Railway Association**, 1974–1986; the government corporation that oversaw the creation of Conrail after the bankruptcy of the Penn Central and other Eastern Railroads.

UTU/United Transportation Union: formed in 1969 from 4 other unions—The Brotherhood of Locomotive Firemen and Engineers, The Brotherhood of Railroad Trainmen, The Order of Railroad Conductors and Brakemen, and The Switchmen's Union of North America.

varnish: Passenger cars, so-called because wooden-sided passenger cars were given a coat of protective and glossy varnish on an annual basis.

WP/Western Pacific Railroad: Running from 1903–1983, a small Class 1 railroad that ran between Salt Lake City, Utah, and Oakland, California. Merged into the Union Pacific Railroad.

Index, Life Along the Tracks

Illustrations are indicated in italics

S

T

U

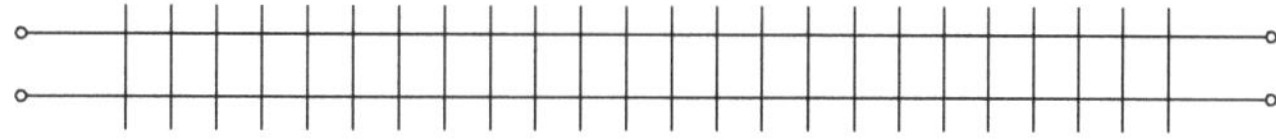

About the Authors

Michael J. McLaughlin was riding switch engines in Seattle in the early 1950s, at age 11. He started off working in maintenance of way, then moved on to signaling for the Great Northern while attending the University of Washington. After graduating, Mike worked for—by his count—seven different railroads across the United States in maintenance of way and signal maintenance. Later in his career he moved into traffic management, working for such major companies as Coors and Leprino Foods, and finished his career as a railroad and transportation consultant. Mike passed away in 2012.

James C. Providenza was born, raised, and has lived most of his life in the San Francisco Bay Area. Having earned both B.A. and J.D. degrees from Santa Clara University, he had a 38-year career in law enforcement, retiring in 2012 as a police captain. Jim is a co-author of *A Compendium of Model Railroad Operations*, published by the Operations Special Interest Group in 2017, as well as the author of 60-plus articles on various aspects of model railroading over the past 30 years. His articles have appeared in *Railroad Model Craftsman*, *Model Railroader*, *Railmodel Journal*, and special interest group quarterly magazines.

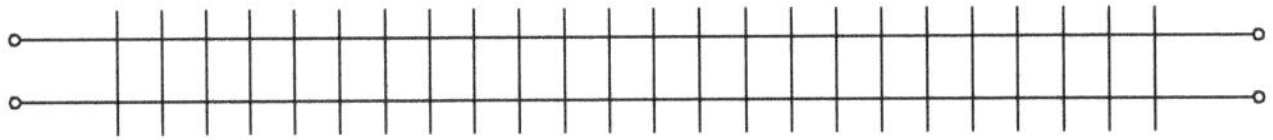